THE DEVIL'S IN THE DRAUGHT LINES

1,000 Years of Women in
Britain's Beer History

Dr CHRISTINA WADE

T0333702

CAMRA
BOOKS

Published by the Campaign for Real Ale Ltd
230 Hatfield Road, St Albans, Hertfordshire AL1 4LW
www.camra.org.uk/books

First published 2024

ISBN 978-1-85249-386-8

A CIP catalogue record for this book is available from the British Library

Printed and bound in the United Kingdom by GPS Colour Graphics Ltd

Managing Editor: Alan Murphy
Design | Typography: Dale Tomlinson
(Set in Elena, *a typeface by Nicole Dotin*)
Sales & Marketing: Toby Langdon
Cover: Tida Bradshaw

Contents

About the author 4

Introduction 5

About the book 11

1 **Of Pints and Plagues** 13

2 **Rules, Regulations, and How to Blithely Ignore Them** 41

3 **This Beer Can Kill You** 63

4 **Homebrewing Housewives** 83

5 **Workin' 9 to Last Orders** 103

6 **'Til Death Do Us Part** 123

7 **Beyond Breweries** 147

Recipes 179
Apple Fritters · Cock Ale · Posset

Bibliography 186

Index 213

Acknowledgements 223

ABOUT THE AUTHOR

Dr CHRISTINA WADE is a beer historian specialising in the hidden histories of women, especially those in the brewing trade. Wade received her doctorate in History from Trinity College Dublin in 2017, for which she was awarded a scholarship. She also holds an M.Phil. in Medieval History from the same institution. Since the completion of her thesis, Wade has spent much of her time posting about women and beer history on her website *braciatrix*, which was shortlisted for the 2022 Irish Food Writing Awards. She has also had her research featured in various other publications including *The Medieval Dublin Series, The Journal of Franco-Irish Studies, TheTaste.ie*, and *Beoir Magazine*. Wade is currently serving on the Beer Culture Center's League of Historians. The Beer Culture Center is a non-profit organisation which is 'dedicated to sharing stories of how beer has shaped humanity, past & present'. As a member of the League of Historians, Wade helps to further the aims of this critically important institution.

A BJCP Certified Beer Judge, Wade is also resident historian, audio editor, and co-host of the *Beer Ladies Podcast*, which was recently featured in *Vinepair* and shortlisted in the podcast category for the 2023 Irish Food Writing Awards. Now in its fourth season, *The Beer Ladies Podcast* talks about everything from beer styles, glassware, to dedicated beer history episodes about the role of women in the trade. Additionally, she founded the Ladies Craft Beer Society of Ireland in 2013, which now has over 1,500 members from all over the world. This organisation seeks to create a safe environment for women who appreciate craft beer, as well as highlighting and empowering women in the brewing industry.

Wade has spoken at a variety of Irish and International conferences during her academic career. Specific to her research on beer history, she has had papers accepted at the International Conference of Medievalists, FoodCon at DIT, The Beverage Research Network Conference in Tallaght, Friends of Medieval Dublin Lunchtime Lecture Series, The FemAle Beer Festival in Cork, Alltech Brews and Food Fair, BrewCon, and the Killarney Beer Festival. And she has been interviewed by *Totally Dublin, 98FM*, and *The Irish Times Women's Podcast, Bean to Barstool Podcast, A New Brew Podcast*, and *Brewing After Hours*.

Introduction

She breweth noppy ale,
And maketh thereof pot-sale,
To travellers, to tinkers,
To sweaters, to swinkers,
And all good ale-drinkers...

JOHN SKELTON, *The Tunning of Elynour Rummyng*, 1517

On a rolling Surrey hill, up past the butcher, the baker, and the candlestick maker, the Devil's sister brewed her ale. Why exactly she was engaged in the trade when she held such lofty infernal connections is anyone's guess. Perhaps, like the demons that possess random kids in our favourite horror movies, she was just bored. In any event, for the very low cost of your favourite rosary (or more accurately, your immortal soul), you too could sample her brews. I wouldn't get too excited, though. For she was famous, or rather infamous, for her bird dropping-laced ales, those brews that she would let ferment while her hens roosted over the vats, blending the resultant concoction with her scabbed fists to create a potion designed to make the drinker appear two or three years younger, and infinitely more desirable.

This is, of course, a mere hint at what she was getting up to: she ripped off her customers, seduced the menfolk, and even kept the company of a witch. All in all, she was a total menace, a woman whose life was utterly devoted to creating chaos. They say that, for some, the bar for good behaviour is so low it's a tavern in Hades, but if such a place were to really exist, it would have been Elynour Rummyng's alehouse.

I doubt she's all that bothered about it, though, because Rummyng is a fictional character. John Skelton's 16th-century poem, *The Tunning of Elynour Rummyng*, told the story of the titular character, a brewing woman who prided herself on her scandalous behaviour. At first glance, she appears to have come from the imaginative musings of Skelton, a lauded poet – he held the much-vaunted position of tutor to a young Henry VIII – and, in his free time, a raging misogynist, though she may, in fact, have been based on a real person: one Alianora Romyng, an alewife at the Running Horse pub in Leatherhead, Surrey. In 1525, like Skelton's Elynour, she got caught ripping off her customers, and was fined tuppence (2d) for selling ale in too small measures. It wasn't a particularly severe fine – equivalent to, say, a gallon of her own ale. The jury is still out on whether she was the muse for Skelton's poem. After all, Alianora Romyng largely disappears from the annals of history after her brush with the law – no magical potions, no seducing customers, and no devilish siblings.

Elinour Rummin, 'a well-known landlady of an ale-house'.

The Running Horse, Bridge Street, Leatherhead, Surrey.

While the real Alianora has largely been forgotten over the centuries, stories like Skelton's live on, spinning us tales of women who brewed during the medieval and early modern periods. In the last several decades we have become entranced with the history of alewives, and many women in the beer industry today find power in these accounts. During Women's History Month, in March, we are inundated with fascinating posts on historical brewing women and their legacies. Around the world, academics have been researching and writing about these women, allowing us to better expand our knowledge on the subject. From tales of Ninkasi in ancient Sumer to Wari women in 10th-century Peru, we are enthralled with their stories. They can make us feel like we are part of a larger tradition; like we are reclaiming a space. This coincides with the beer industry itself becoming more diverse, with higher numbers of people from historically marginalised groups entering the trade in recent years. This is largely due to the tireless work of activists from these communities. And though much more still needs to be done, the last decades in particular have seen more and more women joining the brewing industry globally; women like Seolhee Lee, one of only a few in South Korea to take up the brewing craft, or Madees Khoury of Taybeh Brewery in Palestine, the first female brewer of modern memory in the Middle East.

Perhaps most notably, we have become utterly fascinated with the maligned alewife: the Elynour Rummyngs of history. Every year sees a cascade of new internet articles, podcasts, and YouTube videos telling stories of the connection between alewives and witches. Often, they invite their audiences to believe that medieval European alewives were totally pushed out of brewing because they were accused of witchcraft; even suggesting that the modern stereotype of the witch is based on their garb. This is, of course, a myth – one that we will explore in chapter three – which is often bolstered with tales like that of Skelton's Rummyng.

It makes sense that we are so drawn to these myths. Many of us can relate to feeling like the outsiders, the underdogs, the misunderstood. We know how that feels, and it calls to something deep within us, making the past seem not so very different. Moreover, many women can relate to the gender-based discrimination inherent in these stories, of lives overshadowed by the spectre of misogyny. We can see ourselves in these tales. But instead of mocking and hating figures like Skelton's Rummyng – a woman painted in a terrible light – we have flipped the script and now see her as the victim of the sexism of the time. And so we create a dichotomy of sorts, based on these fictional renderings of medieval and early modern alewives, presenting them as proverbial Davids battling patriarchal Goliaths. However, sometimes in our excitement to see ourselves in these historical women we forget that they were, as we are, flawed. And also sometimes fictional.

The Tunning of Elynour Rummyng is a literary story, certainly reflecting the author's bias. But how close was this depiction to what life was like on the ground for actual brewing women? It's important to look behind the Elynour Rummyngs for the Alianora Romyngs, to find the real story. This is one of the reasons I chose the title of this book 'The Devil's in the Draught Lines'. Like the idiom it's based on – 'the devil is in the details' – our title hints that the history of women in brewing is much more complicated than is often presented – because people are much more complicated than they are often presented.

Years ago, when I was a PhD student, I was part of an organising committee for a conference on medieval women which explored three key themes: Collusion, Subversion, and Survival. I cannot think of a more fitting way to conduct our beer history study. As things began to change in the UK brewing world, and men began to take more interest in the trade, many women sought to survive. They focused on eking out a living and taking care of their families. Others rebelled; they fought against laws, customs or people who sought to oppress them; they stuck their proverbial two fingers up. Still others, well, they were the monsters in people's tales; they oppressed, exploited, and actively harmed people of all genders. But the thing to keep in mind is that many of the women we will be exploring fall into two or more of these categories. Of course, there are exceptions on both sides of the coin, but most humans are a mass of contradictions and hypocrisies. Most of the women in this book will not fit neatly into the categories of hero or villain. It will entirely depend on the context, and perhaps most importantly, who is telling the story.

There are very few records written by the brewing women themselves. Many women only appear in the annals of brewing history when the spotlight of male power shines on them; i.e., when they ran afoul of the law. While the academic in me would love to give you every example of every scenario ever written down, this book would cease to be simply a book and would start being a library. What you see here only scratches the surface. Should you want to study this topic more yourself, I have provided a bibliography of the sources I used for each chapter.

More to the point, women's experiences of brewing differed greatly depending on many other aspects of their identity besides their gender. Class or economic position, race, ethnicity, religion, location, ability, sexuality, time period, and even marital status played a key role in how they would experience the brewing world. Professor Kimberlé Crenshaw coined the term 'intersectionality' nearly 30 years ago to define the ways that people or groups are affected by multiple experiences and identities which shape them and the way they move through the world. Specifically in the history of women's brewing, it wasn't just their gender that impacted their position in the trade, but a confluence of these multiple identities.

*   *   *

As we will see, there are many parallels between historical brewing traditions and the modern industry. As part of our study, alongside the history, there will be interviews with modern women from all aspects of the beer industry and beyond. From this we will be able to look at how certain things may have evolved over the years, while others have remained steadfastly the same. What we will see is that there is no time in the history of brewing in the UK that women are not present.

I will introduce all of the interviewees here as they will pop up at various points throughout the book discussing their experiences. That way, if you want to check on some details, you can just come back here to get a general idea of what they do. All of the women I interviewed for this book are extremely multifaceted, wearing many different hats inside the industry and out. A single sentence introduction won't do any of them proper justice, so I will only mention one small part of what they do here to give you an idea of what we will cover. The rest will be explored as the book progresses.

We will hear from several beer writers and educators: Laura Hadland, Ruvani de Silva, Natalya Watson and Jane Peyton. Of course, beer communication isn't just in written form: Joanne Love and Tori Powell of *A Woman's Brew* and Emma Inch of *Fermentation Beer and Brewing Radio* prove that in every episode. Women's beer groups are very important to our study, so I talked to Nix Prabhu of Glasladies Beer Society and Amélie Tassin of Women in Beer. I also spoke to Women in Beer members Amy Rankine, Sarah Sinclair, and Monica Mendoza, who had much to say about their roles in the beer world. And we can't forget activists like Ash Eliot of the incredibly important Brave Noise. I interviewed Doreen Joy Barber, who has worked in several different places in the industry including behind the bar and in brewery marketing. I talked to Annabel Smith of Dea Latis, a women's beer networking and research group, who got her start working and eventually running pubs. Speaking of drinking spots, we will hear from Jules Gray of Hop Hideout in Sheffield. And, of course we can't forget the breweries. In this book we will learn from Helena Adedipe of Eko Brewery; Lizzie and Lucy Stevens of Closet Brewing; Talia Chain of Sadeh Farm and Lone Goat Brewing Company; Joelle Drummond of Drop Bear Beer Company; Nidhi Sharma of Meantime Brewing Company; Lynsey Campbell, brewer; and Apiwe Nxusani-Mawela of Tolokazi Beer Company.

What follows is in many ways a conversation between historical and modern women.

About the book

The book is organised into chapters that are thematic in nature, though the general direction of the narrative is chronological. We start with the medieval period (500–1500), then progress to the early modern (1500–1800) and work our way up to now.

Chapter One starts with The Plague. The Black Death came to the UK in the 14th century and decimated the population. What happened in its aftermath has led many scholars to suggest it was a kind of flashpoint for the brewing world. We are, unfortunately, quite familiar with the nature of pandemics, and so in the second half of this chapter will we look at how it compares to Covid-19 and its destructive wake through interviews with the brewing industry women who are going through it.

In Chapter Two we take a look at regulations in the medieval and early modern periods. Importantly, we will see that women sometimes cheated their customers, intentionally or otherwise, and how this might have played out in the legal system. Further, we will examine how poor women and those with disabilities turned to brewing as a way to keep themselves out of dire poverty.

Chapter Three focuses on the bad reputations of alewives. By exploring art and literature we will see how alewives were often portrayed negatively, and we will take some time to tease apart the alewife-as-witch myth and find the actual story.

In Chapter Four we see that women never left the brewing world, even if they were no longer dominating the commercial sector in the early modern period. Brewing at home was central to the duties of housewives and servants, and in this chapter we will take a look at how exactly this played out through the writings by and for these women.

Chapter Five explores that most important of institutions: the alehouse. We will look at the role women played in pubs, alehouses, inns and other public drinking establishments, as owners and workers.

Chapter Six explores the change in the brewing world following the Industrial Revolution. Here we will look for where women still brewed or worked in breweries in this new and constantly evolving industry.

In chapter Seven we explore beyond breweries to those women who have helped shape the industry as it is today. Women's beer groups and drinkers, malting women, hop pickers, and beer writers all play a pivotal role in the beer world.

If you are, like me, someone who enjoys a nice beverage and a bite to eat while sinking into a new book, go straight to the appendix, where you will find a few recipes based on those from the very women we will learn about. So, if you are feeling peckish you might want to try your hand at making a little something to help fully immerse yourself in the history presented here.

Our geographical scope will be limited to England, Scotland and Wales. However, according to historian Stuart Laycock, author of *All the Countries We've Ever Invaded: And the Few We Never Got Round to*, at one point or another the British Empire covered at least 200 countries (meaning that it only missed out on 22 of the Earth's nations). The impact of British colonisation and invasion meant that many people from these countries came to the UK, whether by force, desire, economic need, or coercion of some kind. These diasporas certainly had an impact on the brewing trade, and we will discuss this where it is relevant to our story.

About Ale and Beer

The age-old argument of ale versus beer has caused many a heated discussion amongst scholars, but here is what we know: ale is the unhopped malt beverage we are referring to in the medieval period. Ale dominated the brewing trade for centuries prior to the arrival of beer, which was distinguished as a hopped malt-based beverage. They differed in this era by the inclusion – or not – of hops. Now, for a while these two lived side by side, one with hops and one without, but as the centuries wore on, ale would also become hopped, and then the line between them eventually became blurred, until today, where many people now interchange the names ale and beer. The precise hows, whens, and whys are a matter of great debate, and depend a lot on the context. As such, they are well beyond the scope of this book.

OF PINTS AND PLAGUES

The Arrival of the Black Death

The rumours reached their shores long before it did. Whispers carried tales of abandoned villages, decimated towns, and mouldering corpses left to rot in the streets. Armageddon, some said; God's punishment. Others declared it was a miasma, a poison cloud, sweeping through Asia, Africa, and Europe, leaving behind a wake of death, decay and destruction. And it seemed as if all they could do was wait ... and wait; a slow, creeping execution, torturously methodical in its murderous path. Many tried to keep it at bay, offering prayers and processions, pleading with their god and begging their saints for intervention, for succour. But it never came. Instead, death; dressed in black, swollen lymph nodes, fever, weakness, and pain.

The bubonic plague arrived on English soil in the autumn of 1348. It would return again and again over the centuries, killing many before slinking off into obscurity, only to be revived some time in the future. That first arrival in the mid-1300s is, in our modern minds, one of the most infamous instances of this disease: the Black Death. It killed vast swathes of the population – estimates vary from 30–60% – and some towns and villages were all but completely wiped off the map. Mark A. Senn argued that the death toll was so high in London that 'there was a funeral every two and one-half minutes'.

Bubonic plague still exists today around the world, endemic in some places, and is present in, of all things, prairie dogs in the United States.

It still kills, though remains a mere shadow of what it once was, thanks to advancements in modern medicine. Medieval and early modern doctors offered very different remedies to the antibiotics found today. In later plague waves, *The English Huswife*, written in 1615, advocated bisecting live pigeons and applying them to the buboes as a cure. In a marked improvement on that particularly violent remedy, plague water called for a mix of herbs, spices and alcohol, sometimes even ale or beer.

The Black Death forever altered the social, political, and religious fabric of society. There was a profound impact, not only on how people lived, but also how they died. In art and literature death came to the forefront. No longer depicted as passive and peaceful, in images that would make any self-respecting goth squeal with delight, we find death dancing, the *danse macabre*, holding hands with people from all walks of life as they cart them

off to their eternal resting place. Things shifted and people became preoccupied with the idea of dying a good death. The *Ars Moriendi*, the art of dying, and dying well, was a famous book on the topic of how to graciously accept one's fate. There was an ever-present *memento mori*, 'remember that you will die', both in written word and in various art forms, which, for centuries, would grace tombs, churches, even clocks.

Amidst this fascination with death, we can find our brewing women. In Samuel Rowlands' *A Terrible Battell Betweene Two Consumers of the Whole World: Time and Death*, written in 1606, we encounter an alewife. The poem is a somewhat violent conversation between the two characters of Time and Death about the inevitability of

Woodcut from *Ars Moriendi*.
Published by Nicolaus Gotz *c*.1475.

decay and the mortality of humans. They go back and forth, attempting to outdo each other with stories of the ravages they have wreaked upon humanity, before an argument erupts between them. They even talk of the plague in the 1600s and its deaths. But it's our alewife that we must concern ourselves with. Time, in one diatribe against Death, states the following:

> Thy picture stands upon the Ale-house wall,
> Not in the credit of an ancient story,
> But when the old wives guests begin to braule,
> She points, and bids them read *Memento mori*:
> Looke, looke (saies she) what fellow standeth there.
> As women do, when crying Babes they feare.

So, fearing death is a womanly thing, of which Time is quite scornful. But the alewife here is doing her duty to remind people of their impending demise and, therefore, to behave themselves in her house. Judgement awaits all.

Inevitably, the plague impacted brewing during its many reigns. People weren't able to brew, because, well, many of them died. And even if they were alive, fear of the disease spreading could be a deep concern. Quarantines certainly kept people from interacting with local brewing women or accessing resources they needed to make ale. A later resurgence of the bubonic plague in 1578 saw England creating the Plague Orders. These were placed throughout the country and laid out 17 rules, offering clear guidance on how to handle infection for those who sold food or drink. It instructed people that if an alehouse or inn had a spread of infection, its sign was to be removed entirely and patrons were obviously not to go there. Quarantines were strictly enforced; and while people still brewed ale, the business wasn't perhaps quite as lucrative as it had been. The markets were certainly less crowded and there were fewer people to sell to. During these later outbreaks, James Brown of the University of Sheffield, in his aptly titled 'How the bubonic plague changed drinking habits', argued that patterns shifted from drinking in alehouses to drinking at home due to the quarantines and curfews.

To truly understand the long-lasting effects the Black Death had on brewing, we need to rewind a few centuries. In 1203, Maud, wife of Hugh, found herself in some hot water when she was caught red-handed selling a false gallon of ale. She was fined for her sins. This story comes from the *Pleas at Bedford in the Fourth Year of the Reign of King John*, and hers is not an isolated incident. Clarice, wife of Lawrence, also found herself in trouble when she was accused of selling in false measures by one Lambert Miller, who brought a legal suit against her. Clarice, however, did not take these charges lying down, and asserted that she would be taking this in front of the justices when they next came. Lambert, not to be denied, pledged to prosecute her. These are just two of the thousands of instances in the legal records of women brewing in the UK during the medieval period. I could go on (and on and on).

Women dominated the brewing industry in the Middle Ages in England, Scotland and Wales. The ground-breaking work of Judith Bennett, whose 1995 *Ale, Beer, and Brewsters in England: Women's Work in a Changing World, 1300-1600* laid the foundations for the study of English alewives, clearly demonstrated that most brewing was done by married, single, or widowed women, though men certainly participated in the trade as well – either by themselves or more likely alongside their wives in some capacity. In the years since Bennett's book, the research of scholars like Barbara Gleiss, Theresa Vaughan, and Michelle Sauer has further solidified this claim. In Scotland, scholars like Elizabeth Ewan and Nicholas Mayhew have drawn similar conclusions; and the same can be said in Wales, with work by Matthew Frank Stevens and Deborah Youngs demonstrating comparable findings.

This early brewing trade wasn't what we might conceive of as an industry today. Prior to the bubonic plague, Bennett argued that most English brewing women either brewed sporadically, without a set schedule, or brewed when they needed income and sold to their neighbours, which was, perhaps, a bit more regular. There are, of course, exceptions, but this was the general trend. In medieval Scotland, Ewan has found that in some towns, because of the high demand for ale, the powers that be encouraged women to brew more regularly and year-round. During the Welsh Middle Ages, brewing could be well paid. According to scholars like Stevens, poor women started brewing again as soon as they could after times of famine.

Scholarly consensus seems to suggest brewing was an extension of women's household duties – a side gig if you will – a way to supplement their male partner's income if they were married, or, if single or widowed, a way for women to sustain themselves. And though this income stream was important to their households, and could be lucrative for some, it was, generally, a way to make some extra money, as Sauer argued, 'without challenging the public masculine sphere'.

Those who managed to survive the Black Death in the 1300s commanded higher pay and better working conditions since there were significantly fewer people around to work. In *Death, Life and Religious Change in Scottish*

Towns c. 1350–1560, Mairi Cowan argued that in Scotland, because of the reduced population, rents and prices for goods were lower, and wages were higher, which meant that those who were still alive enjoyed a better quality of life than their ancestors. The same can be said for the rest of the UK, though in England it should be noted that elites did seek to restore the balance by issuing *The Ordinance of Labourers* in 1349. It addressed the new working conditions and difficulties faced by landowners trying to hire labour. Among other things, it froze prices for brewers at pre-plague levels. Anyone found behaving contrary to the law was ordered to pay double the amount they received to the injured party. Most scholars view these laws as largely ineffective, and so in 1351 new laws came into play called the *Statues of Labourers*, reiterating that brewers should sell for reasonable prices with only moderate gains, and freezing wages at pre-plague levels. These new laws were very unpopular and contributed significantly to the Peasants Revolt in 1381 when labourers rose up to demand better wages and treatment. This uprising was eventually suppressed, but its legacy lived on, and conditions would improve over time.

In general, those left behind after the plague had more buying power due to higher wages. This meant that those who were on the lowest rungs of the economic ladder could buy more ale than their parents and grand-parents had. According to Bennett, those who managed to survive the pandemic consumed more ale than their ancestors, particularly in England. This, alongside the shift to urbanisation, saw an increased demand for alehouses, public spaces where people could socialise and drink with friends and neighbours. Some scholars like Kristen Burton have even gone as far as to argue that the Black Death was, in many ways, responsible for the creation of the modern public house in England, something that wouldn't appear until centuries later. All of which led to a higher demand for ale; more specifically, a demand for better ale. William Langland's *Piers Plowman*, written in the 1370s, tells us how the labourer won't

> drink any half-penny ale in any circumstances,
> But of the best and the brownest that barmaids sell
> Labourers that have no land to live on but their hands
> Deign not to dine today on last night's cabbage
> No penny ale can please them, nor any piece of bacon

This new beer 'snobbery', and ability to drink more than previously, were key factors that led to some fundamental changes for our alewives, most notably in England (we will get to Scotland and Wales later). We are talking about the professionalisation of the brewing trade.

This trend towards a more commercial and professional trade had existed prior to the plague, particularly in English cities, but the rampant spread of the disease and its after-effects accelerated the change. Gleiss, Bennett, and Sauer have all argued that the growth of urban living led to a reduced role for women in brewing because more people were drinking more ale, which meant that brewers needed to be able to keep up with this higher demand. This increased demand, they found, for more and better ale meant that brewing was becoming quite a lucrative endeavour, which meant that more and more men took notice of a craft that had, traditionally, been carried out mostly by women. All of this meant that brewing changed dramatically. Larger breweries with more capacity were needed to meet this new demand. These scholars contended that these bigger breweries needed more capital to run successfully, and they also needed strong managerial authority to oversee their bigger workforce. In the patriarchal systems of the medieval period, who had access to such things? Men; or more specifically, men from middling and wealthy backgrounds. Because of all this, while single or widowed women could still participate in brewing, it was much easier for their male, or married female, counterparts. Married women could circumvent many of these issues by leaning on their husbands for access to capital and expertise. Of course, there are many exceptions to this general trend, and we will explore these later.

The Introduction of Hops

As we have seen, the knock-on effects of increased demand and professionalisation greatly impacted the brewing world, though this impact would take several centuries more to be fully felt. The Black Death was just one piece of the puzzle, however. For while the plague was busy killing off large swathes of the population, there was one ingredient that was slowly making its way into brewing recipes on the continent: one component of beer, without which many of us would find our modern brews quite lacking. It made its mark more significantly at the end of the 14th and in the early 15th centuries and changed forever the way people brewed. I am, of course, speaking of hops.

When hops entered the brewing scene in Britain, they did not do so to universal acclaim. They came in through the back door so to speak, on ships bearing immigrants who came to England for a new life. The beer, known as Flemish Ale, was imported to those who had ventured far from their own shores and wished for a simple taste of home. It was common cargo, as Richard Unger pointed out. According to Martyn Cornell, the first records of hopped Flemish Ale appear in the middle of the 14th century, when James Dodynessone of Amsterdam paid a toll on the beer at Great Yarmouth in 1361–2. Eventually, hops themselves were imported so that these immigrant communities could recreate their own traditional brews. At first the plant, and the beer it produced, were somewhat tainted by the xenophobic ideologies of the time, but this didn't last long.

John Bull making hop-tea in front of a hop grower and his workers, representing adulteration of beer by brewers. Chromolithograph by T. Merry, 1890, after himself.

By the late 14th and early 15th centuries, immigrants were brewing beer in England for their own communities, and these beer brewers were over-whelmingly male. Unlike ale brewing, which had a mix of men and women working in urban environments, hopped beer was largely male controlled in Britain from the outset. That said, there are some examples of female immigrants who were involved in the brewing trade, albeit indirectly. The *England's Immigrants Database* sheds some light on the medieval women who moved to England in the 14th century; women like Katherine Servaunt, who came from Germany to London and was the servant of John Hert, a brewer; or Katherine Petirson, from Zeeland, who came to Ipswich to work as a servant to Jose Bakker, also a beer brewer. And as we know, Dutch women were still brewing well into the 16th century. Marjolein van Dekken has found that in the Low Countries, because women could inherit guild memberships from their husbands, they could remain in the industry – and, in fact, did. In Haarlem, between 1518 and 1663, 97 out of 536 brewers were women, most of them widows. But regardless of whether they brewed or not, these immigrant women certainly kept the household running so the men they worked for could brew. Of this there can be no debate. Household work enables others to carry out work outside of the home, and without it these men would not have been able to brew, full stop.

The use of hops in brewing would eventually become hugely popular, as evidenced from later contemporary sources. This can be seen in Thomas Tusser's *Five Hundred Points of Good Husbandry … together with a Book of Huswifery*, a book written in verse in 1557 about the roles of a husband and housewife. In it, the author talks about the fun details of hop farming, including instructions on how much to wax the poles, how to dry the hops, where and when to plant them, and when to harvest them (when they look brown). Further, he is clear that brewing should be undertaken by the housewife and that she should be using hops:

> The hop for his profit I thus do exalt,
> It strengtheneth drink and it flavoureth malt;
> And being well-brewed long kept it will last,
> And drawing abide, if ye draw not too fast.

In her master's thesis *The Citie Calls for Beere: The Introduction of Hops and the Foundation of Industrial Brewing in London 1200–1700,* Kristen Burton argued that the introduction of hops, particularly in London, was a key turning point for brewing, and women's role in it. Burton contended that the use of hops in beer enabled brewers to make more money. They reinvested this new income back into their business, and this eventually led to the increased industrialisation of the industry. This meant that brewers wanted, and needed, newer and better equipment with which to brew this new kind of malt beverage. More to the point, because brewers made more money, this increased their social status, something, she argued, that ale brewers never achieved. Burton isn't alone in her arguments about the impact of hops on women's brewing. Bennett's study of alewives and brewing women argued that brewing beer required more money and credit, as well as better commercial networks, which men could access more easily given their experience in the working domain. This impact was felt most acutely in towns and cities; women's experiences were different in rural communities (which we shall explore later).

Hops acted as a preservative for beer, extending its shelf life and thereby allowing brewers to make more money. In contrast, ale was made in smaller batches as it was easily spoiled and generally drunk more quickly. Sauer and Burton argued that the longer shelf life of hopped beer made it more desirable than ale to the military. But there were other benefits for military leaders, who, according to Sauer, 'did not want to deal with women brewsters either in production, or for transport of the goods'. She argued that this was, in part, because male brewers became part of the garrison to some degree, and shipped out with them, but it was also because of prevailing misogynistic ideas about women who brewed. The requirements for brewing beer in ever-larger quantities, and its massive outpacing of ale production, meant that women could not compete on the same level with men alone. Alone is the key word here: women could, and still did, brew as part of a couple and could do so competitively on the market. As widows, and particularly for widows of commercial brewers, they could also find themselves running these increasingly commercial breweries. Even as single women, or within the home, they also continued to brew, though not at the same commercial level as men.

The Formation of Guilds

Ale brewers didn't simply roll over and accept the new dominance of beer straight away. In fact, they didn't take kindly to the new competition. Sometimes this erupted into violent confrontation between the ale brewers' guild and the beer brewers' guild. In 1464, over a century after the Black Death's arrival, the beer brewers of London petitioned to start their own separate guild, distinct from ale brewers. This enraged the ale brewers, who were already sworn enemies of the beer makers. Nearly two decades later, in April of 1481, the ale and beer guilds were officially declared separate entities and no ale brewer was allowed to use hops in their brews (which didn't last, of course). But the issues inherent in these guilds weren't just between beer and ale brewers, they were also between men and women.

The Brewer's Guild of London was officially created in 1438, though there had been some organisation for professional or semi-professional brewers floating around for a while. This supports the argument that professionalisation sped up post-Black Death but certainly wasn't invented then. Indeed, Unger contended that there was a kind of brewers group in London by the end of the 11th century, and this would have certainly involved women to some extent. The Mystery of Free Brewers within the City was founded in 1342 and sought to supervise the making of ale in London. This was the body that incorporated in 1438. In other places, guilds took longer to officially form. There is evidence for guilds forming officially in the 16th century throughout England: there were brewers' organisations of some kind in Norwich, Oxford, Southampton, Winchester, Northampton, Exeter, and Leicester, with evidence of some kind of combined group with bakers in Newcastle dating to 1342.

Married women were admitted into the guilds; or at least the London guild. According to the records of the clerk of the Brewers' Guild in the 15th century, William Porlond, women made up one-third of the members, and by and large these women were married. Some guilds did not include women, or women were only represented by their husbands, which would have been a massive barrier to those who were unmarried. Bennett found that in Chester the guild attempted to curtail widows and older citizens who were trying to make a living in their efforts to monopolise the trade. The Guild of Beer brewers in Hull, from its inception, seemed to be referring only to men. These ordinances were strict and offered clear instructions on how people should brew for sale. Though they did state that people who weren't guild members could brew for their own household use.

An important case study is that of Oxford Brewers' Guild. In the years around the Black Death, women, both married and unmarried, were prominent brewers in the city, and some were quite wealthy (though not necessarily because of their brewing). In time, the numbers of women brewers would fall due the increasing professionalisation of the trade, though some brewer's widows would continue to run their husbands' businesses after their deaths. The Guild continued this trend by forming a brewer's organisation in response to the involvement of the city's university, which had a lot of control over the trade, in the assize of ale. Historians Eleanor Chance, Christina Colvin, Janet Cooper, C. J. Day, T. G. Hassall, Mary Jessup and Nesta Selwy found that in the 15th century Oxford University created a rota specifying which brewers were permitted to brew to prevent the creation of too much ale. This limited the number of people who could brew, creating tension between rich and poor brewers.

It also led to prejudice against women who brewed, with the city eventually moving to limit them from doing so. For example, in 1585 the university issued ordinances that banned women from transporting ale.

Even though some women could become members, either alone or alongside their husbands, the increased importance of these guilds contributed to a decline in the number of female brewers. Over the course of several centuries, the professionalisation of the industry in England, sped up by the rising demand for ale after the Black Death, as well as the use of hops, and the formation of guilds, all led to the rise of the masculinisation of brewing, though the history of this change is, in a word, complicated. In the following chapters we will explore what this looked like for your average woman. As we will learn, there were many exceptions to this overall trend. Women in many rural parts of England experienced this quite differently from those in large urban areas, and the experiences of women from different socio-economic groups also varied greatly.

Brewing in Scotland and Wales

Speaking of differences, the situation in Scotland and Wales, while initially mimicking England in pre-plague times, is slightly different when it comes to professionalisation. The Black Death hit Scotland and Wales with as much ferocity as England and left those who survived in better economic positions than previously. But it didn't push them towards professionalisation at the same rates we can see in England. This could be because the introduction of hops and the formation of guilds didn't happen until much later. Growing hops in Scotland was difficult compared to places like Kent. Because of the difficulty, some scholars have contended that Scotland relied on traditional bittering herbs longer than in England. There was also at one time a small Welsh hop growing industry, but this was quickly overshadowed by the English farmers. Obviously, hops could be imported, but this could be expensive, and logistically difficult.

Hopped beer, and later ale, became quite popular in England during the early modern period. In Scotland it would eventually reach similar levels of consumption, but this was well behind their English counterparts. According to Stephanie Marie Baker, when beer is mentioned in the late medieval and 16th centuries in Scotland, it refers to imported beer, not locally made. In fact, Baker found that hops weren't even mentioned in the Scottish records of Parliament until 1661. As the years went on this would certainly change. As Ron Pattinson has pointed out, hops were being used in Edinburgh breweries as much as in London at least by the 1830s; much later than in England. Baker argued that the delayed popularity of hops in brewing meant that women maintained their positions as brewers for longer.

In Wales, traditional bittering ingredients also dominated brewing for quite some time and lasted, at least in homebrewing circles, well into the 20th century. As for the impact on hops on Welsh brewers, less is known than in Scotland. Like their Scottish counterparts, though, women likely held on longer as brewers here, also due to late professionalisation in the industry. This delay wasn't just because of hops. As was the case in Scotland, the lack of hop use also had the effect of delaying another important factor in the decline of women in brewing: guilds.

In the last decade of the 16th century, the brewers of Edinburgh created an organisation aptly called the Society of Brewers in Edinburgh, which was a source of investment for the brewing community. According to historian Ian Donnachie, it owned the reservoir that supplied the water and a large common brewhouse. But it was different from those in England. While it demonstrated an increasing professionalisation of the industry in Scotland, according to scholars like Baker and Ewan, it didn't have the profound effect that guilds had in England. In fact, as Baker noted, it wasn't until the 17th century that records began to show a male-dominated trade. I haven't found evidence of any guild bodies during the medieval period and into the 16th century in Wales, though this isn't to say there weren't informal organisations. As Welsh historian Deborah Youngs has argued, this is due to a lack of guild ordinances from medieval Wales. We simply don't have the data to study.

Covid-19: A New Pandemic

The arrival of the Black Death was the catalyst for a massive change in the brewing world; one that had a profound effect on the women working in it. This disease had far-reaching consequences, starting the process that saw a home-based neighbourhood trade evolve over the centuries into something large and industrial. But there's a more recent event that has had a similarly profound impact. A global pandemic that effectively stopped the world from working; that closed down breweries and forced the pubs to shutter.

When the Covid-19 pandemic reached South Africa, the government responded in many of the same ways we might be familiar with in the UK: they had lockdowns, enforced quarantines and had strict mask mandates. But they also did something else; something that had a potentially catastrophic impact on their local breweries: they banned alcohol sales entirely.

Apiwe Nxusani-Mawela of Tolokazi Beer Company felt this acutely. She had launched her brewery in March 2020, just as the spread of Covid was beginning to pick up speed globally. Because of the ban, she couldn't sell her beer and was thus unable to pay the bills to keep herself afloat. She didn't have the privilege of amassed capital to fall back on. But though she was down, she was not out. Instead, she decided to innovate.

Posting about her experiences on LinkedIn to her worldwide audience, Nxusani-Mawela caught the attention of Beer52, a UK-based subscription service that sends out various brews to beer geeks all over the world. James Taylor, the chief marketing officer at the company, reached out. How could they help keep Tolokazi in business during the pandemic? And so a plan for collaboration was born.

Under the guidance of Nxusani-Mawela, her sorghum pilsner would be brewed in Croatia and then sent out to Beer52's 100,000 subscribers

Apiwe Nxusani-Mawela, of Tolokazi Beer Company.

across the UK. Thus an alliance was created, something that the UK can look forward to for years to come. Nxusani-Mawela told me that Tolokazi now has a three-year contract with Beer52 to be part of their welcome beer box: 'I am really hoping this will open up more opportunities for the Tolokazi brand to grow not only within the UK market but across Europe as well.' Like her medieval predecessors in plague times, the coronavirus forced Nxusani-Mawela to close her brewery, but unlike the women before her, modern technology and the internet allowed her to keep her business going, and even expand to a new audience.

A quick Google search will show you any number of historians, epidemiologists, social scientists and journalists writing about the parallels between the Black Death and Covid-19 pandemics. Everything from the practices of quarantine to the spread of misinformation to the economic downturn is strikingly similar. We even coped in much the same way it seems. In their comparative study, Thomas J. Roulet and Joel Bothellod found 'four psychological experiences' that we shared with our ancestors, including a 'solidarity breakdown' where people sought scapegoats to blame for the disease, with minority groups, the poor, and immigrants often being those on the receiving end; sometimes with deadly results. They also found several common trends in economic norms, including price-gouging and a long-term shift of power to the workers, and argued that both the Black Death and Covid-19 should not be viewed as one event 'but rather as a series of cascading and intermittent disruptive events'.

The coronavirus certainly has proved to be a series of cascading and disruptive events, and the beer industry has not been spared. As with the arrival of the plague centuries earlier, many breweries initially faced severe problems, with a drop in sales and a shrinking market. This has been the case since the earliest days of the pandemic in 2020. SIBA, The Society for Independent Brewers, conducted the 'Covid-19 Brewing Industry Survey,' a report to Parliament of 282 independent brewers throughout the UK from 9–14 April 2020. Their findings showed that 82% saw a drop in sales, 65% of breweries stopped brewing altogether, 31% said their production slowed, while 3% reported that it remained the same and only 1% noted an increase. Furthermore, 81% said that the government was not doing enough to support them. Despite this setback, breweries adapted quickly. According to the same study, 70% of breweries now had a new takeaway or even delivery service available, with some 61% offering delivery free to local customers. And some 55% saw an increase in online sales.

This innovation would not save all of them, however. We have seen many breweries forced to close their doors in the wake of the pandemic, and the numbers have continued to rise in the ensuing cost of living and energy crises.

How do these closures and crises directly impact women? Or, more to the point, will they, like the Black Death before them, have a greater, long-term impact on women brewers? According to scholars like Bennett, Sauer, and others, the increased masculinisation of the brewing industry in urban England in the wake of the Black Death can be boiled down to a few key factors. Those who survived had a competitive advantage and so demanded higher wages. Further, more people moved to the cities and this increased urbanisation resulted in more customers, and greater demand from people who drank more ale than their ancestors. Because of this, a larger supply of ale needed to be produced. This led to a need for increased capital, more networks, the rise of guilds, and bigger and better equipment. And this was exacerbated by the rising popularity of hopped beer, which in turn led to a greater need for better equipment, larger premises and more capital, all of which was more easily available to men due to the very nature of the society in which they lived. Further, these bigger breweries called for more managerial authority, something that women could not call upon in a patriarchal society. In summary, the Black Death and its long-term impacts, coupled with the introduction of hopped beer and guilds, led to the long-term masculinisation of the commercial brewing industry.

Will this impact be repeated after the coronavirus pandemic? It is, perhaps, too soon to say. The masculinisation of the brewing industry didn't happen overnight, it happened over a long period time. Moreover, we are still very much in the middle of the pandemic. So, much as I would love to be able tell you, I can't predict the future. There are, however, some clues that may hint at longer trends.

Like our medieval counterparts, we were forced to quarantine, forcing us to drink in our own homes or not at all. In May 2020 *New Food Magazine* published an interview with Murdoch MacLennan entitled 'How has Covid-19 impacted the UK brewing and distilling industries'. MacLennan is an expert in distilling and brewing and works at Campbell Dallas as an accounting and business advisor. He found that smaller breweries that didn't have in-house canning or bottling lines might struggle given the new-found increased demand for drinking at home. This requirement for new equipment, and the money to pay for it all, may remind you of what we saw all those centuries ago (i.e., those men with more capital could build bigger and more advanced breweries to keep up with the increasing competition).

It's also the case that those with more money can stay afloat simply by having reserves in place. These tend to be the bigger breweries. In contrast, completely women-owned breweries are smaller affairs, and there aren't that many of those in the UK. While we do see some women in leadership roles in large regional breweries or even in bigger craft breweries, most are still run by men. There are exceptions, of course, and some large regional breweries are also taking a hit from the effects of the lockdowns, but it's generally the smallest breweries that get the short end of the stick. And it's in these smaller breweries where we see more female ownership, either outright or alongside their spouses or siblings. It's also where we see the highest incidence of ownership by historically marginalised groups. MacLennan's assertion that smaller breweries would be more susceptible to Covid closures means that women would be impacted more, just by the nature of their businesses.

But what if your brewery is so small it fits into your spare room? Closet Brewing is, in their own words, 'probably the smallest brewery in Edinburgh'. So small, they describe it as a 'pico brewery'. Run by married couple Lizzie and Lucy Stevens, their 62-ft² licensed brewery was, quite literally, the spare room in their house. They began as homebrewers in 2018 before finally taking the leap to get licensed in 2022. Closet Brewing's small scale meant that they didn't have huge overheads – their energy costs are relatively low – and social distancing wasn't a concern as it was just the pair of them in the brewery. Producing about 40 cans a batch twice a month helped them avoid having to close, and they then used the lockdowns to expand, morphing from homebrewers to professionals. But while they managed to weather the storm, they saw some of their favourite local breweries go under due to the strain of trying to cope with increasing energy costs.

The lockdowns also offered a silver lining to London-based Eko Brewery: a chance to build their community. I interviewed Helena Adedipe, who founded Eko Brewery alongside her husband, Anthony, and asked about her experiences. She told me that the impact of coronavirus was two-fold. Like Closet Brewing, they saw many of their brewing colleagues devastated, and they didn't remain untouched themselves. Eko had just launched their first beer in 2019, and they were getting ready to unveil their second in 2020 when Covid struck and they had to change direction. They had always planned on trading online, but now it was a necessity. And in addition to offering more people access to their brews, going digital provided a way to build a community much more easily than in previous years. Adedipe told me, 'the community that we managed to build and find because of that was incredible. And then we got to the point where you felt like you had known people for such a long time, and a lot of them, we actually met them face to face for the first time last year.'

Helena Adedipe, co-founder and co-owner of Eko Brewery.

It was through these online interactions that Adedipe had access to more people than previously, and she was able to form close connections with them. She told me that during the pandemic people in the industry were able to get to know one another without the usual pressure. So, in some ways, forcing poeople to go online allowed them to build connections with those who were physically distant. It made the world a bit smaller, and, especially for the beer industry, created spaces for people all over the UK to come together to share their experiences and help each other.

Joelle Drummond of Drop Bear Beer Company told me that the devastating effects of Covid on the brewing industry are still playing out: 'I'm seeing closures nearly every day of craft breweries and it's really sad. It's really depressing and it's a loss to the community of craft beer.' Like their English and Scottish counterparts, the Swansea-based brewery is very concerned for the future of craft beer. Drummond has noticed that smaller breweries in particular are more susceptible to closure, breweries that she feels 'bring a lot more diversity and excitement to the industry'. Their absence will leave behind only large macro breweries that 'can charge way less than smaller craft breweries'. This will serve to further alienate customers and lead to the closure of more breweries.

Drummond told me that because they made alcohol-free beer, Covid was a different experience for them: 'we had to be willing to adapt and change course. If we hadn't it would've been catastrophic.' Because they were still in such an early stage of their business, 'we could essentially just completely change our business model'. And that's what they did, shifting to online sales, which worked out well for them as many people were searching online for alcohol-free beer. Drummond said they experienced 'triple digit growth', though that growth came at a higher cost than might have been expected in non-pandemic times. Despite the uncertainty caused by the pandemic, which left many scared for the future, Drop Bear find themselves in an enviable position. The consumption of alcohol-free beer is on the rise, becoming one of the fastest-growing drink trends, not only in the UK but globally. This could set them up well to weather the next storm – the decline in alcohol sales.

In September 2022 vice.com published 'How Alcohol Lost Its Cool', which, as the title suggests, was about how the younger generation is eschewing alcohol altogether. Citing a 2022 Drinkaware survey, which showed that 26% of 16–24-year-olds are now entirely 'tee-total', vice.com found that, increasingly, Gen-Z and even millennials are turned off by drinking. On top of this, people in the UK are also now drinking less beer. Lynsey Campbell told me that during her years working as a brewer, this change in consumer drinking habits has led to craft breweries having to increase their prices 'in order to make any profit'. As for beer specifically, a YouGov survey – 'The British Craft Beer Report' – commissioned by SIBA and conducted in January 2022 found that women in particular are drinking less beer; a drop of 5% compared to a drop of 1% for men from 2020.

Lynsey Campbell, formerly of Whiplash Beer, Dublin, Ireland.

On the positive side, of the women who did drink beer, more than eight out of ten valued where it came from and preferred smaller producers.

From these interviews with brewing women, we can see that ingenuity and resilience are the themes of the day. Their innovation in the face of a global pandemic meant that they were able to weather the storm and continue brewing. Perhaps the forecast is not so gloomy for women in beer? But regardless of the size of your brewery, there are some things you can't avoid, like increased energy costs, or a smaller market share. Hand in hand with this general decrease in beer drinking was the complete lack of pub attendance.

*   *   *

Many of us can surely recall the utter silence that accompanied the coronavirus lockdowns. No loud sounds of big diesel trucks driving by; no screeching tires or muffled engines. In their place were birdsong and peace, a sense of stillness amidst all the tragedy.

> It was just a real serene moment in a time of real stress and anxiety, and it was just surreal to be sat in the Peak District with nobody around.
>
> (JULES GRAY, Hop Hideout)

During the pandemic, Jules Gray and her partner, Will, owners and operators of Hop Hideout, started doing deliveries. And, as she described above, they were often the only ones on the road: 'there was literally nobody about. You'd see the odd person or the odd delivery driver and that was it.' Sheffield sits on the edge of the Peak District, where over a million visitors come every year to take in the landscape and natural beauty. But during Covid, Gray told me, it was empty. As with those 16th-century Plague Orders, we were all in quarantine. Not leaving our houses, and certainly not visiting pubs.

Gray started Hop Hideout with Will in 2013 with around £5,000 from her own savings. Originally, they had a small space in an antique centre on Abbeydale Road, not far from Sheffield city centre. Business was good. Gray described it as a kind of pop-up, hidden among all the antiques. People would wander around the Victorian trunks and old ceramics, and in 'a little bit of a wondrous kind of surprise', they would find Hop Hideaway, an especially fitting name for such place. And what a lovely secret spot it was, with an array of Belgian beers and those from local craft breweries. But what made the location unique was that it was a bottle shop with a specific licence allowing customers to enjoy their brews on the premises, making it one of UK's first drink-in beer shops, if not *the* first. In 2015 they moved into a café space where they really flourished, with cask ale being served on draught alongside their selection of bottled beers from around the world (including a huge range of wild sour ales from Belgium).

Jules Gray, owner and director of Hop Hideout, festival manager of Sheffield Beer Week, festival manager of Indie Beer Feast, freelance writer and blogger.

Then in 2018 they were informed that their landlords would not be renewing their lease. Something that Gray says is a huge fear for small businesses throughout the country. Luckily, Gray found an opportunity to operate out of a food hall in Sheffield city centre. Here she was introduced to a new customer base, those who weren't necessarily familiar with craft beer and wanted to learn more, alongside her regular clientele of beer geeks. The future looked bright once more. And then along came Covid.

The food hall was shut down and, like everyone else, they had to wait in limbo for weeks, glued to the TV every evening to figure out what was going to happen. Gray and her partner followed SIBA, who were reporting on the changes to operations for pubs and breweries. Bottle shops were allowed to be open under the new guidelines, but for safety reasons Gray chose not to. They had another plan. Hop Hideout had created their website in 2015 and were doing some home deliveries. But with the advent of Covid, they jumped from doing about two or three deliveries a month to between 40 and 50 a week, a massive increase for such a small business. They didn't even have the keys to the food hall and could only be let in one day a week. It was on that one single day when they had to process all their orders for delivery, something that had now been made more complicated due to Covid regulations: 'We were sanitising all of the bottles and cans because obviously we were not wanting to spread anything. So things were taking twice as long.'

The Post-Pandemic Impact

Hop Hideout survived the lockdowns, but it faces new challenges in the form of the cost of living and energy crises. Gray doesn't pay a share of the energy bill for using the food hall; instead, she pays a licence fee and a percentage of her drinks sales. However, she is worried that when her contract comes up for renewal she may find herself facing a rent increase to make up for the hike in energy costs: 'Obviously I don't want them to go under. It's a big, costly business to run, but I've only got so much margin that I can invest back, and at the moment, with me working part-time and paying more out in wages, it's quite a difficult thing to balance.'

This is something she has noticed more and more. 'It's actually coming to a point for a lot of people where they can't make a living anymore.' In an article on *The Guardian* website on 18 September 2023, it was reported that 383 pubs had closed in the first six months of 2023, and 386 had closed in

2022. This data comes from Atlus, a commercial real estate analytics firm. Businesses are closing because of soaring energy prices, increased costs for supplies, and what Gray terms the 'ceiling' of what you can charge for a beer before customers forego it altogether. You can only build in a certain increase to your costs before it becomes entirely untenable and no longer makes sense to continue trading.

Gray reports that the years after the pandemic lockdowns have been the worst. Footfall is down because more people are working from home, so she isn't getting the same level of business that she once was. She has also found that because people now work from home more, they don't need to live in larger towns and cities. A study by the London Assembly Housing Committee in 2020 found that 46% of those who wanted to move, wanted to do so outside of the capital, compared with 43% who wanted to stay in London. Similarly, articles such as 'Londoners Leaving City in Droves as Covid Trends Persists', which appeared on Bloomberg.com in August 2022, seemed to support this notion that those who had the financial means to do so were fleeing the cities for the countryside. This is exactly what happened centuries previously during the Black Death. Those with sufficient financial or social status left crowded cities for the purported safety of rural life, leaving behind the very poor and marginalised to die. And though country villages were not immune to the spread of the disease, rural communities did, in general, experience lower levels of death than more populated urban environments. It was only later, after the bubonic plague had ended, that people would flock to the cities.

In today's Britain, people leaving the cities will, of course, reduce potential customers for pubs and breweries with taprooms who rely on a certain level of footfall in order to survive. Rightmove reported a rise of 126% in people wanting to move from cities to a rural location. The cities at the top of that list were London, Edinburgh, Birmingham, Sheffield, and Glasgow. Despite this, city life is still appealing for many, and more recent studies seem to indicate that buyers are back and interested once again in urban living, so this flight might have been a short-lived phenomenon. Perhaps, as in the aftermath of the Black Death, more people will move to the cities.

As we saw earlier, the demand for beer itself is declining. And because of this, the market is more competitive. Gray told me:

Let's be honest, during Covid, and I don't begrudge any business that did this, everyone launched an online web shop. We've gone from a small selection of places that you could buy beer online from to hundreds ... because pretty much every single brewery launched their own online shop.

Now Gray finds herself in direct competition with more of those breweries, many of whom only recently opened online sales. And as she says, there is nothing wrong with this, businesses are doing what they can to survive. The SIBA 2020 report suggested that a tougher trading environment coupled with increased online shopping and government policies would lead to a 'significant fall' in the smaller, independent hospitality sector. In 2022 Daniel Clarke of the University of Dundee's School of Business co-edited a book entitled, *Researching Craft Beer: Understanding Production, Community, and Culture in an Evolving Sector*. In it, he argued, that Covid did pose a big threat to brewers as it made community connections much more vital. This helped people, to some degree, who wanted to buy locally to mitigate against the coronavirus restrictions. The writers also stressed the increasing importance of social media to allow breweries to connect directly with these local customers.

This increased demand for a social media presence can be something that women, and others from marginalised communities, may find more difficult simply because they are statistically subject to more online harassment. A UK survey conducted in 2021 by The Rights of Women found that there has been an increase in harassment of women since Covid restrictions. And because the pandemic caused an increased need for social media presence, this could be detrimental to women in the trade.

How the Pandemic Hit Women Hardest

Globally, women experienced a larger negative economic impact from the pandemic than men. In fact, gender had more of an impact than age, education or rural/urban locality according to 'Gender and COVID-19: What have we learnt, one year later', by Carmen de Paz Nieves, Isis Gaddis and Miriam Muller, in a study for the World Bank Group. Women, especially those who are young, with disabilities, or members of other historically marginalised communities, also reported that they were 'significantly more likely than men to report increased financial precarity as a result of the crisis'. A survey conducted by Close the Gap and Engender, alongside one carried out in 2021 by the UK Women's Budget Group, Fawcett Society,

Women's Equality Network Wales, and Northern Ireland Women's Budget Group, concluded that Covid-19 had a disproportionate impact on women's wellbeing, mental health and financial security. Women reported to have received less support from their employers during lockdown and were twice as likely to say that their employer did not seem to support their wellbeing from the first lockdown.

It isn't just the pub owners who face increasing risks; it's also their workers. Hospitality, as we know, was a field particularly hard hit by the pandemic. It is also a field that employs a lot of women, many of whom found themselves out of a job. Eko Brewery's Adedipe noted that Covid shone a bright light on the way that we treat hospitality workers, and on the sector as a whole:

> But it's like somebody's sick. Come on, pay them. They have an appointment that they need to go to. So be a human being. You need it. They need it. Those are just basic things that you should afford your fellow human beings, right? Especially when someone works for you. So, I feel like a lot of those things came to light as well.

Among the many issues facing women workers that were highlighted by Covid was the fact that they bear the weight of childcare responsibilities. This was echoed by Drummond of Drop Bear, who told me that women are often the ones who take on most of the house and care work. And because of this, women then had to shoulder an even greater load in the home during lockdown. Drummond said: 'Someone needed to look after the children when they weren't allowed to go to school. And I'm not saying all the time, but a lot of the time it was the woman. So, women, even if they stayed employed, they had a lot more responsibility.'

This wasn't restricted to the hospitality industry. Emma Inch of *Fermentation Beer and Brewing Radio* noted that many women had to be responsible for home-schooling, 'And that was a horror, home-schooling was a horror that I hope we never have to go back to.' She told me that women with children might have found it much more difficult to maintain their working positions: 'Women do seem to suffer more in any economic kind of problems.' That survey carried out by Close the Gap and Engender – and mentioned previously – also found this to be true. Women were twice as likely to report less support from their employer in balancing childcare and work. This was echoed by Doreen Joy Barber, project manager at Five Points Brewing Company, who said that women are often the ones expected to take on the management of the household. So, when many people started working from home, it was mostly women who had to do their job on top of all the housework. This resulted in higher stress levels for women during the lockdowns as well as an increased strain on domestic relationships.

It follows that women who work in breweries or pubs would have found themselves with an increased level of stress by trying to manage both their households and their work. That is, if they were even able to maintain their roles through the pandemic and subsequent cost of living crisis. According to the SIBA 2020 report, women working in SIBA breweries made up to 26.1% of the workforce, up from 25.3% in their previous report, though only 11% were employed as brewers. The 2022 SIBA report noted that almost one in three employees in breweries were female, a rise from 26.1% to 30%. However, the percentage of women who were employed as brewers had dropped to 8%. So, we have a rise in the overall number of women workers, but a decrease in those employed as brewers. The same report noted that 26% of female staff worked in administration, with women making up of 62% of all administration staff, and that only 23% of all female staff were full-time.

Over and over again, we find women running social media pages, monitoring accounts, running the finance department or hosting events. As the statistics show us, marketing is incredibly popular with women. It is also way to get yourself involved in the beer industry even if you don't want to be the brewer. Joanne Love of *A Woman's Brew* podcast is an assistant events manager at BarthHaas X, the UK craft arm of BarthHaas, one of the largest hop growers and merchants in the world. Sarah Sinclair has worked at Moonwake Beer Company as a marketing and events manager since their inception. Having worked in the beer industry for over 15 years, Amélie Tassin is now the director of Tipple Marketing, an agency for food and drinks business. She helps breweries (and other businesses) develop a brand strategy, create their branding, and build their businesses online. Tassin describes herself as 'the Swiss Army knife of marketing. Every need they have I can do. They just need to ask, and I have the right tool'. And Doreen Joy Barber has worked for years in marketing roles at breweries throughout the UK, including freelance work for Beak Brewery, marketing and social media for Cloudwater, and various roles at Five Points, where she is currently working as Project Manager.

From their study, SIBA concluded that there was clear gender bias in brewing and that this perpetuated a gender divide. Will this be exacerbated by the coronavirus and the subsequent cost of living crisis? Possibly.

Amélie Tassin, founder of Women in Beer and Women in Beer Festival, founder and director of Tipple Marketing.

As Barber of Five Points noted, in the wake of Covid-19 breweries are cutting back on administrative and marketing departments. Departments, she told me, that are generally dominated by women. These are often the first roles to go when companies are trying to cut costs, so naturally, women will be most affected. In Barber's own experience of working during the pandemic she found that there was a shift from her defined role in social media and external event management to 'you must do everything you can to help this brewery survive'. In the wake of the pandemic the brewery was trying just about everything to keep afloat and so she was expected to become a jack of all trades. 'A lot of breweries don't really know what they want,' she says 'and it can be really hard to imagine what is successful when everybody's just running around like headless chickens.'

There are certainly some differences between women working today and their medieval counterparts. As we have seen, innovation and resilience by breweries has been one way to keep afloat in the wake of these many crises. And there is one avenue in particular that wasn't available to those women centuries ago: global networking. Elicia Gilreath is the founder and principal of Hops4Hire, an international career resource for the craft beer and beverage industry established in 2010. One of the services that Hops4Hire provides is personalised recruitment for craft breweries. Importantly, Gilreath has noted in recent years, and certainly in the wake of the pandemic, that her main clientele are women-owned or women-led craft beer businesses. She told me that 'women leaders tend to reach out and take a hands-on approach to hiring staff, which has resulted in better outcomes in both team engagement and tenure of new hire.' This reflects Gilreath's vision for a more diverse brewing world.

*   *   *

So, will women be pushed out of brewing in the wake of the pandemic? It's too soon to answer one way or the other, but we can make some guesses based on the data that we have. The most profitable and the biggest breweries in the UK are owned mostly by wealthy men, or groups of men. Breweries with women, or other historically marginalised people, at the helm are often more vulnerable because they do not have as much capital, or the same investment opportunities and reach of larger, sometimes multinational breweries. Simply put, they don't have access to the same resources. As Gray told me, those breweries that are most able to weather the continuing storms will be those with a 'big pot of money and those that are able to come up with other ways to make revenue'.

What we will likely see, and what we are already seeing, is a movement away from smaller businesses with less capital to larger breweries with more money. Was the pandemic to blame? At least partly. But other factors – what Roulet and Bothellod referred to as those cascading and disruptive events – such as the war in Ukraine driving up prices, and the current energy and cost of living crises, will continue to have an impact on who can survive. Those who cannot afford to ride the storm will be forced to shut unless some form of intervention takes place. And those who are more likely to shut are those without access to vast amounts of money, investment, or credit – that is, those from historically marginalised or less wealthy back-grounds, including women. Yes, innovation and resilience can possibly offer a way through, as Tolokazi Beer Company, Eko Brewery, Drop Bear Beer Company and Closet Brewing can demonstrate. Changing the way that you operate, as Hop Hideout did, by increasing online sales and deliveries, can also offer a solution in this ever-changing climate. However, you can't simply innovate your way out of systemic inequality.

2

RULES, REGULATIONS, AND HOW TO BLITHELY IGNORE THEM

When Talia Chain and her husband, Josh, decided to brew a beer for their wedding they followed the usual steps – they wrote their recipe, gathered the ingredients, mashed in, and waited for it to ferment. But they had to take one extra step many might not expect. They had the kosher authority come to their garage brewery to certify that the beer was, in fact, kosher. Chain told me: 'We had to all these signs everywhere in health and safety and all this hilarious stuff. And these very orthodox people came to see the garage beer and certified it so we could serve it.'

Since their days of homebrewing, they have adapted to slightly more salubrious surroundings and Chain is now the CEO of Sadeh Farm. *Sadeh* literally means 'field' in Hebrew, and it is quite a fitting name given its location in the rolling Kent countryside. The property itself, a 17th-century manor known as Skeet Hill House, has been an important cultural centre for the local Jewish community for decades. It was purchased in 1943 by the Jewish Youth Fund for the Brady Boys' Club – the first Jewish Boys' club in the UK, founded in 19th-century Whitechapel – in the wake of the Blitz as an escape for boys living in the East End of London. Many of them had never been outside the city, so going to the big manor house would be quite a change with many new things to learn, like rearing goats and growing your own food.

Talia Chain, CEO and founder of Sadeh Farm, the UK's first Jewish farm
and home to Lone Goat Brewing Company.

Nowadays at Sadeh Farm you can still learn about farming, but they can also teach you how to brew. The farm is home to Lone Goat Brewery, run by Josh and Talia, and, as with their wedding beer, everything is based on traditional Jewish practices. They grow their own hops, use farmhouse yeasts, and forage for other ingredients like nettles or elderflowers to use in their brews. This is important to Chain, she says, because Jewish people historically had been forcibly moved so often that it was difficult for them to practise their ancient farming traditions. And because these traditions had been recorded, it is now possible for her to implement them at her own farm. This, in turn, influences their brewing.

Chain introduced me to the concept of *simcha*, or joy. It's both a Jewish commandment and also an invitation to take joy in the everyday – in a beautiful flower, or what we are drinking and eating – and to be grateful for it. This juxtaposition of the spiritual and the mundane can take place in their brewing: 'we can make hops appear on a vine, and then turn them into beer, and that process is amazing and spiritual and practical and all those things together. I think Judaism is so good at taking the practical and spiritual and just having all sides of it.'

Jewish Brewing in Medieval Britain

Sadeh Farm is probably not the first example of Jewish brewing practice in Britain. We know Jewish people were consuming ale in medieval England. Pinchas Roth and Ethan Zadoff, in their 'The Talmudic Community of Thirteenth-Century England', argued that the medieval English Jewish community drank ale because wine was not produced locally in any great amount. Furthermore, there were too few Jewish people in England to import French wine regularly. Instead, the authors argued that 'most the year, they got by with beer,' or, more precisely, ale as we are talking about the un-hopped beverage. But that didn't stop their French neighbours from being concerned about potential Rabbinic Law violations of drinking this brew. In a later article, Roth found that some French Jewish religious men were deeply concerned about English ale being produced by Gentiles, as this led to drinking with Gentiles, and drinking wine with Gentiles was prohibited. In contrast, however, Roth found that Rabbi Elhanan ben Isaac declared there should be no limits on the consumption of ale because doing so might result in what he felt were harmful effects for those Jewish people living in England. Rabbi Elhanan was a Tosafist, a group of rabbi's living between the 12th and 15th centuries in France and Germany who wrote glosses on the Talmud, the primary text for Jewish religious law, so he would have certainly been an expert in this matter.

We can see that Jewish people in England were drinking beer in the medieval period, but what about brewing? The article mentioned above tells us that Jewish people often bought their beer from the local Christian community, hence the fear of drinking alongside them, but it's possible that this was not their only means of getting their beverage of choice. The *Select pleas, stars, and other records from the rolls of the Exchequer of the Jews, A.D. 1220–1284* listed a mandate by King Henry III, issued in 1271, whereby, amongst other things, the king declared, 'Touching persons in the employ of Jews as nurses of children, bakers, brewers and cooks, since Jews and Christians differ in faith, We have provided and decreed, that no Christian man or woman presume to serve them in the said offices.'

Once again, we can find clues as to who may have been brewing through the study of contemporary regulations, and those who flouted them. In this case, we are told that Christians could not serve as brewers in Jewish households, which might have forced those in the Jewish community to become their own brewers. However, we do know that many people flaunted this rule. For example, Licoricia of Winchester, an incredibly wealthy Jewish woman in her own right in the 12th century, was found stabbed to death alongside her Christian servant woman. Furthermore, if there were Jewish people brewing in this period, I would argue that it's quite likely that they were probably women.

Historically, women brewed elsewhere in Jewish communities, and this can be traced to biblical times. Jennie R. Ebeling and Michael M. Homan, in *Baking and Brewing Beer in the Israelite Household: A Study of Women's Cooking Technology*, argued that baking and brewing were deeply connected and that women gained power through this connection. Further, they found that women were the primary brewers in Israelite households. It was part of their domestic duties, an important task, in fact, and closely related to sustaining their families. Could this tradition have carried on through the centuries and in England? The sources seem to suggest a possible yes, though the evidence is scarce.

However, whether Henry's law compelled Jewish women to brew for themselves or not, it leads us to the central theme of the chapter – rules, regulations, and how to blithely ignore them. Brewing women have, for centuries, been subject to a variety of laws designed to keep them honest – or keep them out of business. Through these laws, the government tried to keep brewing under some kind of control. Later, licensing would come into play with mixed results and varied enforcement. But the point to keep in mind is that no matter the laws, while some women would be able to play within the rules, others would sometimes accidently, and sometimes very much on purpose, break them.

Women Fought the Law...
and Sometimes Won

We all love an underdog. We root for the ones who don't quite get a fair shake. We grew up on tales of Robin Hood and his Merry Men, who out-manoeuvred the corrupt Sheriff of Nottingham and saved the starving people of that city. These kinds of stories have left a profound imprint on the way we view the world. And what do we like more than the story of a rebellious woman who told the world precisely where they can shove their notions?

Often histories of brewing women create stories of alewives pitted against the powers that be. But real life often isn't so straightforward and history is, in many ways, a grey area. The records of medieval brewing are full of cases of women who fought against regulations and tighter controls. In 13th-century Ravenesfeud (in present-day West Yorkshire), Juliana brewed and sold her ale in direct violation of the local assize, the standard by which ale is meant to be brewed and sold. When the local aletasters, those men appointed to taste the locally brewed ale and set the price, confronted her about this, the records stated that she said, 'she would sell ale against the will of them and of the bailiffs, in despite of the Earl'. Basically, that she's going to go ahead and do what she wants. She was fined 12 pence, and because of her antics the whole town found themselves in hot water. The next entry shows that the entire township of Normanton was fined four shillings as punishment for hiding the fact that they had covered up for Juliana and others who brewed against the regulations. These aren't particularly large fines, but they do send a message. Though our first instincts may be to applaud Juliana for sticking it to the man, there was a reason for these regulations, at least in theory; to prevent customers getting ripped off. Of course, in practice they could be used by those in charge to force certain people out of the industry. The authorities were, after all, corruptible. However, that said, some of those fined could very well be happily cheating their customers and defying regulations simply because it suited them to do so, whether driven by greed or a desire to just do what they wanted.

Blithely ignoring the laws, deliberately, or unintentionally, breaking them, and blatantly sticking a middle finger up at the enforcers when caught was not beyond the bounds of possibility in medieval and 16th-century England. Judith Bennett's exhaustive study has proved this, so there is no need to go into too much detail here, though one further example is worth mentioning. According to *The History of the Country of Cambridge and the Isle of Ely*, we are told that the abbey's court was usually responsible for handling various civil and criminal matters, including those pertaining to alewives and enforcing the assize. Apparently, in 1435 the court amerced an alewife for making ale with bad water. And another in 1440 for removing her ale-stake while still having ale left to sell to customers. An ale-stake is a pole (or stake) often accompanied by a kind of garland or bush at the end of it, that was hung outside an alehouse to let people know ale was available for sale inside. We can see here in these abbey court records that the religious court oversaw the local women brewers and kept things in line. But like their Jewish counterparts, medieval Christians also placed a high importance on ale, not just in their secular lives but also in their houses of worship. In fact, ale was a critical part of the daily diet for religious communities.

*   *   *

At Ankerwyke Priory in 1441, the prioress, Dame Clemence Medforde, and her nuns were just not getting along. Dame Clemence accused the nuns of being generally up to no good and drinking to excess almost every day. The house itself was in peril as, apparently, some six nuns had left it in apostasy. The nuns countered that the prioress was the problem, stirring up all kinds of trouble and behaving badly. They also alleged that she had been getting up to shenanigans with the priory's receipts, as well as dressing very expensively and dripping in gold and precious stones. Among their grievances were issues regarding the brewhouse and ale in general. The nuns reported that there were no serving people in the brewhouse from the festival of the Nativity of St John the Baptist (24 June) in the previous year all the way until Michaelmas (29 September) the following year. Things were so bad, in fact, that Dame Juane Messangere complained that she and her sisters had to prepare the ale and food themselves and serve the other nuns. The absolute *horror* of it all.

The priory was given some rules to obey in order to prevent such a thing happening again. The list of injunctions was large, and most fell under pain of excommunication. If you died without it being repealed, you would find yourself damned to hell for all eternity, so, in theory, it was a severe malediction only to be used in the direst of cases. In practice, people got excommunicated for upsetting the wrong people, or as Rosalind Hill found, in the case of the entire deanery of 14th-century Newport Pagnell, hiding a runaway falcon. Perhaps unsurprisingly, the church was very much susceptible to corruption. More to the point, these new rules included a few relating directly to ale and brewing, specifically that the prioress had to provide sufficient meat and drink for her sisters. Additionally, under that same pain of excommunication, they were to have 'an honest woman servant' in their brewhouse, as well as in the kitchen and dairy house. And we already know that servant women were brewing and helping in the brewhouse, and that these roles were held, and supervised, by women.

Not everyone could brew and live a religious life, of course. In Sir David Lyndesay's *c.*1535 *Ane Satyre of the Thrie Estaits*, a different prioress tells readers that it is better to marry a good man and brew good ale than to take up the veil:

> Bot I sall do the best I can,
> And marie sum gude honest man,
> And brew gude aill and tun.
> Mariage, be my opinioun,
> It is better Religioun.

Many women *did* brew and live a religious life. In 1438 Margary Kempe, a famous Christian mystic, wrote in her aptly titled work, *The Book of Margery Kempe*, that her servants taught her to brew. At first, she was fairly good at it. In fact, she says she rose to be one of the best brewers in town. But she got greedy, and she was too inexperienced. She tells us that her servants were very knowledgeable, but when she went to brew, 'the head would fall away, and all the ale would be lost one brew after another'. Things got so bad that her servants became embarrassed and left, so she stopped brewing altogether.

*   *   *

Sadeh Farm shows us that the links between the past and present aren't so very far away. They use ancient traditions to inform their practices, carrying on traditional, millennia-old farming techniques, which would have also been available to their medieval counterparts. Equally, they demonstrate the importance between brewing beer and the links with religion. As our Christian and Jewish medieval communities demonstrated, beer was critical to their maintenance, while also playing an important part in their actual customs. But though there are many similarities between the modern practices and historical traditions, there are some clear differences. I don't think many brewers these days would get away with giving the two-fingered salute to HM Revenue and Customs, for example. But breaking regulations, although perhaps not quite in the dramatic way Juliana did, was quite common. So common, in fact, that some scholars have argued that these fines in England were more like a tax; a cost of doing business if you will. But what of Scotland and Wales? Were things very different there?

Regulations in Scotland and Wales

According the *Liber Albus*, the first book of English Common Law, women faced fines of 40 pence at the first offence of serving ale in the incorrect measurement, then an increased fine to half a mark in the second (approximately 6½ shillings), rising finally to 20 shillings. *The York Civic Ordinances 1301* stated that the measure would be burned if any brewer or alewife sold by some false measure, against the assize. Scholars like Elizabeth Ewan and Nicholas Mayhew have contended that in Scotland the fines were much more serious, and, therefore, intended to be proper penalties.

As in England, women dominated the brewing industry in Scotland in the medieval period and into the early modern era. We know this because the regulations clearly spell it out. The *Leges Quatour Burgiorum*, covering Berwick, Edinburgh, Roxburgh and Stirling, was created under the reign of King David I *c.*1124-1154. Here, the law referred only to women, those who 'brew ale to sell'. The alewife was instructed to brew according to the custom of the town, and if she failed to do so, on the first offence she was suspended from the trade for a year and a day. If she again made 'evil ale' then she was fined eight shillings or put on the cuckstool and the ale divided between the poor people of the town and the local hospital. A cuckstool, or later ducking stool (though this is a specific subtype), was a chair used in the punishment of – especially – women, but also tradesmen. Some were simple chairs, while others could be larger devices used to dunk the victim in water. They were used as a form of humiliation, with the guilty party strapped to them and paraded around the town, or left outside their home, or even set up where the offence allegedly took place.

The Aberdeen Council Registers is a series of volumes regarding the legalities and inner workings of the city of Aberdeen. It has recently been digitised through painstaking work. It is a wonderful resource which I cannot recommend highly enough if you have any interest at all in the history of brewing in Scotland. Everything about Aberdeen in the early modern period will have come from this resource.

In 1511 *The Aberdeen Registers* lists the names of all the people in the town's four quarters who brewed for profit. Of the 136 names listed, 135 are women (the one ambiguously identified man is only known as 'the maltman'). Many of these women are only referred to as the wife or widow of so and so, which reflects the legal practice of coverture, whereby married women were subsumed legally under their husbands' names. But still, 135 women were brewing in Aberdeen in 1511. As elsewhere, the regulations for brewing were clearly set out to prevent cheating and nefarious behaviour. The assize was strictly set and enforced by the aletasters (who were mentioned previously), and the penalties for violating these measures could be quite severe. Women could have their brewing equipment destroyed, or could be banned from the business altogether. However, this did not stop Scottish women from thumbing their noses at the regulations and doing whatever they wanted. Records of such illegal shenanigans were also included in the *Aberdeen Registers*.

We do have to wonder how just how strictly enforced these bans and penalties were. A close examination of those women who found themselves in hot water with the aletasters reveals some serial offenders. In 1506/07 the wife of Androw Louson was convicted at least five times of brewing ale contrary the common ordinance, including selling false measures. In theory, she should have been barred from brewing, or at least had her equipment destroyed, but just how much of a deterrent these punishments were is highly debatable. Many of the women I found were repeat offenders. In 1493 the wife of James Strathathin, sometimes also called Ebe Raneson, was charged on no fewer than seven occasions with breaking the brewing laws. But this didn't seem to stop her as she was still listed amongst the brewers in 1511. The wife of Cristy Prat is another one frequently in trouble, appearing in the *Aberdeen Registers* six times, while Margaret Litstar runs afoul four times, and the wife, later widow, of Richerd Waus was convicted multiple times of breaking the assize. The list goes on and on … and on.

But women brewers didn't limit themselves to violating the assize. There was also the old trick of selling in false measures. On 28 March 1506 some 25 women were convicted of selling in false measures, and on 14 January 1510 all the brewsters from three of the towns' quarters were convicted of violating the assize and common ordinance and selling ale at a higher price than permitted. This was again the case, for all the town's brewers, on 16 April 1510, and throughout that year.

It wasn't just married women or widows who brewed; single women are also present in the *Aberdeen Registers*, though in much smaller numbers.

Katherin Wrquhard is a particularly interesting case. She is mentioned on three occasions as breaking the assize or brewing and selling for more than set down in the ordinances. She is also included on the list of brewers in 1511, on her own, which, in all probability, makes her a single woman. We can assume that she was not a widow, because widowed women are listed as such. Another single woman, Canny Waus, was also convicted of breaking the common ordinances multiple times. Like Katherine, she still appears on the list of brewers in 1511, so perhaps this was not a huge deterrent. Canny and Katherine were, however, exceptions to the general rule; single women were vastly outnumbered by married women in the brewing trade.

In fairness to our alewives, breaking the assize was not particularly difficult, and, in many cases, was unavoidable. As Judith Bennett pointed out, in England, keeping up with these regulations might have been difficult for women without access to proper measures and equipment, so much of the so-called cheating could have been inadvertent. It was also, as Bennett has argued, hard to enforce these regulations (though that didn't stop the authorities from trying).

In medieval Wales, finding records of brewing women proves much more difficult than Scotland or England, simply because very few documents have survived. According to Llinos Beverly Smith in 'In Search of an Urban Identity: Aspects of Urban Society in Late Medieval Wales', while efforts were made to create brewing monopolies in urban centres, unofficial markets still flourished. Most importantly for our purposes, Smith argued that women continued to dominate the brewing trade in late medieval Wales. This was echoed by Deborah Youngs in 'The Townswomen of Wales: Singlewomen, Work and Service, c.1300–c.1550'. She found that for Welsh women in this period, victualing and brewing were the most common ventures easily available, with women dominating the trade and helping out their families by providing extra income. As we saw in England, she argued that widows, married women, and single women all participated in the trade, but married women were in the majority. Youngs also contended that brewing was favoured by wealthy women.

That brewing was a preferred activity for wealthy women has been argued by other scholars. There is a set of court rolls from Dyffryn Clwyd, a Marcher Lordship covering 15 miles and encompassing Denbighshire (aka medieval Ruthin), which may grant us more insight. Matthew Frank Stevens was able to examine these sources specifically for women who brewed in Ruthin (a town of about 600 people) from 1294–1654 and his conclusions are a fascinating glimpse into what brewing life might have been like, with women dominating the industry. He found these women – as we have in England and Scotland – when they ran afoul of the regulations. He isn't the only scholar to notice this link. Lizabeth Johnson, in her study of sex workers in late medieval Wales, found that in Ruthin by the end of the 1400s brewing was still an important industry, one where women still operated in large numbers, and certainly amongst those who engaged in concubinage. In 1418 the Great Court of Ruthin records that Joan, concubine of Geoffery, was a brewing woman who broke the assize of ale and was fined three pence. Returning to Stevens' study, he concluded that wealthy women controlled the markets, especially in famine times, though women from other socio-economic groups did offer competition when times weren't quite as lean. This must mean that profits from brewing could be healthy, which challenges our idea from Chapter One that much of brewing was poorly paid work in the pre-plague medieval period. It clearly was not. In fact, it was a desirable role in some contexts, and one that wealthy women took pride in taking on. And taking over.

So, who was responsible for deciding that these women broke the law? This was the job of the aletasters, who set the regulations on how beer was to be made and enforced them. What they didn't do, as popular myth would claim, was sit in soggy trousers sticking to benches to magically determine good beer. Instead, they decided if the ale was good in the time-honoured and proven way: they drank it. In the medieval period, this was an almost entirely male profession (Judith Bennett did find one example of a female aletaster in England but I have not been able to locate one in Wales or Scotland thus far), and it would remain male dominated for centuries.

In our modern world we don't have men running around people's houses and pubs tasting all the beer, making sure it's brewed to their assize standard, and destroying brew kit and issuing fines if not. And though we do have Untappd reviewers and beer bloggers who might picture themselves in that role, we are, thankfully, a long way from that. We do, however, have quality control officers and beer inspectors working for breweries to make sure their brews are up to standard. This has certainly been a role that includes women, at least from the 20th century onwards. For example, in September 1974 Pauline Hunt of the *Cambridge Daily News* interviewed Fiona McNish, a 21-year-old working as a beer taster at Paine & Co of St Neots, sharing with readers some of her beer knowledge and closing with relating Fiona's penchant for 'real ale'. And one of our interviewees,

Annabel Smith, co-founder of Dea Latis, a women's networking and research group, was, at one time, the only woman beer inspector for Cask Marque, a non-profit trust for brewers, ensuring that the quality of cask ale is up to scratch. Contrary to what happened historically, most beer inspectors now officially work in-house for brewers, judging the beer quality at the pubs

Annabel Smith, co-founder of Dea Latis and passionate beer educator, Beer Sommelier, and a director for the *British Guild of Beer Writers*.

themselves, though local government health and safety inspectors do also play an important role in this process. But centuries before we had quality control departments, the existence of aletasters was one of the ways in which women could be held to a certain standard of brewing. Another would unfold as the years went by: the introduction of licensing.

Licensed to Brew

Intoxicants and Early Modernity: England, 1580–1740 is a collaborative research project between the University of Sheffield's Department of History, the Victoria and Albert Museum, and the Digital Humanities Institute at Sheffield. The project has compiled hundreds of primary sources relating to intoxicants and intoxication. Searching through these records, I was able to locate many women who brewed, some of whom were certainly poor, or at least had now become so. The examples given below of women petitioning for licences are sourced from this archive, unless stated otherwise.

When Jane Smith's husband, Adam, got locked up in Lancaster gaol, she turned to brewing to support herself. In 1646 she petitioned to be granted a licence to brew so that she could feed herself and her four small children while also being able to provide some relief for her imprisoned spouse. She asked the justices if they would grant her a licence until the next assizes, when she hoped her husband would be released.

For so many, brewing was a relatively easy way to earn income and did not require a massive investment. It was, therefore, an effective way for many women to keep poverty at bay. That is, if their licences were granted in the first place, or were not subsequently revoked. If we look at the granting of these licences, we can find evidence of interference, particularly by men, with women's abilities to provide for themselves and their families.

Licensing came into effect, officially, on a national level in England and Wales in the 16th century. According to a 1522 Act, only those who had consent of the local Justices of the Peace were able to sell ale and beer. To get this permission they had to enter into an agreement to maintain a good reputation, good behaviour, and abide by certain rules, otherwise they might be fined, or lose their licence. According to the *Glamorgan Calendar Rolls and Gaol Files: 1542–94*, Margaret Collyns of Roth was charged in 1585 for selling ale, likely without a licence. In 1584 the very aptly named Dionysia, wife of Thomas Wyndham of Cardiff, was charged, along with six others, with selling beer, again likely without a proper licence. It was not a new idea for those that brewed to require licences; it was merely the nationalisation of an already existing local process, and an attempt to create a central licensing system.

We have seen from the Welsh records that brewing could be profitable for wealthy citizens, but it was also a way for the poor and disenfranchised, especially women, to sustain themselves well into the 17th century. According to the *Corporation of Lincoln Registers*, a law was enacted on 3 May 1628 which stated that no one could keep an alehouse or tippling house except 'freemen', and that those who had a licence could not have it renewed when it expired until they purchased their freedom. However, on 27 April the following year, this was changed to some degree:

> for that it appeareth that divers poor men and widows, not freemen,
> have no other means of livelihood but by keeping of alehouses,
> it is agreed that such as shall be approved by the justices may be
> re-admitted, but that none hereafter be newly admitted until they
> be first sworn freemen.

In 1628 an appeal was made by Susan Lunt, who used to brew but had somehow lost her licence. She tells us that, after being abandoned by her husband, she brewed and kept an alehouse in Deansgate in Manchester to provide for herself and her three small children. She brewed 'without any charge to the town,' but was ordered to stop, so then petitioned for a licence to continue brewing and provide for her children. It is a desperate appeal, and the language seems distraught. She is in danger of not being able to sustain herself if she doesn't start bringing in money.

Women such as Susan Lunt who found themselves in untenable situations turned to brewing as a way to make money. This was how many women saved themselves from destitution. Another petition, from 14 January 1650, made by the Widow Rosbotham in Ashton-in-Makerfield, Lancashire, tells us that her husband died recently of sickness and that she has been in great misery since. She has no estate to help her and so asks to be granted a licence to brew and bake to sustain herself and her child.

While brewing was perhaps accessible for women, it was not without its perils. According to the coroner's reports compiled by Steven Gunn from the 16th century, accidents around the mash tun could prove fatal. In 1546 Edith Randell, Dorset, was brewing beer in her house when she 'fell asleep by the oven and suddenly her head and part of her body slipped into boiling water so that she was suffocated and drowned'. In 1571 Clemency Cox was brewing beer for her employer. She was pouring water from a one vessel into the copper when she slipped and fell into the mash vat full of scalding water. She languished for several days before succumbing to her injuries. Jane Dowe, in 1538, also fell into the mash vat and was scalded and died.

Regardless of the dangers, women still petitioned to brew, sometimes because they had no alternative due to their age or disability. Cicely Collier, a widow from Shaving Lane in Worsley, filed a petition in 1655 stating that she was 85 years old, and, because of her age, had not been able to work and had fallen on hard times. She asked for permission to brew, sell ale or beer, and to provide lodging and victuals to travellers in her home. She specifically requested this avenue of income because it was an accessible job she could do regardless of her age or infirmities.

From Collier's petition, we can assume that her age has given her some form of disability that inhibits her capacity to work in other jobs. Brewing, and accommodating people in her home, would, therefore, be a viable option for her. Brewing was an obvious choice for women in this position, if they were granted the rights to do so. It was something that they knew how to do, and they already had the necessary equipment. The idea of age potentially creating disabilities that prevented women from finding other work is clearly apparent in the sources.

When I tell people that elderly women with disabilities turned to brewing centuries ago as a way to make a living, most are slightly shocked. I don't think many of us would consider brewing commercially as particularly accessible to elderly women with disabilities, even with our modern technology. As Doreen Joy Barber told me, 'you have to be … like Hercules … to lift a 20-kg malt sack over your head'. Originally from the US, having been born in the Philippines and grown up for some time in Japan, Barber came to the UK to do a Master's of Anthropology of Food. She then worked in pubs for a while before landing her first brewery gig at Five Points Brewing Company. She has worked in the brewing industry for years, and has found herself in various roles in the brewing industry at places like Cloudwater and working behind the bar at local pubs like the Jolly Butcher. She returned to Five Points as project manager in 2023. In other words, she knows what she's talking about.

When we think of commercial brewing, we might picture those huge sacks of malt having to be lifted up into giant metal containers. This doesn't quite fit with something 85-year-old Collier could be getting up to in her spare time. But if we remove our modern conceptions, things begin to

Doreen Joy Barber, project manager at Five Points Brewing Company, and experienced event management, marketing and communications professional in the craft beer industry.

change. Instead of huge stainless-steel mash tuns, picture a stove top with a pot, and instead of huge bags of malt, picture a woman carrying only what she needs, much like modern homebrewing. This is not to say that it wasn't hard work. Any homebrewer will tell you stove-top brewing has its own difficulties, but it was not quite as physical as we envision brewing today. Which is why it offered a way out of poverty for many women.

Collier's petition to save herself was not an isolated incident. In 1667 Dorothy Hall, also a widow, from Heap in Lancashire, had people petitioning on her behalf for similar reasons. Apparently, some people had conspired to ruin her out of sheer malice, simply because they didn't like her. We are told that Hall had spent most of her life caring for her mother, but that during this time she 'lived honestly and in good repute' by brewing and selling ale from a house that she rents. If she is not granted a further licence to sell and brew ale, she won't be able to pay her landlord. Like Collier, she stated in her petition that she was an old woman, and 'by reason of the infirmities that accompany old age she is not able to take pains as formerly, and so is altogether void of any means for her subsistence, and likely to fall into extreme want'. Once more, brewing is seen as the type of work that is accessible to those experiencing some kind of disability due to old age or otherwise.

*   *   *

Today, we still have some way to go to making the brewing industry an accessible place to work. Nidhi Sharma of Meantime Brewing Company told me that just communicating that brewing is an option for people is an important first step. Lynsey Campbell, a long-time commercial brewer, said that automation may help the industry become more accessible; while Barber asserted that it is important for breweries to make themselves accessible to neurodivergent people. Additionally, Barber stressed the importance of accessability for people with learning disabilities, something she personally advocates for, bringing in a member of Mencap to talk to the Friends & Family & Beer Industry Expo after listening to the wonderful brewer Jaega Wise speaking with one of their workers on this topic. She told me that there are a lot of opportunities for part-time work:

> it'll give people in the community who don't often get jobs ...
> a means of employment. Something that they can be proud of,
> because not having a job, as I know, can be a really significant
> blow in this capitalistic society where a lot of people identify
> themselves with their workplace.

This echoes the arguments put forth by Cicely Collier and Dorothy Hall. They wanted a job to be able to pay their bills; to be able to afford to live. People with disabilities are often not paid the same as their non-disabled colleagues. Prior to the coronavirus 52.3% of people with some form of disability were working, with a pay gap of 28.8% compared to non-disabled workers. This gap has increased due to Covid. Some breweries have been stepping up to acknowledge this lack of accessibility; Ignition Brewery in South London hires and trains people with learning disabilities how to brew, and, most importantly, pays their workers the Living Wage.

As we can see from the historical records, women with disabilities sought licences to brew in order to keep themselves afloat. But getting a licence wasn't always straightforward. In some instances, men stepped in to try and prevent women from getting them altogether.

In 1667 Anne Core petitioned to be allowed to keep an alehouse and brew. Core had been in the business for years, selling and brewing ale in her orderly house. That is, until Nicholas Halliwell flew into a rage and decided to try and ruin her life. Core had lent Halliwell some money, but, naturally, he never paid it back. When Core brought a suit against him to recoup her missing funds, an incensed Halliwell decided to retaliate by embarking on a one-man crusade to 'suppress' her, that is, prevent her from keeping her alehouse. So, he attacked her character and maligned her business. As we have learned, the reputation of the women who kept these alehouses was crucial. Halliwell took his false charges to the magistrate to prevent Core from gaining her licence. But she would not be deterred. She asked the magistrates to take into account that the charges against her had no grounds other than 'malice and desire of revenge, as is very well known to the entire neighbourhood'. She was able to provide witnesses to prove that Halliwell was just an angry, entitled man bent on revenge because she asked him to pay back the money he owed.

Not all the examples, however, were so blatantly ridiculous. Women could keep alehouses that didn't have, shall we say, the best reputation. There are plenty of examples, but one of the more interesting ones involves Katherine Blomiley of Chorlton and the two men, John Harrison and Joshua Taylor, who took up against her in 1656. They wanted the justices to revoke her licence and deem her unfit to brew. They wrote to inform the justices of the 'miscarriages' that she had committed. These include not having stabling for horses, and providing accommodation for humans that is not 'convenient'. Worst of all, she serves booze on Sundays, including during sermon times, until people are wasted drunk instead of attending church. This was a serious offence at the time, one that would continue to be so throughout the 19th century. The rest of the charges could be laid at the door of many a modern nightclub:

she hath entertained gamesters at unlawful hours; she hath entertained thieves and vagabonds; she hath had stolen goods found in her hands; she hath entertained persons and granted them liberty to drink in her house till they have been so distempered that they have fought and wounded each other; she hath kept music at unseasonable times; her mother-in-law being dead in the house yet her revelling ceased not; she was once by your worships fined ... but the business was so carried by Richard Heawood of Withington Churchwarden that she was rather encouraged rather than discouraged to offend again; she hath concealed poor labouring men when their poor wives and children with weeping eyes have come to enquire for them and hath by ill words and throwing of fire at them abused some of them.

It must be said, however, that not stopping the party when her dead mother-in-law lay within was probably an unwise decision.

Katherine did not take these charges lying down and spoke up in her own defence. She began by telling the justices that her husband was a soldier under the command of Captain James Scholfield and was faithful to Parliament during 'the time of these late unhappy wars'. Her husband had since died, leaving her a widow and having to care for her three small children. She explains that the trades are 'decaying' and that there is 'very little to be gotten with work', so she decided to brew ale and beer to sell, for which she was arrested and sent to jail. She was then released until her father, Robert Wild, was granted a licence to brew and employed her as brewer, seller and deliverer of the ale. So, basically, her dad got the licence, but she was the one doing all the work. In any event, she tells us that she just wanted to provide for herself and her children, but, because a warrant had been issued for her arrest she was forced 'to flee for security and her poor children'.

As we shall see in the later chapters, men sometimes sought to interfere with the ability of women to brew or work in breweries, and also to work in and run alehouses. This can be attributed in part to the deep-seated sexism in society, but also because of personal grievances. It should be noted that, in some cases, women were in direct competition for jobs with men, some of whom resorted to extreme measures to remove them, often exploiting sexist societal norms that dictated women's behaviour. That is not to say that some of these charges weren't true – cheating customers or selling false measures did take place – but men got up to the same things.

Regulations, as many scholars like Bennett have argued, were applied more strictly to women, for no other reason than, by and large, men were simply wealthier, had better connections, had a more privileged position in society, and more authority.

In Wales, brewing was also a way for poor women to sustain themselves well into the 19th century, though regulations made this increasingly difficult. In Wilma R. Thomas' thesis, 'Women in the rural society of south-west Wales, c.1780–1870', she discusses at length the practice of *cwrw bach*, literally meaning small beer, whereby a person – often a woman – brewed and sold ale out of their house to raise money for those in greatest need. Thomas found several examples, including William Rees' daughter, who, after she was abandoned by her child's father, got her friends together to brew ale to raise some money for her. In this way, brewing for women in Wales could be a communal event designed to support each other. And it wasn't just women who gathered round in times of hardship. Couples would brew beer to sell at their wedding, according to Thomas. She found an instance of one woman in Solva who illegally brewed her beer for just that purpose. But brewing for your wedding isn't some lost, ancient custom, as we saw in our story about Sadeh Farm.

*   *   *

We'll finish this chapter with one of my favourite literary cases: the story of Puggy, the ale-drinking cow, the lawsuit an alewife brought against her, and how all this related to long-standing Scottish customs. The 17th-century work entitled *Northern Memoirs* contains this lively tale told between two characters, Theophilius and Arnoldus. The story starts by introducing our lead character, the 'ancient Brewster wife', who was the best ale brewer in the town of Forfar. But it was just after she had brewed 'a cauldron of stinging stuff' for some 'jolly good fellows' that things go epically sideways.

As a busy woman, our excellent alewife trusted her maid, Moggy, to mind the coolers, open air vessels where she put the ale she had just made to 'ripen and prepare it for a present Draught', which sounds like she puts them there to ferment, and similar to processes used in making lambic-style Belgian ales. Unfortunately, our maid, Moggy, got a tiny bit distracted. Enter Puggy the cow, who was completely overwhelmed by the lovely smells coming from the ale coolers, and lost control:

and the poor cow as if invaded by some feverish Indisposition, and because knowing no Law of Limitation, seem'd wholly uncapable to satisfy herself, so long as any Ale was left in the Cooler; for she drank, and puff'd, and then took Wind, and too't again, so long, and so oft, till at last she surveyed the Dimensions of the Tub, where the Liquor in a short time was almost consumed.

So Puggy drank the ale down to the last drop. Which caused Theo and Arnaldo to discuss what made the cow drink it all. Was she just thirsty or was it something unnatural? In any event, the alewife was incredibly angry and attacked the unfortunate Puggy. The cow, having drunk so much she couldn't move a muscle, was forced to bear the brunt of the assault. At this point, Puggy's owner, Billy Pringle, entered the scene. He attempted save Puggy from the alewife, but only served to enrage her further and she turned on him 'like George at the Dragon'. The argument apparently created such a stir that spectators gathered and there was a risk of a riot. Things got so out of hand that the provost intervened and told the alewife to take her case to court.

So now we have the legal case of Alewife v. Puggy. The alewife pushed for satisfaction, but there was no precedent for punishing a cow for drinking ale 'sitting or standing', and more to the point, it was remarked that Puggy 'never call'd for't, and *Doh and Doris* is the Custom of our Country; Where note, a standing-Drink was never yet paid for'. 'Doh and Doris' here is *Deoch-an-doris*, meaning 'drink of the door', which is a custom of providing guests with one drink, free of charge, before they head off to wherever they are going. So, if Puggy was standing when she was drinking and didn't ask for the beer, well, that's her free *Deoch-an-doris*. And so it fell to the provost to solve the matter. He asked the alewife:

how the Cow took the Liquor, whether she took it sitting, or if she took it standing? To which the Brewster-Wife, after a little pause, answered, by making this reply; In guid fa Sir, quo the Wife, the Cow took it standing. Then, quo the Provost, your e'en words condemn ye, to seek Satisfaction for a standing-Drink. This annihilates the Custom of *Doh and Doris*. For truly sike another ill Precedent as this, were enough to obliterate so famous a Custom, as stark Love and Kindness for evermare. Where note, guid Wife, ye have wronged Billy Pringle, for prosecuting the guid Man contrary to Law; and have done mickle Damage to Puggy his Cow, because to chastise her but for a standing-Drink.

Basically, the provost asked the alewife if Puggy was drinking the ale sitting or standing. The alewife replied that cow was standing, to which the provost then exclaimed that she has condemned herself by her own words, and began to berate her for ignoring the practice of *Deoch-an-doris*, which is a sign of love and kindness. How dare she think herself so above the customs of the land. Furthermore, the alewife had done much damage to poor Puggy when the cow was clearly just having one for the road.

I love the story of poor Puggy. I think it demonstrates that some alewife stories were told with levity and sarcasm and were meant to be shared and understood with humour. Unfortunately for our alewives, this wasn't always the case. Our next chapter will take a closer look at how brewing women were depicted in art and literature; how they were often maligned and represented as unsavoury characters engaging in all sorts of unscrupulous activities. Some have argued this might have had more sinister consequences for women in society as a whole, leading to some being executed for witchcraft. But is this true?

The image of Mother Louse (pictured here) is often used as evidence to support the alewife-as-witch argument (see p.68).

CHAPTER

3

THIS BEER
CAN KILL YOU

When you think of damnation, what do you envision? Fiery pits with a plethora of demons cackling manically as they torment lost souls? A deep, empty oblivion, dark and choking; perpetuity spent abandoned to decay, our only companion the relentless nothingness? In Irish Christian folklore, we are told that heaven might involve beer, a giant lake of it to be precise, presided over by one of the most famous brewers from that country, Saint Brigid. In English, Welsh, and Scottish theology, however, the alewife might find herself in that other place: Hell. Brewing women are often depicted in the very depths of that eternal inferno. In both literary portrayals and artistic works, alewives are found cavorting with the devil, bound in holy matrimony with demons, and generally getting up to no good; though, in fairness, many of them seem to be having the best time.

One of my favourite examples of the alewife-with-demon motif is found in St Laurence's Church in Ludlow. Here, among the vaulted ceilings and beautiful stained-glass work is a misericord, which is a 'mercy seat' meant to help someone long at prayer take a bit of a rest. Created between 1425 and 1447, it's one of 28 to be found around the church. This one, though, is rather remarkable. It features a naked alewife with an elaborate horned headdress waving an ale mug being carted off to Hell while serenaded by a bagpipe-playing demon. Alewives were also often depicted in doom paintings in England, such as those at Holy Trinity Church in Coventry and St Thomas's Church in Salisbury. Norwich Cathedral is host to a carving of another naked alewife happily perched atop a wheel-barrow-carting demon. In context, these artworks would have been understood as a warning to those who might venture down the wrong path, but to our modern eye it looks like a massive party. These alewives are all generally carved or painted in a similar manner: naked with elaborate headdresses holding a tankard of ale. Miriam Gill, an expert in medieval wall paintings and art, contended that this design showed quite clearly the sins of the alewife. Specifically, that they were liars and thieves who sold their ale in false measures. They were lustful creatures, as signified by their nudity, and the ale trade itself inspired the deadly sin of gluttony. There are a few caveats to this, namely, not all representations of alewives were entirely negative. In some, they are portrayed just getting on with their work, though these instances are decidedly rarer.

It's also worth noting that alewives were not the only ones who bore the brunt of accusations of cheating their customers. There was a general anxiety towards victuallers, and bakers, millers and others received similar treatment. James Davis explored these fears in depth, and argued this mentality was clearly evident in poems like John Lydgate's aptly titled 'Put Thieving Millers and Bakers in the Pillory'. Here, Lydgate contended that millers and bakers should build their guild chapel under the pillory because so many of their members would end up there anyway. It's simply a time-saving measure. Such distrust was not unique to women who brewed, though alewives received more than their fair share of such misogyny.

Not all alewives were particularly thrilled about their new set of circumstances: that is, spending eternity in hell. At least that is what the *Chester Mystery Plays* tell us. Written in the medieval period, these are various tales of different people and professions in their town. *The Cookes Plaie* tells the story of a scandalous alewife who cheated her customers, broke the assize, sold in false measures, and went a bit rogue with her grain bill, substituting malt with things like ashes. She begins by telling us that she dwells with Satan in Hell and is subject to 'endles paines and sorowe cruell'. However, things might be looking up for our alewife. After her diatribe, she is the recipient of a heartfelt demonic marriage proposal; Satan calls her 'deare darling', and a second demon mentions her false measures of ale, proclaiming that they will have a feast and an endless ball with dice, cards and small cups of the ill-gotten ale.

How did these alewives cheat their customers (besides selling in false measures)? William Harrison's *Description of Elizabethan England* tells us that alewives would mix their drink with 'rosen' and salt. Rosen here likely means rosin, a distillation of crude turpentine used in things like waxes, glue, inks and varnishes. In powdered form it was used as a medicine to treat things like coughs and arthritis. Why were these substances added? Salt serves to make the drinker thirsty, so they drink more. But the rosen? Perhaps it was thought to serve a similar purpose, though it must have had a very distinct flavour so I am not quite sure how anyone got away with that.

Adding dodgy stuff to ale or trying to induce thirst was not an uncommon practice. William Dunbar, the famous Scottish poet of late-medieval and early 16th century fame, wrote a work called *The Devil's Inquest*, which had the alewife knowingly brewing with ill malt and subsequently finding herself tempted by the devil. The examples just keep coming. From Betty the Brewster to the John Lydgate's *Ballad on an Ale-seller*, alewives are represented as selling befouled and adulterated ales in illegal measures and generally lying and seducing their way through late-medieval and early-modern society, particularly in England. This, in some way, reflected the lived reality we saw in the first chapter, whereby cheating alewives and breakers of the assize ended up on the wrong side of the law. In short, alewives represented in art and literature became something of a catalyst for a more general misogynistic ideology that became increasingly prevalent in the Middle Ages and early modern periods.

We have seen that alewives are often associated with all things hellish and demonic. Skelton alleged that his alewife Rummyng was perhaps kin to the devil himself. However, he goes a step further and tells us that she accepted payment from a woman who seemed to be a witch, one that was said to make a charm with good

Witches giving babies to the devil. Woodcut, 1720.

ale yeast. This link with alewives and witches has captured the imagination of journalists and readers alike for the last decade. Dozens (and dozens) of articles, blog posts, podcasts, videos and the like have been released, all echoing one theory: women in Europe were pushed out of brewing *en masse* by men who accused them of being witches, because brewing itself, when done by women, was viewed as witchcraft. Further, because of this alleged connection, the stereotypical modern depiction of a witch is based on the garb and kit of medieval ale-brewing women. Are either of these assertions true? Or is it just another example of modern folklore?

The Woman-Brewer-as-Witch Myth

Many of us grew up with our parents or teachers reading tales of the fantastical to thrill and scare us. And we loved it. We clung to these stories, giving them our rapt attention as the legends unfolded, revealing accounts of heroes and villains. It shouldn't come as much of a surprise to know that just a few centuries ago, kids loved the same things. Stories about all manner of outlandish creatures – mermaids, dragons, and, of course, witches – graced the pages of books. In fact, that modern stereotype of the tall-pointy-hatted witch, dressed all in black, complete with black cat, perhaps even riding on a broomstick, probably has its origins in these late 17th- and early 18th-century children's books. Not, as many would perhaps like to tell you, with alewives.

I first debunked the link between the popular witch stereotype and alewives back in 2017 and since then have been working hard in digging deeper into the myth. Let's start with the cat. Cats were associated with heretics long before they came to be seen as familiars in witch trials. They were commonly linked with the devil. Kathleen Walker-Meikle cites an example of the 12th-century French Theologian Alan de Lille who 'claimed the very name Cathars came from cats and that they worshipped a black cat, the devil in disguise, and would kiss its bottom during service'. Of course, such outrageous claims about the Cathars were largely propaganda designed to terrify the general population about a heretical threat. And it wasn't limited to this group. The Knights Templar suffered similar treatment during their trial in the Middle Ages when they were accused of worshipping a cat. Walker-Meikle contended that the association with cats and heresy (and eventually witchcraft in the early modern period) has to do with the animals being both domestic and wild, and an inherently disloyal animal owing to its natural instincts. This is highlighted in the writings of Hildegarde von Bingen, who referred to them as unfaithful, and in Chaucer's 'Manciples Tale' (from his 14th-century story collection, *The Canterbury Tales*) in which the cat is depicted as one who could enjoy the most luxurious of trappings but would still abandon its owner to chase a mouse. Moreover, witches' familiars, or indeed animals they could morph into, could be anything from a dog to a bat, toad, or ferret. In a witchcraft pamphlet from 1653, Anne Bodenham was apparently turning into a cat, a mastiff, a black lion, a white bear, a wolf, a horse, a bull, and a calf.

Witches were depicted riding all manner of inanimate objects such as pitchforks, brooms, stakes, and staffs, even the devil-powered wind. They are also shown riding animals; for example, in the 1613 painting by Pierre de Lancre, 'Tableau de L'inconstance des Mauvais Anges et Demons'. The belief that witches could actually fly was, typically, denounced in medieval thought, and was not necessarily mentioned in English witch trials. Instead, it was believed this was a hallucination brought about by the devil. So why the broom? Brian Levack, in *The Witch-hunt in Early Modern Europe*, argued that the broomstick was associated with women, and its use 'might therefore reflect nothing more than the preponderance of female witches'.

Witchcraft beliefs differed greatly from country to country. Scottish people believed in large gatherings of witches at so-called Sabbaths and pacts with the devil. This idea did not take hold in England or Wales to any large extent, and, as we shall see later, greatly impacted the number of trials in the respective countries. Further, there is not a link between the alestake and flight. In fact, I have found no references to witches riding alestakes in my research. As for the cauldron, people could use all manner of things in which to brew ale, including cauldrons, but also wooden buckets, brewing pans and troughs. The link between the cauldron and the alewife is a bit of a non-starter. Many wills and inventories of brewing equipment are clear in their mention of pans and troughs.

The pointy hat has been at the centre of a lot of scholarly debate, but it's not derived from alewives. Rosemary Guiley, in her *The Encyclopedia of Witches, Witchcraft and Wicca*, offered a broad range of arguments for the witch hat origins. Some scholars have argued it came from medieval dunce caps, others from a conflation with the goddess Diana, and still others that it represented Quakerism. For me, the one of the most convincing arguments made by scholars is: that it originated from rampant and horrific anti-Semitism, as contended by Peter Burke. Burke argued that the portrayal of the witch

The history of witches and wizards: giving a true account of all their tryals in England, Scotland, Swedeland, France, and New England; with their confession and condemnation. Collected from Bishop Hall, Bishop Morton, Sir Matthew Hale, etc. By W. P.

was a 'migration of stereotypes' because it absorbed contemporary depictions of Jewish people, including the hooked nose and hat, concluded that this was a 'visual code expressive of sub-humanity'.

Finally, some other scholars argue that it was simply a version of a hat in fashion sometime earlier, specifically the phrygian or capotain hat, both of which look very similar to the modern stereotypical witch hat. In contrast, witches in the early modern and medieval periods were depicted in common garb, and prior to the inclusion in children's books did not wear a pointed hat. They were often shown bareheaded, or with a devil's snare, a two-pronged headpiece common in the period and associated with vanity (think Maleficent), or simply wearing the hats of the period. There wasn't some sort of pan-European millinery for alewives. The idea commonly touted that all women brewers throughout Europe wore tall hats in the marketplace to attract customers is patently false.

The Dutch Anna Boudaen Courten wearing a ta[ ]capotain hat, painted by Salomon Mesdach, 161[ ]

Many of the articles supporting the supposed alewife/witch link might point to one specific woman, Mother Louse, as the source for their argument. Louse was, apparently, a small alehouse-keeper running 'Louse Hall' at the bottom of Headington Hill near Oxford. Famously depicted in a print by David Loggan in the 17th century, and written about by Anthony Wood in 1673, she lived some 273 years after the medieval period. But let's just say the alewife-as-witch proponents mixed up their dates. So, is there anything to be said about Mother Louse and her links to witches and brewing? Interestingly, some point to her garb as indication of witchcraft because she is depicted in a tall hat, like those capotian hats famous from previous generations. But this is not some witch-based link. Instead, she's depicted thus because she's meant to be the last woman in England wearing a ruff. Therefore, she's supposed to be viewed as old fashioned and an object of scorn and mockery because of her very unfashionable hat and ruff. And remember, she was depicted like this before anyone associated witches with tall, pointy hats.

I can understand why this idea that the modern witch stereotype comes from alewives is inviting. On the surface, it seems like it could be true. After all, there are credible links between alewives and demons/hell in literature and art. But this was likely because there was a general anxiety of cheating amongst victuallers, and, as stated previously, bakers, millers and others received similar treatment. Though, as said before, stories of alewives were also laced with a hefty dose of misogyny. As we saw with Elynour Rummyng, there were allusions to witchcraft in her description and the company she kept. And we see similar associations in a later story from the 1600s of Mother Red Cap, also known as 'Mother Damnable', who was possibly based on a real woman who ran an alehouse while also maintaining a side gig as a healer and prognosticator in Kentish Town. As pointed out by academic James Brown, Mother Red Cap was said to have eyes that couldn't shed a tear, a charge that was also commonly made against alleged witches. Of course, these are fictional stories. What about the real-life women?

To be clear, those who were accused of witchcraft in this period were not 'evil witches'. With few exceptions, they were, by and large, innocent people who were caught up in the terror of the day. Did some people practise magick? (NB In those circles of people who practise witchcraft, many use magick with a 'k' to differentiate it from magic with a 'c' done by magicians in Vegas shows.) Absolutely. Folk magick was popular among common people and was not incompatible with their Christianity. In fact, as we shall see, magick was practised to ward off witches and appease them. Brian Hoggard's study, 'The Archaeology of Counter-Witchcraft and Popular Magic', revealed many material examples of magick practice in early modern Britain, including charms and witch bottles. However, just because someone perhaps practised folk magick, or magick of any kind, did not mean that they would have self-described as a witch. Though some did confess to practising malevolent witchcraft, many under severe torture and duress, most early modern or medieval people accused would not have identified themselves with the term 'witch'.

Further, the witch hunts as we conceptualise them today are not medieval, but largely early modern in nature. To clarify, the medieval period roughly dates from AD500–1500, and the early modern era runs from 1500–1800. Witchcraft trials generally took place from the later 16th century through to the 18th century, with the bulk happening in the latter half of the 16th and through the 17th centuries. These trials were extremely rare occurrences in some towns and villages, and there are, in fact, entire counties where none took place. In Wales, for example, Richard Suggett found existing evidence for around 35 trials, producing eight guilty verdicts and five executions. There may have been more trials, but the evidence does not exist. I think we can safely say that the 35 Welsh witchcraft trials do not show a wholesale accusation against alewives, and they probably had very little impact on brewing. Why were the numbers so low? Well, apparently, according to Suggett, the Welsh were too preoccupied with hanging thieves to have much time worrying about witches. In fact, the Welsh thief trials numbered in the thousands and subsequent executions in the hundreds. Quite a contrast to the alleged witch trials. There are, though, some beer-related links in the Welsh witch trials, but perhaps not what you might imagine.

*   *   *

Most of us have found ourselves sipping away at our favourite pint when along comes some kind of bug that decides to go for a little swim in our glass. However, I don't think any of us have used it as evidence of witchcraft. Gwen ferch Ellis was one of the first Welsh witches tried. She was, apparently, known to be a cunning woman, and had garnered a long reputation for *maleficium*, or harmful witchcraft. From Suggett's translations of this court case, we can see that there were several instances over the years that led her neighbours in Denbighshire to suspect that she was up to no good, none of which involved brewing. These accusations culminated a home invasion, whereby a group of men marched into her house and demanded that she serve them ale. After much pushing and harassing, she was finally forced to bring them their ale, but sitting on top of one of the drinks was a fly. Not only that, but a fly so huge and so totally monstrous that it could only have been her familiar, and thus proof of her evil witchery. Did Gwen brew the ale herself? It is possible. But the ale itself wasn't viewed as dangerous or magically evil. The only link with the ale is the giant fly. Gwen isn't accused of witchcraft because she brewed ale, and her serving ale wasn't particularly strange. Rather, this story highlights the ubiquity of ale in early modern Welsh society.

A few centuries later, in the 1800s, Elizabeth Isabella Spence, writing in her *Summer Excursions through parts of Oxfordshire, Gloucestershire, Warwickshire, Staffordshire, Herefordshire, Derbyshire and South Wales*, regaled her readers with the story of 'old Margaret'. Spence's guide at Dinefwr Castle, near

Llandeilo in Carmarthenshire, told the tale to her. Margaret, who had recently died, was said to be a witch who 'was the terror of the neighbouring farmers'. Allegedly, she had such a penchant for ruining people's brewing that they had to cast a spell before every mash-in to 'prevent her malicious machinations'. Whether this story is true or merely a folk tale doesn't really matter. The fear is that a witch will interfere with brewing, not that brewing women were witches. We can conclude that in Wales there is likely no link between women who brewed being accused of witchcraft simply because they brewed.

Things might have been different elsewhere in Britain, however. In 1588 Joan Prentice was a resident at the Alms House of Hinningham Sibble in England when she found herself accused of witchcraft. One night, around 10 o'clock we are told, the devil, in the guise of a ferret, appeared before her and demanded her immortal soul. Of course, she refused. After all, he wasn't offering her anything in return. He relented, and changed his request, asking for some of her blood instead, which she readily gave him to drink even though he still didn't seem to offer anything in exchange. Then he vanished into the ether, returning a month later, once again as a ferret, seeking her blood. This time, he offered her a favour in return. Was there something she wanted done? In reply, she told the devil that she and William Adam's wife had had a massive falling out, and that she wanted him to spoil the beer that Adam's wife was brewing. So, off he went to do just that.

In England, trials like Prentice's were more common than in Wales, leading to – possibly – some 500 executions over a period of several centuries. And then there are those who were accused and convicted but not executed, and those who were acquitted. However, while at first glance this number may appear very high, it is, actually, quite low when put into context. In 1662 John Graunt published a pamphlet called *Natural and Political Observations mentioned in a flowing index and made upon the Bills of Mortality*, which is a long-winded way of saying he catalogued the records of deaths and births in London between 1629 and 1660, a period that coincides with our witch trials. According to Graunt, over the course of this period 14,236 people died of diseases of the teeth and worms, 10,363 died of convulsions (seizures), 1,389 people died of colic and wind, and some 7,787 died of bloody flux. The biggest killers of adults – 46,583 and 23,615 respectively – were consumption and ague or fever. Coming in right behind that was the plague. Further down the list of causes were grief, which killed 279 people; 86 people were murdered, 243 were found dead on the streets, and 1,021 were 'killed by several accidents'. There are, though, many issues with how this data was collected. Graunt was a haberdasher by trade, and, as Will Stahl-Timmins and John Appleby, analysts of the aforementioned data, have stated, 'many deaths would have gone unreported'. So, we should take these numbers with a pinch of salt, given the issues of lack of reporting and misunderstanding of medical causes. But though these numbers may not be totally accurate, they do help to put the number of executions into some perspective. Assuming that they were dispersed evenly (which they were not), executions as result of witch trials killed on average around 2.5 people per year (500 people over the course of say 200 years). By comparison, in 1650 an entry only named 'wolf' killed eight people in London. As Stahl-Timmins and Appleby stated, this fact raises more questions than answers.

However, these figures are skewed by a period with many more witch trials. In the introduction to *The Lancashire Witches: Histories and Stories*, James Sharpe argued that, with the exception of the East Anglia Hunt in 1645 led by the witch-finder general Matthew Hopkins, which killed well over a hundred people, the trials in England were 'sporadic and few'. Most often they featured a single person or a group of three or four, and the acquittal rate was relatively high. In fact, higher estimates of Hopkins' murderous spree put him as responsible for 200–300 deaths. So, outside of his particular reign of terror, the odds of being tried and executed drop significantly further. Malcolm Gaskill argued that, even during the worst of it in England, most trials didn't result in conviction or execution because providing proof was quite difficult and the trials themselves were probably expensive. Therefore, while we have a higher rate of witch trials and subsequent executions than in Wales, these were not so frequent and widespread that they would have stopped women brewing.

The reasons why women were accused of witchcraft varied greatly. Most scholars would argue that the trials differed in context and were caused by a myriad of factors. For example, historian Robert Poole argued that one of the key causes for the Lancashire trials was that the local authorities were trying to curry favour with King James I. In short, none of the reasons given for the occurrence of witch trials show a coordinated campaign against alewives. There was no national trend of accusing women who brewed ale of witchcraft simply because they brewed ale. Scholars argue that the reasons were complex and very much context specific. And while economic motivations could have been a factor, that doesn't explain the full situation. None of the trials demonstrate an innate hostility towards women who brewed. Neither do they show that men viewed women brewing as something inherently suspicious and worthy of a possible witchcraft accusation. In fact, as we saw with Prentice's case, those women who brewed were often the victims of the supposed malicious magick.

In Thorpe, Essex, Margaret Grevell apparently kept in her care four infernal imps, called Robin, Jack, William and Puppet (or Mamet), 'two of them were hees and the other two were shees, & were like unto Blacke Cats'. At least that is what Alice Manfielde claimed that Grevell had revealed to her some 12 years prior to her trial in March of 1558. Lugging these imps around all day was quite the task, and Grevell was worried she would be found out unless she could find someone to mind them for her. So, she enlisted Manfielde's help to watch them and feed them, which she did, with bread and beer. And what did these infernal imps get up to? Manfielde told examiners that Grevell used them to destroy the beer of several other brewers: 'she saith a brewē at Reades, a brewē at Carters, and a brewē of three or foure bushelles of malte at Brewses.'

That wasn't the end of Grevell's antics, however. On the same day of Manfielde's confession, John Carver testified that Grevell came to him asking for 'Godesgood', meaning yeast, which he refused her. In retaliation, Carver accused Grevell of cursing his family's brewing. He said that 'his folkes tried to brew, but of two brewinges after they coulde make no beere,' so they opted to shoot the brewing vat with a bow and arrow, as you do. His son 'beeing a tall and lustie man' shot the brewing vat twice and the arrow wouldn't stick, but on the third go it worked and penetrated the vat. This seemingly lifted the curse and they were able to brew as before.

Grevell wasn't the only one cursing people's brewing in Essex. Similar accusations were made against Annis Herde who Andrewe West and his wife, Anne, accused of cursing Anne's brewing. Edmond Osbourne and his wife, Godlife, also said that Annis had cursed Godlife's brewing after she ran into some trouble with her. Godlife recalled to the court that she was able to mash in the first time with no problems, but the second time the beer wouldn't ferment and apparently stank so badly they had to put it in the swill tub.

Noxious beer caused by *maleficium* apparently continued well into the 17th century, at least if we believe the confessions of Thomas and Mary Everard, who were tried and executed at Bury St Edmunds on 27 August 1645. The couple were both working at a brewhouse in Halesworth, Suffolk.

Thomas was employed as a cooper, but we aren't told what Mary was getting up to, besides the witchcraft that is. According to a contemporary account, they 'freely confessed' to bewitching the beer at the brewhouse to the degree that 'the odiousnesse of the infectious stinke of it was such & so intolerable that by the noysomnesse of the smel or tast many people dyed'. This sounds like fabrication, unless they literally poisoned the beer, which is possible.

* * *

I've had some badly infected beers during my beer judging days, but none has thus far managed to kill me. However, my sample size of one isn't quite big enough to dismiss this possibility outright so I asked the brewers I interviewed for this book if they had ever made a beer so bad that the smell of it was liable to kill someone. Surprisingly, one brewery told me they had got close.

When they were learning to make alcohol-free beer in their 'tiny kitchen', Sarah McNena and Joelle Drummond experimented with different methods, including heat evaporation, which Drummond told me is not the way their beers are made now. They had a 'really rubbish little hob' that took forever to get to the right temperatures (the boiling point of ethanol is in the high 70s centigrade). In any event, it took hours and hours. While they were waiting, they attempted to make the room as hot as possible, 'we had all the windows shut, all the doors shut,' but the ethanol wouldn't boil off. It was only later that she realised they had been breathing pure ethanol fumes for a while, and were, in their words, 'absolutely hammered'. 'We'd hot boxed ourselves and if there had been any gas, it would've gone bang. So that was a close call, nearly killed by Drop Bear.'

For most of the others I spoke to, while their beers hadn't quite managed to kill them off entirely, they had made some dreadfully infected brews; as I'm sure any of us who have tried our hands at homebrewing can relate to. Closet Brewing's first brew on a kit, on Lucy's 18th birthday, was drinkable, which inspired her to try again. This time, though, she went a bit rogue with her recipe and the resulting beer was infected. Emma Inch brewed a California Common, an ale brewed with lager yeast but fermented at ale temperatures. It's a tricky one to be sure. One morning she came down the stairs to an 'awful sulphurus smell' infecting the whole house. She immediately became worried that the dog had taken ill and would need to be rushed to the vet. But no: the culprit was malodourous lager yeast. And unlike those who came into contact with the deadly 17th-century brew mentioned above, Inch is still very much breathing.

*   *   *

Lethal beers, however, are not beyond the realms of possibility. Around the year 1900, some 6,000 people were poisoned and 70 died due to the unintentional addition of arsenic in beer. One case was a two-year-old girl who developed poisoning after her father, who owned a pub, gave her small sips of the beer, according to Dr Kelynack and William Kirby who wrote about this poisoning case a year later in 1901, in *Arsenical Poisoning in Beer Drinkers*. In this instance, it was determined that the arsenic had been added via sugar contaminated with sulphuric acid at the brewing stage. Ernest Reynolds, a doctor, made the connection, which was eventually traced to the brewers of Bostock and Co who had purchased sulphuric acid from Nicholson & Sons to make the sugar. Nicholson initially gave them arsenic-free sulphuric acid, but later decided to send them the arsenic-laden variety, claiming they hadn't known what it was being used for, and that they would have given them 'arsenic-free acid' if the brewery had asked for it. So, it is possible that our 17th-century husband and wife had created their poisonous brew by accident. Or, indeed, that the beer had nothing to do with people getting sick or dying.

Accounts of accusations of witchcraft against women who were allegedly cursing or messing around with other women's brewing are not restricted to certain parts of the country. Examples the trials resulting from these accounts can be found in various witchcraft pamphlets, and while these were written contemporaneously, they are not without their issues. In 'Publishing for the Masses: Early Modern English Witchcraft Pamphlets', Carla Suhr argued that these pamphlets are one of the 'few windows into the everyday lives of regular people', and as such they were written for the 'unlearned masses', who were more worried about the 'material hurt' the alleged witch had

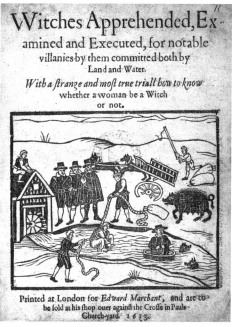

Despite the popular misconception that numerous witch trials took place throughout the late 16th and 17th centuries, these were, in fact, few and far between, and resulted in very few executions.

caused to his or her neighbours. Many of these pamphlets focused on the loss of property or animals, or beer. Though most of the earlier examples were based on trial proceedings, and thus can be assumed to be more accurate, there are still things written in them that don't exactly stack up. As the 17th century progressed, they took on more of a literary flair, which calls into question their veracity. Despite this, when we look at pamphlets from the earlier and later periods, we can see that patterns emerge, none of which demonstrate an obvious attack on alewives specifically for the act of brewing ale or beer.

That said, I did find two examples of brewing people explicitly accused of witchcraft. In the first, in 1560 in Essex, the brewer in question was actually a man. The Essex Assizes, held at Chelmsford on 4 July 1560, included the indictment of John Samond, alias John Smythe. Samond was noted to be a 'common wizard' and a 'berebruer'. The second example is from a database called the *Physicians and Irregular Medical Practitioners in London 1550-1640*. Among the people listed here, we find Catherine Chaire, an alewife who practised some kind of medicine from around 1588 to 1608. Catherine did find herself in trouble with the law on a few occasions. In a hearing on 4 August 1598, she was charged by a Mrs Bridgman for giving purging medicines and tansies. She didn't bother to appear at this hearing but showed up to the next one on 19 August, where she confessed to administering the tansy. None of which appears to have worried Chaire, who told the court that she could diagnose pregnancy from washing clothes with 'red rose water and soap'. The court ordered her to cease this behaviour at once and give back the money she had taken for her cures. And that was the end of it. In neither of these cases involving brewers was there any mention of witchcraft or magick related to their brewing, and both brewers were free to carry on brewing afterwards. In fact, brewing was mentioned purely in the context of being their occupation and had nothing to do with the trials.

As we have seen, women brewing was not inherently associated with witchcraft. Rather, beer and ale were such a part of everyday life that they were obvious targets for any demonic shenanigans carried out by those people believed to be witches. Accusations of witchcraft were made by those whose daily chores were being interrupted or their farm animals harmed. Annis Herde, for example, aside from cursing people's brews, apparently had time to bewitch pigs, swine, lambs and sheep, as well as causing the loss of milk and cream. Cyssey Celles bewitched Richard Rosses' horse and beasts and had her imps burn down his barn. In short, cursed brewing was simply part of a more general cursing of various foodstuffs and beverages and farm animals that went on during the 16th and 17th centuries.

Another important point to mention here is, as Gaskill argued, that witch trials in England were expensive to organise and not always guaranteed to lead to a guilty verdict. Men – and women – did not need to resort to a trial as a means of committing commercial sabotage. There were much easier ways to do this. The witch trials, as we saw in the previous chapter, mostly happened during the era of licensing, which began with the 1522 Act. Those wishing to get rid of the competition could besmirch the reputation of a rival and thus ensure that their licence wouldn't be granted to brew and sell ale. And if the woman in question already had one, it could be revoked. This wasn't a simple process, and as we saw in the previous chapter, it wasn't always successful, but it was easier than having to go through the expense and uncertainty of an entire witchcraft trial. This is particularly the case with men, who could accuse women brewers of ripping off their customers or selling against the assize, irrespective of whether or not it was true, simply because of their place in society and the advantages that it afforded them.

Witch Trials in Scotland

As in Wales and England, the reasons behind the trials in Scotland were varied and complex. However, they differed because they were more frequent, and more deadly. Estimates on the University of Edinburgh *Survey of Scottish Witches* website indicates that 3,212 people were tried for witchcraft. About 305 cases resulted in a conviction: 205 of these were executed, 27 banished, 11 became fugitives, six were excommunicated, two outlawed, one was kept in prison, and one was publicly humiliated. A further 98 fled persecution, which sounds like a wise choice. So, of those accused of witchcraft in Scotland, some 67% were executed, though this figure is, in the words of Edinburgh University, 'not very accurate'.

Regardless of the precise numbers, the survey is an excellent resource for finding out about specific trials. I combed through the database looking for any mentions of ale, beer and brewing and found some interesting results. Marable Coupe, who was accused of witchcraft in Kirkwall, Orkney, in July 1624, testified that she appeased a woman she believed to be a witch with ale to stop her from plaguing her household. Coupe in turn was accused of destroying the ale of others, as well as crops and animals. This was not her first time. She had apparently been tried for witchcraft earlier and banished but refused to leave. Coupe was found guilty and subsequently executed by strangling and burning. Margaret Finlasoun, aged 35, was also implicated by another witch. These cases all form part of a larger category of grievance; what the University of Edinburgh called 'neighbourhood disputes' and which include disputes over land, buying and selling, and childminding. For Finlasoun, there are mentions in her trial about attempted appeasement with ale, though we don't know what the trial outcome was, or if she lived or died. Appeasement in this case meant that people tried to ward off an alleged witch's seemingly wicked intentions by offering up goods, or in this case ale. It was a way to try and quite literally 'appease' the person into overlooking them and finding other victims.

Agnes Finnie, a shopkeeper, was accused in 1644 of demonic *maleficium*; specifically, she had been trying to remove the 'witches' malice' by offering ale as appeasement, among other things. Finnie was summarily executed. According to John Bickerdyke in his *Curiousities of Ale and Beer,* a set of Scotch ale instructions from 1793 included the following passage: 'I throw a little dry malt, which is left on purpose, on the top of the mash, with a handful of salt, to keep the witches from it, and then cover it up.' This could function as a bit of a counter spell to ward off any witch's malicious intentions. A bit of good magick if you will. Bickerdyke himself wondered if 'perhaps the idea that witches could spoil the ale by their evil charms gave rise to the phrase "water bewitched," signifying very weak beer or other liquor'.

Ale could also be used for good or bad, cursing or blessing, depending on the user. As in the English records, people accused of witchcraft in Scotland were also thought to have destroyed ale brewing. In 1597 Johnnet Wischert was accused by another apparent witch of many things, including spoiling an entire brew of ale and poisoning a child. In another instance, Bessie Wright, around 1626-1628, was supposedly using various cures to help people in the area. She was told to refrain from doing so, but chose to ignore this demand, with dire consequences. One of her supposed victims accused her of causing pains in his limbs and spoiling his ale. Isobell Young, c.1616-1629, was accused of spoiling or ruining ale and was executed by burning in Aberdeen. Again, it is worth noting that the women doing the brewing were not accused of witchcraft because they were brewing. The crime in question is destroying the brew, not creating it in the first place.

In around 1607 Issobel Griersoune was accused of witchcraft, and amongst her crimes, we are told, was cursing others, including a woman who had called her a witch in public. She was also involved in spoiling people's ale. In 1688 Catharin Mactargett was accused of putting salt in ale to make it go off (so not exactly the work of a witch), but we are also told that she bewitched people and then offered to cure the bewitchments. One of her alleged cures involved an egg mixed with ale. She was basically running a scam, cursing people only so that she could later remove the curse.

The Healing Properties of Ale

Ale was commonly used in magick spells. Not because it possesses magickal qualities that lend themselves to spell making, but simply because it was so ubiquitous in everyday life. Ale was often cited in witch trials, but so were eggs, crops like hemp, corn and flax, milk, bannock (a type of flatbread), dairy products, and animals. There are records showing that cheese was used as a ritual object, and during a cursory search I found many involving eggs, salt and bannock.

The use of ale in spell work has a long and storied history, one that stretches back millennia and still exists to this day. There are some commercial breweries dedicated to brewing beers with magical intentions, for example, those from Breakside Brewery in Portland, Oregon, who made a magick-infused beer called Basic Witch. But you don't need to even brew to use beer in your spell work. Anaïs Alexandre's popular book, *Potions, Elixirs & Brews: A Modern Witches' Grimoire of Drinkable Spells*, features beer in her recipes, as well as lists of messages telling readers that it is perfect for protection and healing, among other things. Scott Cunningham's *Encyclopedia of Magical Herbs*, often described as one of the go-to books for practitioners of magick, tells readers that barley is good for love, healing and protection spells, and can be thrown on the ground to 'keep evil and negativity away'

The use of beer in healing is not limited to magickal practices. In fact, women commonly used ale or beer in everyday medicines for centuries, though the line between medicine and magick in this period is often blurry at best. Women's private notebooks, and even published volumes, contain recipes for medicines involving ale and beer before, during, and after the witch trials in Britain. There are many such books containing recipes with ale and beer, but perhaps my favourite non-published recipe collection comes from either Scotland or northern England (the experts aren't quite sure). This 17th-century manuscript of recipes (currently housed in the Folger Shakespeare Library) was written by an educated woman of some means, according to the description on their website. Although this contains recipes calling for ale, including a posset, the one I will share with you is a medicinal recipe, which also makes for one of the strangest uses of ale I have seen. Ever.

Keep in mind that the language used here is early modern and not my own. This cure is for what the author called 'convulsion fitts', also known in modern language as seizures. For this you're going to need a human skull. If you are a man you're going to need a woman's skull and if you're a woman you're going to need a man's skull (if you fall outside this gender binary, you're apparently out of luck). But there are even more caveats on the skull, because you can't just use any old skull you may have lying around. No, unless the person died a horrific death, the skull cannot be used. The recipe is clear that death by disease is no good either. It has to have been a violent death; strangulation is ideal. Best practice is probably to go dig up the grave of a condemned and executed criminal, preferably one who was hanged. So now you have your skull, but you aren't quite there yet. We all know that this free-range skull might have some, er, organic matter still on it, which we are told is not desired. So our author tells us we need to shove it in a linen cloth and stick it by the fire so it dehydrates. After it's completely dried out, you pulverise it. Then add 2, 3, or 4 grains of the pulverised skull, depending on how old our patient is, to the ale and mix it in. The resultant concoction is then drunk for several mornings. Needless to say, don't try this at home. In fact, don't try any of these medicinal recipes at home.

In books written for and by women, beer and ale were commonly used as medicinal ingredients: for boils, bumps and sore boobs, broken bones, consumption, colic, cough – and, in 1608's *A Closet for Ladies and Gentlewomen*, 'for winde and shootings in your head'. They were included in cures for just about anything you can think of.

In Wales, Merryell Williams' *Book of Recipes*, from the end of the 17th and early 18th century, includes a 'Syrop of Malt for a great Cough', which required 'four quarts of the running of the malt of the strongest wort you can get'. An English gentlewoman, Johanna St John, living between 1631 and 1705, wrote a book of her various medicines, in which ale features prominently. You can read the entire text at the Lydiard Archive (see bibliography) and it provides a fascinating insight into beer as medicine. For example, she included Dr Brown's Clary Water for the Back. This required three gallons of strong ale or beer to which various herbs, as well as raisins, brandy and anise seeds, were added. The cure for the bite of 'a mad dog' also required a bottle of strong ale. And we have another medicine for 'convulsion fitts' requiring, once again, a dead man's skull (also from someone who has met a violent and untimely end). A cordial ale for the head is also found, and an ale cough syrup that contains, among other things, strong ale and poppy. She also includes Dr Coxes' Cock Ale, which, we are told, is 'good for the cough inward unless consumptions'. St John also recorded a purging ale, something which pops up with some frequency in these books. These recipes certainly would not pass inspection by our modern medical community. For example, in a cure for sore eyes perfect for our Elynour Rummyng and her penchant for *fowl* ingredients, St John tells us to use dried hen's dung and powdered ginger and sugar and blow it into the eye. And if you don't have hen's dung, or ginger and sugar, you can just use breast milk. Another 'cure' requires holding a live pigeon on top of a child suffering from seizures until it dies (the pigeon, not the child) and is then replaced with a new pigeon until the child is no longer seizing. (We have gone full circle back to the plague pigeons.)

Just a few years later, in 1727, *The Complete Housewife*, written by Eliza Smith, featured medicinal beers for fits of wind, a pain in the stomach, consumptive cough, dropsy, sore boobs, the bite of a mad dog, a purging diet, and several others. Her book also contained certain medicines involving ale to stimulate menses or menstrual bleeding; i.e., an abortion. At the opposite end of the spectrum is a recipe to promote 'breeding', which features three pints of good ale as the base to which all manner of spices, herbs and fruits are added. The user is then told to drink a small wine glass of the potion at bedtime and to 'accompany not with your husband during the taking, or some time before, be very chear ful, and let nothing disquiet you'.

Ale continued to be used as a form of medicine well into the 19th and 20th centuries. This concept of beer as medicine is clearly evident in the malt tonics of the time. These were derived from malt and hops, and often in a thick, syrup-like consistency. They also contained all sorts of things that were alleged to help keep the drinker healthy, such as quinine, cod liver oil, and even strychnine. Yes, strychnine. That ingredient commonly used to murder rats, pests, and victims in crime novels, was also used as a medicine not so very long ago. These malt tonics were often advertised to tired housewives or working mothers as a cure for all their maladies.

We might seem very far removed from drinking skull beers and malt syrup for coughs, but the notion of the medicinal properties of beer, particularly for women, continued to be touted. In Samuel and Isabella Beeton's

Englishwoman's Domestic Magazine, Version 6, from 1858, the connection between nursing mothers and stout is firmly established. In 'A Surgeon's Advice to Mothers' the surgeon in question recommended that a mixture of stout and porter be given to nursing mothers, decrying any substitutes, including other kinds of beer. And this is not an isolated incident. David Hughes's book *"A Bottle of Guinness Please": The Colourful History of Guinness,* studied the use of the famous stout as medicine. Hughes found that a man called Dr Lumsden, one of 122 doctors who allowed Guinness to use their views on its medicinal qualities, had been prescribing it since the 1890s for nursing mothers. He also concluded that UK hospitals used Guinness to treat blood disorders, the flu, boils, insomnia, and everything in between. Stouts as nursing aids are sometimes still suggested, even though this has been debunked.

Today, a quick internet search will bring up a host of articles touting beer as a useful medicine. For example, a feature on NBCnews.com entitled '7 Science-backed reasons beer may be good for you', had the tagline 'a pint of beer a day may come with a host of health benefits'. Beer is hyped as having a myriad of healthy properties, from antioxidant levels to beneficial vitamins, and we remain fascinated by the potential use of beer for our health. An article on thedrinksbusiness.com, on 17 September 2020, featured a story about Fungtn, a vegan and gluten-free beer brand founded by Zoey Henderson, which uses medicinal mushrooms, those classified as having health benefits. Others have tried to find a way to fit beer into their healthy lifestyles. For example, Thrillist.com ran a story in 2020 about the benefits of using a low-ABV beer as a post-workout drink, and *Men's Health* ran a similar one in 2021.

*   *   *

As we have seen, beer or ale have long been used as central ingredients in cures for many diseases and ailments. Well into the 20th century, doctors were prescribing stout for nursing mothers and malt tonics for tired house-wives, and even now we try to find ways to link beer with good health. It is also important to note that the first medical recipe books and journals, written for and by women, were written during the witch trials. We can see from this chapter that women who brewed weren't accused of witchcraft because they brewed. In fact, as we shall see, women would continue to be encouraged to brew. It was the domain of the housewife after all.

HOMEBREWING HOUSEWIVES

BOOM! A deafening blast rents the air. A moment of panic and fear descends before realisation kicks in. There goes the homebrew.

In the 1970s a group of researchers from the University of Exeter, led by P. Thompson and P. Lummis, interviewed older people who grew up in the late 1800s and early 1900s about their childhoods and families. Called *Family Life and Work Experience Before 1918*, participants were asked questions about their parents, their activities, and also about homebrewing.

Robert Bracken, born in 1902, told the interviewers that his mother made beer at home for the family, 'in a big yellow mug'. This beer featured nettles and herbs and she used to sell it on Sunday mornings to people who would come by her house. Apparently, it was very popular and well-loved in Manchester where they lived. Bracken's mother was not the only one still selling homebrew. Mrs Charlotte Harris of Sandsfields, Wales, born in 1901, tells us that her mother also used to make and sell small beer – quite a lot of it, in fact. Mrs Elizabeth Eade's family used to run a boarding house where they would take in evacuees from London during the war. She told researchers that her mother made all the beer for the household and her father didn't go to the pub because of that. And, like today, she said that brewing beer was inexpensive: 'all it cost was the sugar, which was quite cheap in those days, and a bit of yeast. We didn't get yeast in those days, we got barm, which you'd get from brewers.'

Some of the interviewees told stories of brewing mishaps. Florence Kate Johnson, born in 1892, told a researcher that her aunt's ginger beer made quite the impression: 'It went off in the cupboard with a loud explosion. Frightened the life out of us. It was rather horrid actually.'

I'm sure many of us can remember our last terrifying encounters with exploding homebrewed beers: the sound of glass shattering behind the cupboard door and contents sprayed everywhere. I'm still finding spots of stout in random places in my kitchen. When Emma Inch, podcaster extraordinaire at *Fermentation Beer and Brewing Radio*, was at university she brewed in her student accommodation. In one instance the beer she had bottled managed to explode inside her wardrobe. Undeterred, Inch has continued to brew at home, using ingredients like rose tea, peanut butter, or pear. Now, of course, those halcyon days of student brews in cupboards and wardrobes have been replaced with a dedicated shed and a Grainfather.

Miss Slamon, a single woman from Llantrisant, told interviewers that her mother made *diod faen*, which is Welsh for small beer, and sometimes used nettles or dandelions. Many of the Welsh participants told stories of their mothers brewing *diod faen*, and these brews often used nettles, elderflower or dandelions. Mrs Harris, born in 1904 in Heol Gerrig, Merthyr Tydfil, also stated that her mother made *diod faen*, which, she told researchers, was 'quite lovely'. Mrs Mainwarning recalled that her mother sometimes made *diod faen*, and also ginger beer and elderberry wine. She goes on to tell us that that they would use blackcurrant leaves, nettles, elder and dandelions in the *died faen*, and also add ginger, making a kind of ginger beer/*diod faen* hybrid drink. Mr Griffiths of Howell Griffith, Hollybush Estate, also tells us that his family made *diod faen* with dandelions, 'oh, aye, small beer we used to make no end of that, always had plenty of that in the house. Lord alive, aye'.

Almost all of the breweries I spoke to for this book got their start in homebrewing and stories of kitchen brews and bath-tub beers abound. Closet Brewing started brewing in their kitchen, as did Drop Bear Beer Company, while Talia Chain at Lone Goat told me that their first effort wasn't far off a bath-tub beer, and Eko Brewery began homebrewing on a small plastic kit. Even the women I interviewed who aren't brewers had at least dabbled in homebrewing themselves at some point, like Ruvani de Silva who got more into it during the coronavirus lockdowns. Though we might assume that such homebrewing experiences, good and bad, are a more modern occurrence, women have been brewing in their homes for themselves and their families for centuries. And so, homebrewed beers have been exploding in cupboards for a very long time.

A Woman's Place

When we get home from a long day at work, the last thing most of us want to do is household chores. The unrelenting list of monotonous tasks that never seems to end, making us feel a bit like Sisyphus, rolling that damn rock up the hill for eternity. On our list of household chores we find the usual suspects: cooking, tidying up, and maybe taking the bins out. But what about brewing? I don't think many of us would consider that a chore, never mind something we regularly need to do. However, there was a time when brewing would have been part and parcel of these household duties, albeit one that could bring in some money. A potential side hustle, if you will.

For centuries, brewing was the domain of the housewife, and – if she had them – her servants. This situation prevailed well into the 19th century, alongside the increasingly male-dominated commercial beer industry. You see, women didn't actually stop brewing when men attempted to take over the trade; they just kept doing it at home.

Firstly, though, what do I mean by housewife? Contrary to the 1950's image you may have in your head, the housewife in the early modern Britain was not a middle-class woman wearing Dior's new look, vacuuming her house with a vacant smile on her face. Of course, that woman didn't really exist either; she was just another construct of sexist advertising pushing impossible and ridiculous standards onto women. Back to my point: the word housewife is rooted in medieval social structure. A parallel term to the husbandman, with each referring to the female and male heads of the household respectively. Husbandman, along with yeoman farmers, in the 16th and 17th centuries were middling sorts of people, and within these groups people could be more or less wealthy. Eventually, the term housewife would broaden over time to include other social groups.

*   *   *

As we move further into the 16th, 17th and 18th centuries we encounter an increasingly diverse Britain, not just in terms of immigrants from other countries in Europe, as we saw in the first chapter, but from around the world. And though there had, for centuries, always been an immigrant population living here – for example during the Roman period – from the 16th century onward we see Britain becoming more multicultural, with people from Africa, North and South America, Oceania, and Asia arriving and settling here, particularly in the cities and seaports. For instance, Thomas L. Blair found that by the 18th century there were an estimated 5,000 Black women in London.

These immigrants from around the world settled into various roles as working women, wives, and mothers. Some were heiresses, like Dido Elizabeth Belle, a Black British gentlewoman and daughter of Sir John Lindsey. We know a lot about her, mainly because of her social rank and family connections, not to mention the famous painting by David Martin that immortalised her. For the daily lives of less famous women, however, finding them in the records can prove more difficult, though this is made easier thanks to the tireless work of a team of researchers, archivists and academics who created *Switching the Lens – Rediscovering Londoners of African, Caribbean, Asian and Indigenous Heritage 1561 to 1840*. It is a critical database resource that allows us to find out more about these women's lives. Women like Ann Tatary, likely from Mongolia, who worked as a servant in the 18th century, Susannah York from Bombay, another 18th-century woman who worked in domestic service, Maria Morton, an indigenous woman from New South Wales who worked as a servant in the 19th century, Elizabeth (no last name), originally from Ethiopia, who was a servant in the 17th century to a Mr Soper, a surgeon, and Sophia Young, who also worked as a servant and who was born in Africa (specifically where on the continent isn't clear) in 1787. As we can see from this brief sample, many of these women worked as servants to housewives or in households, while some others were the head of their own households of servants.

Women arriving in Britain brought with them their own brewing traditions from countries and continents where they dominated the practice. In West Africa, for example, women for centuries brewed a variety of beers, including those made from sorghum and millet. Nomkhubulwane is the Zulu goddess of rain, agriculture and fertility, and the creator of beer. Also known as Mbaba Mwana Waresa, or Lady Rainbow, so named for her house in the sky made of rainbow colours, she is credited with teaching Zulu women how to brew. The goddess Yasigi of the Dogon in Mali has women who brew for her and is often represented carrying a ladle to serve beer. During the African diaspora, women and men likely brought with them their brewing skills, passing them down through their families, or learning new ones along the way. Theresa McCulla recently wrote a James Beard award-winning article on Patsy Young, a woman who escaped her enslaver in the United States and maintained herself in part by brewing.

McCulla found that through her beer-making skills, alongside cooking, weaving, baking cakes and sewing, Young was able to provide for herself as a free woman for almost 15 years. But Young's story is not an isolated incident. Enslaved people as well as household servants were often responsible for brewing in this period.

Beer and Ale in Recipe Books

As we shall see, women who worked in domestic service had a key role in the history of brewing. Alongside their employers, these women worked to brew beer and ale for the households as well as for sale. This was so prevalent, in fact, that books were written as guides to help them create a perfect home environment, and these how-to guides were an incredibly popular form of reading and writing.

Doughnuts are perhaps not the kind of thing you might expect to find in a 17th-century recipe book. How about cheesecake? Lemonade? Rock candy? But you can find all these and more in Merryell Williams' *Book of Recipes* dating to the end of 17th and early 18th centuries. We were introduced to Williams' book in the last chapter with her malt cough syrup, but she also recorded all manner of recipes, including one for beer doughnuts, or more specifically doughnuts made with ale yeast. Merryell Williams was the daughter of Richard and Elizabeth Powell of Worthern in Shrewsbury. Born in 1629, she would go on to marry John Williams, a wealthy Welsh aristocrat. Her *Book of Recipes* included many examples of foods or drinks calling for ale as a central ingredient. The doughnuts themselves offer a clue into ale production in this period because they suggest that ale yeast would have been readily available on a rural estate, which means brewing would have been carried out close by. Williams also has any number of recipes for how to make all kinds of wines – raspberry, apricot and the like, as well as elderflower and birch, which are arguably closer to beer than wine.

I'd like to draw attention to Merryell's recipes for spiced ale drinks, such as posset, a hot milk beverage often made with eggs, sugar, and warming spices like nutmeg, cloves, cinnamon and ginger. Or her recipe for a braggot, which is ale mixed with honey and warming spices then refermented. We still love to mix those kinds of spices into our beer, though this proves quite controversial in certain quarters. The annual appearance of pumpkin beer always seems to enrage certain people who then take to social media to rant about it. As Tori Powell from *A Woman's Brew* says:

> The one thing that does impact me within the beer world is I feel like there are certain flavours of things that I like that are very much frowned upon, like pumpkin spice. If you breathe pumpkin spice, people are like, how dare you contaminate this beer with cinnamon? And I'm like, more cinnamon. Give it to me. Injection of cinnamon, please.

People have been adding warming spices to their brews for a long time. Indeed, most recipes for hot beer or ale call for some combination of them. Your pumpkin spice ale has much more in common with a medieval braggot than merely following a modern fad. And using pumpkin itself in beer is also centuries old. We can thank Native Americans for that introduction to the queen of the squash. Throughout North and South America many different tribes have been cultivating the pumpkin for millennia, with evidence dating back to over 7,000 years in some places.

These kinds of spiced ale drinks are not unique to Meryell's book. They are extremely popular across the board from the 1500s. In England, Hannah Woolley (or Wolley) wrote several books on cooking and homemaking. In her *The Queen-like Closet* we find a recipe 'To make ale to drink within a week'.

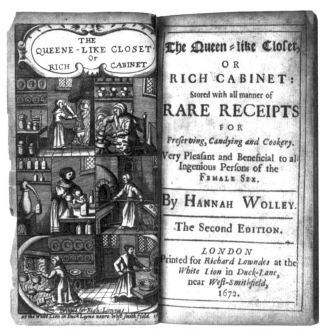

Engraved frontispiece showing five cooking scenes and title page of
Hannah Woolley, or Wolley's *The Queen-like Closet*, 1672.

This involves tunning your ale into a vessel, adding some ginger, an orange stuck with cloves, sugar, and mixing it up. Then decant it into bottles with a sugar lump in each, cork it, turn it upside down, and a week later you can drink it. In Woolley's 1675 *The Accomplish'd Lady's Delight in Preserving, Physick, Beautifying, and Cookery* we see many more recipes that call for ale and beer, and we also learn how to make strong liquor. She gives clear instructions on how to make wormwood water, spirit of honey and balm water, all of which are distilled spirits. As well beery gingerbread, caudle, almond caudle, and one of my favourite drink recipes to recreate, cock ale, which involves boiling a rooster in ale with some raisins, dates, and spices (see page 182).

Ale and beer were used in stews, soups, batters, in sauces for all kinds of meat, and often found their way into desserts. Most women's cookbooks I found had several recipes calling for ale to be used. The *Good Huswifes Jewell*, written by Thomas Dawson *c.*1587, had all kinds of lovely recipes for foods that required ale, including stewed steak, spinach fritters, and caudle. This tradition continues today. Melissa Cole's recent book, *The Beer Kitchen*, contains recipes for beer-poached chicken and beer-brined pork chops, and would be right at home next to Woolley's 1664 *The Cook's Guide*, which includes two recipes for fritters using ale. Beer (or ale) fritters feature frequently in these cookbooks, especially those made with apples. I have made fritters from recipes dating back to the 1300s, which are tasty. (If you want to try some, the recipe is on page 180.)

But what about brewing specifically? Sir Hugh Plat's late 16th- or early 17th-century *Delights for ladies to adorn their persons, tables, closets, and distillatories, with beauties, banquets, perfumes, and waters* is one of the few books I've found that actually tells us the basics of ale and beer making. Plat told his female audience how to bottle beer properly (when your beer is about 10 or 12 days old and is 'reasonably clear'). This may also indicate the relative newness of this kind of beverage and why it might be included here. Plat is very specific on cleanliness. He also emphasises that it is critical that your corks fit the bottles to stop them very closely and that you should not drink the beer until 'they begin to work again'; i.e., secondary fermentation in the bottles. He also explains in some depth why bottled ale is 'windy and muddy, thundering and smoking upon opening the bottle', because it's usually bottled the same day. Therefore, he instructs readers to wait a bit before bottling their beer or ale. Plat also tells his female readers that in order to prevent musty beer bottles they should put them in the oven after the bread has been taken out and leave them there until morning, or, alternatively, to scald them in hot liquor until 'they be sweet'. Further, we are actually given a specific recipe for ale in this book. Under the heading 'divers excellent kind of bottle-ale', Plat describes a sage-ale and how to make it, telling us, 'But if you will make a right Gossips cup, that shall farre exceed all the Ale that ever mother Bunch made in her life time,' referring of course to that infamous alewife Mother Bunch.

The Closet of Sir Kenelm Digby Knight Opened not only has many recipes for various alcoholic beverages but also tells us whose recipes they are. Nestled among the Countess of Bullingbrook's White Metheglin and Lady Morice's Sisters Mead, we find Lady Holmbey's Scotch Ale. The latter is a very detailed recipe for how to make the brew, starting from the mash-in and finishing with the bottling and cellaring. It includes fascinating tidbits such as heating water to just below boiling and adding the malt a little at a time. We are also told to let it mash for several hours, and to keep the pot warm with 'coverlets and blankets'. At this point it is, apparently, a 'thin syrup'. Next, we are to boil it in a cauldron and then decant to a wooden vessel to cool it down for about 40 hours. It even details a precise, and very long, way to add the yeast so it doesn't get shocked. Finally, it should be cellared for a year at a very low temperature, after which it's ready to drink.

The Closet represents an exchange of ideas between women who would trade recipes or find them in various sources and write them down in their own recipe books for their own households. These private recipe collections were passed down through families. The National Library of Scotland has a collection of recipes from the Fletcher family of Saltoun, compiled by a Mrs Johnston *c.*1700, which contains instructions for making hopped ale. This is only one such Scottish source. There is also the famous *Recipe Book of Janet Maule*, written around 1701, which is part of the collection at the National Library of Scotland. While this contains multiple recipes with ale, including a mutton pie, a salmon pie, and those fritters again, Maule also includes a recipe for 'Diverse excelled kinds of bottled aile', which sounds very similar to another recipe discussed here. The line, 'but if ye make a right gossops cup that shal far exceed at the aile that ever mother punch made in her lifetime', is almost identical to the phrase Hugh Plat used in his recipe for sage ale. In fact, it is most certainly the same recipe, virtually word for word, which speaks to the diffusion of these recipes over the centuries.

So, people in times gone by could get together with friends and swap beer recipes, much like they do now. Many of the women I interviewed who homebrewed collaborated with other women. Ruvani de Silva often troubleshoots recipes with the woman who runs her local homebrew shop. Jane Peyton and Emma Inch came together to brew a rose pale ale in honour of International Women's Collaboration Brew Day. Speaking of which, I don't think there's a better example of women collaborating on a brew. Most of the women I spoke to had participated in some way in International Women's Collaboration Brew Day.

*   *   *

Moving swiftly into the 18th century, we can see a more in-depth knowledge of beer brewing in women's books, specifically, Eliza Smith's *The Complete Housewife: Or, Accomplished Gentlewoman's Companion. Being a Collection of Upwards of Seven Hundred of the Most Approved Receipts*, which was written in 1727. In between her various recipes for beery foods like rump of beef and ale-battered fish, cock ale, and caudles, we have actual beer recipes. She has instructions for making barley wine involving boiling French barley and adding to it things like white wine, clary water, lemon juice, red rose water, and sugar. She also tells readers how to make a strong beer (which is basically making beer in beer; i.e., you mash in your malt in beer instead of water, and to this you add hops and rosemary). Most importantly for us, she has an entire chapter on how to make beer and ale and troubleshooting bad brews. Smith is here to set us straight with advice that would make any modern brewer nod in approval. She begins her beer chapter with the following (which is as apt now as it ever was), 'It is granted on all hands, that, according to the common saying, good eating deserves good drinking.' She states that many ladies are 'fond of superintending the affairs of brewing, keeping, bottling' their beer and ale, and goes on to say that she can't think of a better way to conclude than how to make strong and small beer and bottle it. Clearly then, the women she is writing for are of an upper or upper-middle socio-economic status. They are not necessarily brewing themselves but are certainly supervising, and so would want to be knowledgeable in order to properly manage their household.

I won't go into all the details of what Smith tells us because, frankly, it's a lot. We have instructions and tips for small ale, strong ale, just ale, pretty strong ale, and bottled ale. She tells us that beer is important for families, for servants, and also for keeping the apothecary's bills down. As mentioned previously, beer and ale were considered as vital medicines. Smith instructs her readers that if the small beer isn't good, it will hamper workers, as it is an essential ingredient to nourish the body and a key part of the diet. She talks in detail about types of malts and gives advice on the best kinds of hops. The best kind of water for brewing, she says, is river water, but that 'all water which will mix with soap is fit for brewing'. Smith talks about the best months in which to brew, provides instructions on how to preserve yeast, and on the best types of wood for casks. She even gives a detailed rundown on the various kinds of clay that make for the best beer cellar and where precisely one should build one.

I think perhaps my favourite bit of advice from Smith is about using oyster shells to cure a bad and stale brew. She tells us that if a brew becomes thick and sour, to open the bung of the cask for several days. If this still does not stop the fermentation, then take 2–3lb of oyster shells, dry them out in an oven after washing them, then grind them up into a very fine powder and add them to your beer. This will 'presently settle the drink, make it fine and take off the sharp taste of it'. This reminds us of the origins of oyster stout. There is much debate about when oysters first came to be used in beer, and there is a clear difference between oyster meat being used in brewing and oyster shells being used to improve beer or ale. And though many articles attribute the latter practice to the late 1800s, Smith clearly shows that it was in use much earlier.

Like any good BJCP beer judge, Smith also identifies why a beer might have gone off. She relates the case of several gentlemen from the same town brewing with the same malt, the same hops and the same water. They all brewed in the same month and sampled their beer at the same time, 'yet one has had beer extremely fine, strong and well tasted, while the others have hardly had any worth drinking'. The three men could not understand why. Smith offers three possibilities: one, that the weather impacted the brews; two, that the yeast or barm was different; and three, that the cellars weren't all to the same standard, with one being of better quality than the others. Smith, it seems, is wiser than these brewing gentlemen.

Smith's book shows us that women certainly still knew how to brew with expertise in this period, and that this knowledge was deemed important enough to pass on. The women Smith was addressing were referred to as 'ladies' which denotes a specific class of women. Smith tells us that she herself was employed for some 30 years in 'fashionable and noble families', which is where she gained her expertise in housekeeping.

She tells us that she has read a great many cookbooks, but the authors have largely failed because they are 'impractical, other whimsical, other unpalatable, unless to depraved palates'. Instead, Smith compiled a book full of practical advice and useful recipes. She tells us that the medicinal recipes are perfect for 'those generous, charitable, and Christian gentle-women' who are in service to their 'poor country neighbours'. This seems to show that she is writing for gentlewomen, which could imply either aristocracy or gentry, but her audience was likely much larger than that. But brewing housewives were not just confined to guidebooks and how-tos. Written sources accounting the day-to-day activities of the periods clearly demonstrate that women continued to brew at home.

William Lily was an astrologer who frequently wrote to his patron, Elias Ashmole, also an astrologer, as well as antiquary, freemason and founder of the Ashmolean Museum in Oxford. Lily wrote to Ashmole a lot, often sending effusive gratitude but also regularly oversharing the details of his life. He wrote frequently about his wife's ale brewing and bottling, and one of the most entertaining of these tales is related here. Lily tells Ashmole that 'my Gallant' – his wife – is most grateful for his letter but cannot reply at the moment as she is indisposed. He then goes on to explain in detail everything you never wanted to know about why this may be. You see, his 'Gallant' apparently intended to cozen her maid; i.e., she wanted to trick her maid into drinking some purging ale. As we know already, these purging ales were very popular, though sometimes with rather unpleasant results. Lily's wife usually took some *syrup spinae cervinae*, probably for her rheumatism. This syrup was supposed to be served warm in a posset-ale. But it seems the universe was not best pleased with Lily's wife's dastardly intentions, for she mixed up her ales and drank the purging ale herself instead. As Lily relayed to his patron, 'that Sunday, shee shitt abomination at least 7 or 8 tymes if not more'. Delighted for her.

William Harrison's *Description of Elizabethan England* provides us with another fascinating insight into brewing women at the time. Harrison spends a decent portion of a chapter talking about malting and brewing, though he tells us he is not that great a maltster or brewer himself. It is his wife and her maidservants who carry out the brewing, once a month, and so she told him everything he knows. His detailed accounting of her brewing revealed that she was making beer and not ale, as she added English hops, bayberries and arras. This was a clear personal preference as he noted that other people prefer to add long pepper instead of bay and arras. In the *Household Account Book of Sarah Fell of Swarthmoor Hall*, dating to the 17th century, this trend of women brewing is again abundantly clear.

In an entry from October 1673, Fell tells us that her family paid Greaves' wife for ale. This happens again in November of the same year. On 16 February that year she had paid Greaves' wife for ale for her sister, Mary Lower, and the same for her other two sisters living at Swarthmoor Hall, Susannah and Rachel. Over and over, money is paid out for ale for the various sisters, as well as for her mother, and sometimes even the animals. Apparently, the cows and horses were also drinking pints of ale when they were unwell. Puggy would be so proud.

These sources aren't exceptions; they are the rule. Women continued to brew in great numbers throughout the 16th and 17th centuries, some even well into the 18th and, in lesser numbers, throughout the 19th and even into the early 20th centuries, depending on location and context. But you don't need to take my word for it. Many studies have been carried out by experts on this phenomenon. According to Darron Dean, Andrew Hann, Mark Overton and Jane Whittle, in *Production and Consumption in English Households 1600-1700*, the making of alcohol in the home declined over time in Cornwall, from 50% of households making it in 1600–29 to 28% after 1660. Meanwhile, Kent witnessed a steady rise in households brewing, rising to 79% by 1720–49. Most of this alcohol was ale and beer, followed by cider and then spirits. Most significantly, the authors' argued that this brewing in the private sphere was 'likely to have been dominated by women'. And they weren't the only ones to make this argument. Pamela Sambrook, in her study *Country House Brewing in England 1500-1900*, argued that brewing was part of women's duties alongside tasks like dairying, baking, and food preservation.

Women would persist in brewing at home during the 19th century. Samuel and Isabella Beeton were the editors of *The Englishwoman's Domestic Magazine* in the mid-19th century. Initially, the very popular magazine was sold cheaply at about 2d (tuppence) and written for young women of middling social status. In 1860 the Beetons upped their prices and changed their audience, switching to a wealthier group of women. But regardless of the magazine's demographic, we can gain insight into the fact that these young women still had a close relationship with beer, perhaps even with brewing. The magazine contained recipes, as well as answers to reader's letters and fictional stories. One such story comes from Vol. 1 and was called 'Paul's Impromptu'. In the tale the titular character is set on wooing Miss Miranda, though we care less about the love life of this man than the brewing theme of the story. Paul tells us that he is thirsty at the thought of his Aunt Tabitha's nice beer, but 'I rejected the idea of Miranda being engaged in brewing beer with the utmost disdain'. It appears the character has a negative view of women brewers, because they are closely associated with his aunt, or perhaps because brewing is labour intensive and something he didn't want to picture his paramour doing.

The magazine also provides an excellent source of factual information on beer and brewing, with all manner of recipes and handy tips. In order to wave their hair, for example, the readers are instructed to wet it with beer and to plait it overnight. In the post-1860 editions, written for a wealthier audience, we can discern a knowledge of brewing amongst the readership. We are told of the 'model housewife who is studying the science of things', who writes in to ask what vinegar is and how is it 'propagated'. To which the magazine answers in depth about the 'fungus' it deems is the cause of the vinegar: 'growth in saccharine liquids at moderate temperatures converts them into vinegar'. The reply further explains that it is closely related with the 'yeast plant, which by its vegetation at high temperature, causes fermentation in bread and beer', and then goes on to talk about how best to make vinegar in fermenting liquids. What this tells us is that at least some of the readership were keen to learn the science behind matters such as fermentation.

An 1857 volume of the magazine included six recipes for ginger beer, some of which called for fresh beer yeast, which again assumes a certain level of knowledge and access to the stuff. One of these recipes also talks in length about finings which it defines as 'isinglass picked and steeped in beer'. Beer also featured in food recipes. To cure sweet hams, for instance, the audience is told to boil one in strong beer, sugar, salt and bay salt. And there are yet more drinks recipes, such as one for shandy. There are two recipes for malt wine: one involving adding sugar, ginger, a Seville orange, half a lemon, and a gallon of 'good beer'; the other, a very similar process but with 'sweet wort'. So again, there is an assumption that women readers were familiar with the intricacies of brewing.

*   *   *

The decline in women brewing at home was not linear; it did not happen in the same way throughout Britain. What this tells us, and I cannot stress this enough, is that brewing trends were very much context specific. Changes could be made in one town that were not implemented in another. While there are certainly national trends, the day-to-day life of brewing – who was brewing, what they were brewing, how they were brewing, and who drank what and where – could differ greatly depending on location, social status and time period. But, as we see from the Beetons, women did not stop brewing in the 19th century.

The Englishwoman's Domestic Magazine isn't our only source for home-brewing women in this period. The author Jane Austen wrote in a letter to her sister, Cassandra Austen, on 7 October 1808, that spruce beer is being brewed because Martha has arrived. They make this spruce beer again, as she told her sister in a letter of 9 December that same year, in which she tells Cassandra that she is the one with the great cask, 'for we are brewing Spruce Beer again'. Was Jane herself brewing? Perhaps, but it is equally possible that the servants on the estate were brewing and she or some other female member of the household supervised the roles, or even helped alongside them. Indeed, she tells Cassandra in a letter of 9 March 1814 that 'I am so pleased that the Mead is brewed! – Love to all.' This does seem to indicate some pride on her part and perhaps a more direct involvement. So, even prolific female writers were possibly brewing in their spare time.

The letter from Jane Austen raises an important point. Just precisely who was doing the brewing? So far, a lot of these sources have been written for the landowning class: people who were upper middling sorts (middle class in more modern parlance), or entirely upper class. While housewives certainly brewed for their households, they often did so alongside their servants, who were possibly doing the bulk of the actual brewing.

We saw hints of this in Eliza Smith's book. She was a housekeeper after all. Hannah Glasse, who was a contemporary of Smith, wrote in *The Art of Cookery Made Plain and Easy* that she used plain language so that her work could be understood by servants. Again, reiterating that the people reading these books were not just ladies but also servants and possibly other women in the middle socio-economic group. Glasse also wrote about beer and ale and shared her tips about how to preserve yeast for brewing. A similar case can be found in Hannah Woolley's 17th-century *The Compleat Servant-maid*. As the title suggests, she wrote this for women who worked or wanted to work as servants. She included medicinal beer recipes, diet drinks and drinks to cleanse the blood, and while there were no specific instructions for brewing, she did mention different kinds of beer such as small beer, good stale beer, and strong beer. This tells us that these servants were expected to be familiar with beer and implies some knowledge of brewing.

There is also plenty of evidence beyond these books of servants brewing. Jane Whittle's study 'Housewives and Servants in Rural England, 1440–1650: Evidence of Women's Work from Probate Documents', supports the argument that brewing was something that female servants would do. In her study of the Kent inventories from the first half of the 17th century, she found that the four most common forms of women's work in servant employment patterns were dairying, spinning, baking and brewing. This is also the case in Wales. Wilma Thomas, in her thesis, *Women in the Rural Society of South-West Wales, c.1780-1870*, found that female servants in farms such as those of the Nanteaos estate and the Golden Grove estate would have to take on duties like herding sheep, spinning, and assisting in brewing. Thomas argues that this continued through the early years of the 20th century. Scotland was similar, where, in 1708, Lanarkshire wages were set out by the justices for female servants. They stated that 'a strong and sufficient' woman servant who engaged in the tasks of 'brewing, baking, washing and other necessary work within and without the house' is be paid £14 Scots a year 'and no more'.

Working as a servant brewing for others could come with its own dangers. Returning to the *Intoxicants and Early Modernity* database, on 11 May, 1685, Sarah Heyman, a brewer for Mrs Poole testified against Mr Poole, who was apparently an abusive monster to Heyman and every other woman in his vicinity. We are told in one instance that, without provocation, he came up to her, struck her and ripped the tongs out of her hands and stated that he would, 'knock out her brains'. She was incredibly afraid and stated that she would not brew in the said brewhouse because she was so scared of him and what he was capable of doing. This was echoed by Mrs Jane Poole, who also described Mr Poole as belligerent, mean, and violent. He swore and cursed at her and called her a whore, and told her that he would plague her as long as she lived in her house. Apparently, Jane Poole testified that he was incredibly abusive to her servants, and that Sarah Heyman was Jane Poole's brewer who 'dares not brew for this deponent for fear of some harm to be done to her'. We can see here the trend of exploitation and abuse of female servants. Sadly, this was not particularly uncommon.

While most of our sources are concerned with rural or suburban environments, women also continued to brew as servants in urban homes well into the 19th century, albeit in smaller numbers. There is also less evidence of this. According to one example from *Old Bailey Proceedings*:

Accounts of Criminal Trials, found in the *London Lives 1690–1800: Crime Poverty and Social Policy in the Metropolis* project, household servants were still brewing in the 19th century in London. In 1817 George Fawcett was accused of stealing a few items from Eliza Stoddart. Ann Jones, the servant to Stoddart, was sworn in to testify against him. She tells us that she was brewing at the time. In fact, Fawcett actually came to the 'grains-in' as she called it (aka mashing in), and it was then that he stole the spoon and claimed it must have fallen into the mash.

It is also of note that some places deliberately did not brew and let their would-be servants know this. An advert for a maid servant in the *Oxford Journal* on 4 May 1776 stated that they were looking for a middle-aged woman who was able to cook 'in a plain way', and went on to state, 'No Brewing at Home, nor Washing of large Cloaths'. This may have been an attraction of the post, telling their potential employees that the labour would be less intensive and that they would not need to bring this specific skill set. By declaring up front that this skill was not required, it may also suggest that this task would have been commonly expected.

So, we know that women brewed in households well into the 19th century. They brewed for their families or for their employers. Sometimes they brewed beer to sell and earn a bit of money on the side, or to provide nutrition. They swapped recipes and wrote down ones they found in books or in newspapers. As immigrants, they perhaps brought with them traditions and methods from their home countries. They wrote letters to each other and would troubleshoot how to make their brews better. They even published books on the topic, writing in minute detail about everything from how to build a beer cellar to adding oysters to help fix a beer. In short, women were still a significant part of the story of brewing and continued to help shape the history of beer.

*   *   *

Our families are often the first place many of us were introduced to beer. Perhaps we grew up watching our relatives enjoy a few pints at the dinner table or in the local pub. And maybe those beers made it into a few of our most treasured foods; secret recipes passed down through the generations to create the mythic family dishes we all wait to savour just a few times a year. As we have seen in this chapter, some of these traditional staples have been in families for centuries, handed down from mother to daughter to granddaughter over the years. For many of us, drinking beer, or cooking with it, is something we have learned from our upbringing. It feels familiar to us – and it's comforting.

This is certainly the case for Helena Adedipe of Eko Brewery. The women she grew up around in the Congo tended to drink beer more than other alcoholic beverages: 'Beer is definitely the drink that was passed around a lot more, you know, growing up at gatherings and festivities or whatnot.' Beer itself has always been important in her life. 'Beer is very much part of our culture and actually part of our history', she told me. Her husband, Anthony, who has Nigerian roots, had similar experiences. His great grandmother had a stout every single night. These core memories have greatly influenced their love for these styles, and, in fact, their first beer was a porter.

However, it's not just drinking beer. It's the juxtaposition of beer and food that Adedipe recalls so fondly. She grew up watching her mother make crêpes with lager, and now her family uses her own beers in their cooking. Her sister used one of Eko's porters to make those family crêpes and Adedipe herself has tried her hand at adding one of her lagers to beer batter for fish (a dish we saw crop up in Eliza Smith's 18th-century recipe book). Primarily though, she likes to experiment with sweet dishes. In an echo of Merryell Williams' doughnuts, Adedipe tells me that using beer 'basically acts like yeast, so it's just wonderful', and it makes a perfect addition to many recipes.

After growing up and living in different countries in Africa, she tells me that you can't really go out to drink there 'without there being a massive plate of food'. And we're not just talking about snacks; she tells me that it's usually a 'full-blown meal'. Because of this custom, they designed their beers around food pairing. In fact, restaurants were their first customers, with their beers replacing macro-brewed options on their menus.

Like the historical women we learned about in this chapter, Eko Brewery has its origins in homebrewing, starting with a 'tiny kind of plastic kit that probably wasn't sanitary'. According to Adedipe, her husband did more of the hands-on brewing, while she did the troubleshooting, consulting books, figuring out ingredients, and suggesting techniques. To be clear, though, she does also brew.

'I'm a big history buff,' Adedipe, tells me. And it was history that led to her love of beer and brewing, both through her family's history and the history of African brewing traditions. 'I started to read a lot more into the history of brewing and different civilisations, especially African civilisation, and how women were so influential in brewing,' she told me, adding that throughout Africa women are still brewing in villages and for their households, as they have done for centuries.

As we have already seen in this chapter, Black women were a part of the brewing history of Britain, starting in small numbers from the 16th century onwards. African women immigrants brought with them their diverse traditional techniques when they first came to these shores, passing them down through their families, though sourcing traditional ingredients in Britain would have been difficult. Black and African women have been a part of the cultural fabric of UK society for generations, albeit in relatively small numbers, and, as servants, housewives, and heiresses, would likely have been familiar with brewing as part of their duties in the household. So, in many ways, the reintroduction of African beers and brewing techniques can be seen as echoing the past. (Today, Eko Brewery and Rock Leopard are the only two fully Black-owned breweries in the UK.)

Like their historical Welsh counterparts who used nettles and dandelions because of their proximity and cultural significance to create *diod faen*, Adedipe and Anthony decided to mesh the differing elements from Congolese and Nigerian culture into the beers they were making. This is why, while they are also British, it was important for them to brew a beer that was 'connected to our heritage somehow', even though 'Nigerian and Congolese cultures are quite different, but still we thought it would be nice to kind of bring it back to Africa'. She told me that palm wine is an important drink in many different West or Central African countries, so they thought about taking the components of that product and then adding them into their beer. This inspired them to use coconut palm sugar in several of their beers, including a New England IPA and a pilsner. From there they started using other kinds of African staples in their brews, like cassava, Madagascan vanilla, sorghum, yam and Zambian coffee beans.

They have also experimented with South African hops, which are hard to find outside that country. This is something that Apiwe Nxusani-Mawela of Tolokazi Beer Company has experienced herself when she was making her beer for Beer52 in Croatia. She ran into difficulties sourcing South African hops. Like Eko Brewery, Nxusani-Mawela also credits different traditional African brewing practices to be a huge influence on the beers she makes and how she makes them. In fact, her beer brand itself, Tolokazi, is actually her clan name. She told me that 'when a woman brews a beer, as a sign of respect she would typically be called by her clan name'. So her brand itself is about 'paying homage to the female African brewers, those who came before me and those who will come after me'. Speaking of her experiences as a brewer, Nxusani-Mawela told me, 'I often tell people that I would like to be remembered as a great brewer who just happened to be Black and happened to be female.' She goes on to say that 'for me to be the first Black female in South Africa to own a brewery and operate one is really a great privilege that I don't take lightly'. Her love of using traditional and indigenous ingredients like sorghum and rooibos in her beers has had a profound impact on her brewing. In fact, after completing her Diploma in Brewing qualification in 2008 she returned home to brew:

> I remember being asked by my dad to go back home in the village and brew *Mqombothi*, our traditional African beer, to thank the ancestors for all the blessings. I recall being in awe as I watched my mom and aunts brew, in how the brewing principles and methodologies were similar to what I had studied. At the same time I was sad that I didn't know how to brew a beer of my own people and my tradition. Over the years, not only have I learnt and mastered the art of traditional African brewing but have also incorporated this into my Tolokazi beer range.

We can see, in the stories of Eko and Tolokazi breweries, that family plays an important role in carrying on tradition. It's watching your great grandmother drink stout at dinner, or your mum and aunt's brew, and passing these stories and recipes down over the generations, keeping the history alive. But there's another place that often represents the stuff of family legends: the pub.

BEER STREET.

Beer, happy Produce of our Isle
Can sinewy Strength impart,
And wearied with Fatigue and Toil
Can chear each manly Heart.

Labour and Art upheld by Thee
Successfully advance,
We quaff Thy balmy Juice with Glee
And Water leave to France.

Genius of Health, thy grateful Taste
Rivals the Cup of Jove,
And warms each English generous Breast
With Liberty and Love.

Beer Street, by William Hogarth, 1751, illustrates that the alehouse, or public house as it became known, was considered an important social space, and that women were a key part of these places.

5

WORKIN' 9 TO LAST ORDERS

The local: that most sacred of spaces. What do you see when you imagine yours in your mind? Perhaps antique wood panelling stretches up from the floors, interspersed with bookshelves bearing titles no one has bothered reading in decades. Maybe photographs line the walls, pictures of regulars or local haunts frame red-patterned carpets and a mismatched collection of weathered tables and chairs? Or perhaps those walls boast mid-20th-century adverts beckoning punters to try their beers with dark-leather-trimmed benches, a sleek oak bar, dim lighting, and an ancient stone fireplace? Possibly it's something completely different. A craft beer bar boasting 30 taps bearing badges of local and international brews; loud music, neon lights, and metal stools completing the look. Each of these places can function as a kind of home from home: a spot to meet with life-long friends, to make new ones, to commiserate our losses, to celebrate our successes, to meet a partner, or even lose one. And so, we turn to that most important of places: the pub.

The pub is much more than the sum of its parts. Annabel Smith, co-founder of Dea Latis, started her career pulling pints behind the bar and quickly fell in love with the people and the atmosphere. This love for the community that the pub created catapulted her straight into her decision to take over the licence, and the rest, as they say, is history. She told me that in the pub 'You see all forms of human behaviour. So, in addition to all the other skills that you learn as a publican, you become an informal anthropologist because you're studying human behaviour all the time.'

In the medieval period, public drinking spots could be temporary or more permanent spaces. It could be anything from a designated tavern to a few tables in your neighbour's house. And a whole lot in between. Historian Kristen Burton argued that much as brewing expanded in the wake of the Black Death, so too did the alehouse, as more people wanted to drink in public. Not only did more people want to drink, but as we have seen, they had more money to do so and were drinking more than their predecessors. So, the alehouse itself became a more important social centre, what we often refer to as the 'third place', neither home nor work but another thing entirely. A centre for community perhaps. Peter Clark contended that from the 15th century 'fully-fledged alehouses' appear. These were markedly different to the spaces where women sold ale from their houses. It was much later, in the latter half of the 17th and early 18th centuries, that we see the introduction of the term 'public house', which is then abbreviated to the more familiar 'pub' in the 19th century. Over the years, these pubs, alehouses, even inns, positioned themselves as another kind of home, and though they have changed markedly over time, women have remained a key part of these spaces well into our modern period.

Pubs continue to function as important cultural spaces. In his award-winning book *Desi Pubs: A Guide to British-Indian Pubs, Food & Culture*, author David Jesudason showed readers that Desi pubs were set up to become 'community hubs', allowing local people to escape the racist discrimination they were experiencing elsewhere while also serving as a source for legal services and even finding employment. He also spoke of the role of women as publicans and staff in these spaces. Emma Inch, in 'Passion, Pride and Protests', told listeners of the important history of LGBTQ+ pubs and their purpose as community centres. Laura Hadland talked to me about her piece 'Portraits from the Pub' for the Women on Tap Festival, where she interviewed women who attended, owned or worked in such places. One person she spoke with was currently being supported by a local pub she had never gone to, but nonetheless they were providing her and her grandson with meals to help them during lockdown. Hadland told me, 'She had had no other means of support during lockdown, no mental health support, no kind of tangible support with food and resources and that kind of thing. And this pub stepped in and helped her.' Further, she also shared with me the story of an Irish pub that served as a community space for new immigrants and the local Traveller community.

Now, as in times past, the pub isn't just a place to go and have a pint, it's also very much somewhere you can find your people, where you can access support. These places can be life-saving in a very literal sense. But for the women who have worked in them, and those who have owned them, pubs and alehouses can be something of a double-edged sword. In certain contexts they can be a safe and supportive space for community, a place to gather with friends and allies, but in other situations they can be a source of pain and unmitigated abuse.

Licensing Laws

On 18 February 1576 Joan Walley, an alehousekeeper in Tarporley, Cheshire, appeared in court as a plaintiff in her defamation case against Henry Dawson. You see, Dawson had been running around accusing Walley of all sorts, referring to her as an 'old, burned arse whore' whose house smelt of pox, and generally making a nuisance of himself. As we touched on earlier, in 1552 the Alehouse Act saw national licensing come into effect for these kinds of premises. In order to gain permission to run an alehouse, a person had to enter into an agreement to maintain a good reputation, respectable behaviour, and to abide by certain rules, otherwise they might lose their licence or be fined. Defending that good reputation was essential to stay in business, so Walley took out a case against Dawson. She enlisted the help of witnesses and her neighbours, who testified that prior to these accusations she had been a woman of 'honest fame'. Walley defended herself and her reputation so that she could keep her business. This story – from the *Intoxicants and Early Modernity* database – is one of many in which women appear in the courts in defamation suits to defend their honour. Another from this database dates to 1670, when Ursula Malpas took out a case against Alice Litler after the latter called her a 'whore' because she permitted her husband to drink at her alehouse. And on and on it goes.

Sometimes, though, the requirement to maintain a good reputation could be laxly enforced, as scholar A. Lynn Martin found. It seems it was generally up to whoever was in charge at the time. A prime example of this is the story of Jane Ashton, employee at the alehouse belonging to her mother, who was also called Jane Ashton. The elder Ashton apparently had a reputation for being a woman of loose morals, 'a profane swearer and cursor, a brawler, a liar, a drunken woman and cheater', who permitted 'infamous people to drink and tipple in her house on the Sabbath days and at other unreasonable times'. Yet her place of business was allowed to continue. It is important to note that this particular case dates from 1718, so things were perhaps a bit different than they had been just a century before. And in the interest of fairness, it must be noted that women could defame men's businesses. John Withers filed a defamation suit against Elizabeth Radley for calling him, amongst other things, a 'broken rouge' who would 'run this country before the next Assizes,' and that he was 'not worth a groat'. Both ran drinking establishments and Withers testified that Radley's slanderous words had 'blemished' his reputation. So it certainly worked both ways.

Regardless of occasional lax enforcement, licences were generally required. In the Middlesex Sessions of September 1717, Alice Mitchell and Alice Goodman were convicted for selling ale without a licence and keeping common tippling houses. Also from the Middlesex Sessions, in 1708, Mary Newberry of Enfield allegedly liked disorder in her house. We are told that the justices concluded, 'we have thought that to Suppress her from any longer keeping an alehouse or Tipling house or using commonly Selling of ale, Beer, Brandy or other distalled liquors'. Of course, women could be successful in their petitions to run alehouses. In January 1718, from these same Middlesex Sessions, Elizabeth Drury and Ann Neale were to be granted licences for the selling of beer and ale by retail in their respective houses. And it wasn't just women's businesses that were shut down because of bad behaviour. Again, from the Middlesex Sessions, this time in October 1697, there was petition from the inhabitants of Hendon against Ann Clarke, Daniell Mills and Timothy Smyth, who continued to sell beer and ale even though they had caused 'great disturbance in the said parish'. Because the people of the town were not happy, it was deemed necessary that no person in the parish could be allowed a licence to sell beer and ale without the consent of the neighbouring justices.

Sex work

Maintaining a good reputation wasn't the only issue facing women who kept or worked in alehouses. Staying safe and out of danger was also a real concern. Margaret Fiske infamously said in 1578, 'there cannot be any alewife thrive without she be a whore or have a whore in her house'. This link between women who worked in alehouses and sex work, whether real or imagined, meant that women could find themselves in very dangerous situations. As we saw in Chapter Three, there was a societal fear, expressed through art and literature, that women who worked in alehouses or sold ale were not good people. They were linked with the devil, they were thought to sell in false measures, and they were known for licentious behaviour. And maybe in some part, because of these beliefs, men have tried to control women who work in alehouses and sell ale.

As well as licensing, the years from 1500 to 1800 saw the introduction of regulations specifically targeting women who sold ale. In 1540 in Chester, for example, a bylaw was passed stating that no woman from 14 to 40 years of age was allowed to sell ale. Unlike those earlier fines for English alewives selling in false measures – which were generally seen as the cost of doing business – these later laws were anything but lax. At least according to Judith Bennett, who argued that this law was repeated in later doctrines and 'firmly' enforced. This was not just aimed at women who brewed but extended to women who sold ale. And Chester was not an isolated example. In Beverly, East Yorkshire, a bylaw was introduced in 1405 stating that no brewster, or female seller called a tippler, could allow strangers to remain after 9pm. In 1492 in Coventry, officials tried to prevent sex workers from working as barmaids by banning women with 'evil name, fame or condition'. In London several regulations were issued in an attempt to ban sex workers from taverns and alehouses altogether.

There was clearly a general anxiety about women who worked in these spaces being associated with sex work. However, scholars like Barbara Gleiss have argued that this reflected the reality for women working in the trade, i.e., that women working in alehouses needed to be seen as kind, funny and entertaining, but had to tread a fine line between displaying these qualities and being accused of being sex workers. Much like today, women were expected to be pretty, but not too pretty, funny, but not too funny, kind, but not too kind, and flirty, but not too flirty. This line changed depending on who the woman was talking to, what she was wearing, and frankly just the way the wind happened to blow that day. And though men and women participated in such flirtatious behaviour, it was women who were largely blamed for any negative experiences, and therefore were the ones at risk of being put in danger.

In James Brown's study of the public houses and alehouses in Southampton in the early modern period, he argued that single women who worked in alehouses, or later in public houses, could often be perceived to be sex workers, irrespective of whether they were engaged in the trade.

The Ale-House Door, from 'World in Miniature' by Thomas Rowlandson, showing the common perception of how women behaved in alehouses.

Regardless of their consent in the matter, they were viewed as always sexually available. And so single women who worked in alehouses, sex workers and non-sex workers alike, faced harassment, abuse, assault, rape, and even murder.

This also extended to young girls who worked in these places. In a particularly chilling account, Brown recalled the story of 12-year-old Margaret Smith, who, in 1577, was working at an alehouse operated by a French woman living in Southampton. Smith reported that she was making beds in the morning when a French man accosted her and tried to force himself on her. Smith was able to resist him and ran to tell her mistress who promptly kicked him out. These sorts of stories were all too common. As Brown discovered, sometimes the people these women worked for did not defend them. In fact, they did the very opposite, exploiting them sexually and putting them in positions to be raped, often repeatedly. For example, Brown came across the case, in 1587, of Jacqueline Corbin, who worked for the Rowse family of tipplers. Apparently, she had been attacked by the son, but Mrs Rowse then led her into a dangerous position with a group of drunken men.

These cases are not limited to Brown's study. Barbara Hanawalt found that women in taverns were 'at risk of being pimped by their masters and mistresses for the sexual satisfaction of the male customers'; such as the owner of the Bushe Tavern who did so to his two servants, Mandeyleyn and Alice. Hanawalt found that this was not limited to men; female alehouse owners would also engage in this practice.

A. Lynn Martin contended that in some cases barmaids and female tavern keepers would supplement their incomes by engaging in sex work. She found many instances of women who were convicted for selling sex as well as drink. For example, Joanna Skeppere in Brandon, Suffolk, in 1471 apparently drew in 'lecherous men'. I want to stress that how much agency these women had in these situations is often unknown. Some were not sex workers at all but were trafficked. The realities of sex work in the medieval and early modern periods are becoming more evident now that work has been done to uncover the stories from the perspective of the workers themselves. Historians like Kate Lister with her book *A Curious History of Sex*, and the *Whores of Yore* research project have done immense work on helping to illuminate these accounts.

Sexual harassment and assault were only one facet of the mistreatment that women could face in alehouses. Verbal abuse could also be commonplace. In 1680, in Thurstaston, Cheshire, Margaret Burscough, aged 25, testified against John Groome, a rector, who hurled all manner of abuse at her when he visited her alehouse. She told the court, 'he called her ill names and abused her much with his tongue'. He notably also refused to pay her until she was able to get her neighbours to shame him into it.

Despite all this, women continued to run alehouses, often alongside their husbands. However, finding women who owned, or who worked in alehouses can be quite a challenge, as Alexandra Shepard encountered in her study. Shepard examined 13,500 witness reports from the dioceses of Canterbury, Chester, Chichester, Ely, London, Salisbury and York, the archdeaconries of Lewes and Richmond, and the Cambridge University courts, dating to 1550-1728. These witnesses had to state for the record what job they did or how they made money, as well as their financial status or worth. From this study, she concluded that many women didn't define themselves with a specific job. Instead, they listed the tasks that they carried out, making it very difficult to ascertain what they did for a living. Consequently, women who worked in alehouses, or who brewed, might list that as something they did and not as their actual occupation. This was in stark contrast to their husbands who, Shepard found, would identify themselves with the titles of brewer or innkeeper, jobs that they were supported in by their wives.

Returning to those entries in the *Intoxicants and Early Modernity* database, we have many examples of families working in drinking establishments. Margaret Maddock ran an alehouse, likely alongside her husband, Richard, a husbandman. She comes to our attention when she reported a theft of money from her premises. In 1667 Catherine Holland worked in her father's alehouse serving ale. She testified about a parish clerk who would sneak out when the minister was in the pulpit to have a penny worth of ale before slinking back to the church later.

We have scholarly consensus that women ran alehouses, inns, and pubs alongside their husbands in the early modern period. After the death of their husbands, most widows would continue the trade. In 1623 Anne Woosencroft of Manchester, a widow and alehousekeeper, found herself on the wrong side of the law when she was charged with permitting John Radcliffe and Nicholas Moorton to remain in her tippling house, contrary to the statues. Widow Kirks sold ale at the Sign of Pigeon in Eastgate Street in Chester in 1713. When her servant, Ann Lloyd, was serving ale to her female customers she witnessed a fight that eventually ended up in court. A further example can be found in the will of William Dreede of Banbury, an inn holder, who was buried on 12 April 1639. Dreede left his wife almost everything, other than some money he willed to his daughters, and a malt mill and brewing vessel. He and his wife probably brewed ale for sale to their customers. When he died, his widow continued the family business.

Women didn't need to sell ale in alehouses or taverns; they could sell at a market as hucksters or regrators. But with the rise of guilds and increasing commercialisation, these hucksters would find themselves as targets, with the guilds accusing them of selling ale at more expensive rates, or not in the right quantities. This kind of discrimination was rife in the early modern period}, as we saw from the bans on women and girls selling ale, but it was not restricted to sex or gender. In the 18th century, attempts were made to ban entire groups from selling ale or beer and keeping alehouses on religious grounds. In the Middlesex Sessions of December 1716, we see an example of this. There is a call for 'papists', i.e., Catholics, to be banned from keeping alehouses, or selling ale, beer, or other liquors, because 'they have an opportunity to debauch the minds and alienate the affections of his majesties good servants'. This effectively banned Catholic women and men from owning alehouses and selling ale and beer.

As we have seen in this early modern period, owning and working in alehouses could be dangerous and unpleasant for women. However, it must be stressed that there were women who very much enjoyed their work regardless of the potential risks involved. We saw stories of women who successfully petitioned for licences to run their own places, and widows who kept working after the death of their spouses. And though it may be the case that this was out of need rather than a desire to do the work, we can venture that at least some women did enjoy working in or owning these kinds of establishments.

Into the 19th Century

Located behind enemy lines, The British Hotel was a haven for soldiers wanting to escape the horrors of the Crimean War, if even just for a moment. Providing food and refreshment to those who came to her doors, Mary Seacole served French beer, champagne and ham sandwiches. But Seacole is perhaps best remembered as a nurse, and a hugely influential one at that. When the war broke out in the 1850s, Seacole went to the British government to volunteer her services, knowing she could do immense good on the frontlines, but she was denied passage (no doubt because of their racial prejudice). That did not deter her, however, and she went on her own, knowing she was needed to attend the wounded and sick soldiers. During her lifetime, Seacole garnered a huge following and was widely praised for her courage, kindness, and compassion to the soldiers, and her nursing expertise was unparalleled. She was recently voted the greatest Black Briton in history.

We are fortunate that Seacole wrote down her experiences so that we know from her own words what she was undertaking. Amongst all the stories of her heroism in taking care of the sick and wounded, we can find tales of ale. At the British Hotel, one of her best customers was the Turkish Pacha who loved bottled beer, sherry and champagne. We also learn that Seacole made a mean claret cup, adding lemon peel, sugar, nutmeg and ice to water or claret; and her cider cup was also very popular. Jane Robinson's work on Seacole highlighted her hotel's importance to the soldiers of the time, and their need for comfort and refreshment. And while Seacole's contributions to the history of nursing is unparalleled, she is also an important figure in the history of inns, pubs, and alehouses. As we saw earlier in this chapter, such places, often women-owned, can be vital for the survival of communities.

Statue of Mary Seacole, by Martin Jennings, in front of St Thomas' Hospital, London.

* * *

In the 19th century many women in the UK ran pubs and alehouses. According to data extrapolated by Robert J. Bennett, Harry Smith, Piero Montebruno and Carry van Lieshout from the corresponding census', there were around 24,652 women serving as proprietors in 'refreshment' in 1851 compared to 48,533 men; 28,263 women compared to 56,833 men in 1861; and by 1881 there were 43,168 women and 71,299 men. Bennett, Smith, Montebruno and van Lieshout contended that, between 1851 and 1881, women became more involved and took ownership of more establishments than men. The pages of brewers' magazines are littered with examples of women owning pubs, alehouses and inns. In a 20 June 1893 edition of the *Brewer's Guardian*, we learn of a Miss Macraie who owned and operated a beerhouse called the 'Woodman' on Devonshire Street, in Mile End Old Town, and a Miss Woods who owned one on Iden Street in Liverpool. A *Brewer's Guardian* article from 20 February 1871 tells us of Mrs Sarah Coplestone of the Clifton Hotel, Liverpool, who also had a licensed house at Norton Street. She had made the mistake of thinking one licence would cover both premises, but she needed one for each.

Some records of women's alehouse ownership, though, reflect the potential dangers that were present for women working in the trade. On 24 April 1871 we are told of the tragic story of a woman called Martin who died from suffocation in the cellar of a public house in Loughborough after it was ruled that carbonic acid fumes from a vat of fermenting ale created a poisonous environment and killed her. It was determined that the closed cellar door allowed the fumes to concentrate enough to cause the poison. The article goes on to say that the landlady of the public house and another woman were 'rendered insensible', as were some of the men who attempted to rescue them.

While we have seen many instances of men moving to legally bar women from selling ale in previous centuries, some of the legal moves made during the 19th century made it easier for women to do so. In 1828 the Alehouses Act was brought into play, followed quickly by the Beerhouse Act in 1830. These made it significantly easier for people to apply for licences, and also eased regulations on beer sellers. This resulted in an increase of those spaces where a person could drink in public and inevitably impacted on the number of women who could access ownership of these kinds of businesses.

However, despite these new regulations, some men still viewed the presence of women in public houses as unseemly and tried to have them removed from the trade. An issue of the *Brewer's Guardian* of 18 September 1871 investigated the Annual Licensing Meeting at Marlborough, where several licences were 'adjourned', including those of Mrs Watts of Axford and Mrs Rose of Bedwyn. This was done because it was argued by the magistrates that it was improper for women to run public houses and that, in the future, women should only be able to have a public house licence for a year after her husband's death. The writer of the article quite clearly disagreed strongly with this stance, stating that it would be a 'great hardship' for those widows, and contending that they had probably been in the business a long time alongside their former spouses and so would have been extremely competent.

Less than a month later, the *Brewer's Guardian* reported on a raid against widowed publicans in Marlborough. The journal cited an article in the *Morning Advertiser* which defended women against these claims, stating that these raids should 'arouse every right-minded woman to resistance, and enlist the sympathies of every manly and true-hearted man'. The writer argued that women, 'either wives or widows', 'are some of the best managers of inns, hotels, and public houses in the United Kingdom'. The writer goes on to extol the virtues of landladies and women who manage public houses for their husbands, brothers, fathers or employers, arguing that the raids were cruel and ridiculous. It is clear that the decision of the Marlborough magistrates was not popular with the readership of the *Brewer's Guardian* or the *Morning Advertiser*. The latter went on to describe in detail about how foolish and wicked they were, describing their decision as 'utter, ludicrous, and most unparalleled absurdity'. They went on to state that the magistrates were inflicting this on 'the weaker sex at their weakest moment' – so a big dose of paternalism there – but ended with a strong message:

> We urge the womanhood of England to take up the cause of those widows, disfranchised not of political but social rights, and deprived of their livelihood, their means of existence, their commercial rights, and their reversionary interests by a dictum as senseless as it is arbitrary, as cruel as it is unjust.

Unfortunately, the difficulties faced by the women publicans of Marlborough were not isolated incidents.

It must be stated, however, that women sometimes got into trouble of their own making. In Scotland, shebeens were an ongoing issue throughout the 19th century. (Shebeens were clandestine drinking establishments.) An issue of *The Country Brewer's Gazette* dated 1 October 1877 discussed the prosecutions going on in Scotland of those who had set up these surreptitious drinking locals. The majority of these were set up by women: 168 in Edinburgh, 239 in Glasgow, 92 in Dundee and 21 in Aberdeen during the years 1874–1876. Punishment ranged from a fine to six months' imprisonment.

An issue of the *Brewer's Guardian* from 20 March 1871 tells us the story of William John Craig, a 'well-known shebeener', who ran his establishment alongside his wife. His house was raided by officers who found three men and four women inside. Craig was found lying abed and told officers it was his wife, referred to only as Mrs Craig, who had the run of the house. Mrs Craig lied to try and get out of trouble, telling officers that there was not a drop of drink in the house (except for the three or four jars of whisky and a number of beer bottles that had been summarily smashed). This was not her first run-in with the law, however. She was apparently the same person who kept 'no fewer than three brothels in property belonging to the City Improvements Trust,' and who was expelled from those houses for keeping the brothels. We also learn of Catherine Duffoi's shebeen, where the three people discovered drinking there remarked to officers that they merely 'came for ham and eggs'. A final example is a Mrs Agnes Clark, or Hill (the authors weren't quite sure which), of the George Hotel, Gourock, who was charged on 6 April 1871 with selling 'trafficked in excisable liquors without having a licence'. This was apparently her third such offence. She was fined £230 or face six months in prison. She was able to pay the fine, but the justices remarked that they wished they could have sent her straight to jail, to which she is said to have remarked, 'Then why did you take away my licence without a cause? I'll keep my door open now every Sunday after this — that's the size o't. It's been a dear Gourock to me.'

Serving beer or ale without a licence was not the only shenanigans women were getting up to; they were also accused of cheating their customers. But this time, instead of the brewers themselves being the alleged culprits, we have publicans. According to a July 1893 article in the *Brewer's Guardian*, a Mrs Catharine Margaret Young of the 'Chapman Arms', Lower Chapman Street, St George's, had been engaging in the time-honoured tradition of diluting her beer, amongst other things, and was fined £25. We learn of a similar tale in an issue of *The Country Brewer's Gazette* from 1 October 1877, in which a woman who worked as a publican found herself in court for adulterating her beer. In Birmingham, Eliza Bradbury, landlady of the Duke of York, was adding salt to her beer in order to 'excite thirst'. She ended up being fined 40 shillings and ordered to pay costs. She wasn't the only woman who had apparently been adding salt to her ale. A *Brewer's Guardian* article on 3 April 1871 tells of Thomas Watkiss and his wife, who were charged with adulterating ale with salt at the George Inn. However, in this instance the case was dismissed.

The 20th Century

In 1930s' Bolton a pub landlady found herself presiding over a rather strange happening when a group of her regulars brought in a foal to show her. The adorable animal was paraded around the taproom before being taken to the kitchens where the women working there fawned over how cute it was. The regulars were struck with the idea that such an animal ought to be christened. And so it was, with a sign of the cross in beer on its forehead and naming it after the landlady. Afterwards, everyone stayed to have a few rounds of drinks. Apparently, they liked it so much they wanted to do it again, which was fine by the landlady because it made her quite a bit of cash.

This story came from The Mass-Observation Study, *The Pub and The People*, conducted in 1938 and situated in a place they call Worktown, but which is none other than Bolton. While there are certainly flaws in the study, like observer bias, it is a remarkable window into the lives of women who worked and owned pubs. Much like in previous centuries, women in these spaces were in precarious or sometimes dangerous positions. However, unlike before, help was on the way.

The suffragettes, a group of women traversing class, race, ethnic, and religious boundaries, famously took up the cause of barmaids. According to the 1851 General Census of Great Britain, 53,000 women were employed in the food, drink and lodging industry; and the census in 1901 found that there were 27,701 barmaids working in the UK. Many suffragettes themselves were barmaids or worked in the brewing industry and were therefore knowledgeable about what needed to be done. For example, Charlotte Drake, a seamstress and barmaid, was on the front line of women's suffrage. Mary Elizabeth Phillips (b. 15 July 1880, d. 21 June 1969), was a suffragette, a socialist, a feminist, and editor of a brewing trade news service from around 1928 to 1955.

In the late 19th century, Eliza Orme, Clara E. Collet, May E. Abraham and Margaret H. Irwin compiled a ground-breaking report on barmaids for the Royal Commission in Labour. Orme was a leading member of the suffrage movement in the 1870s and 1880s. She famously argued that women should not be excluded from any kind of workplace, regardless of the danger. During the course of this work, Orme visited some 150 pubs and bars. According to her reports, there was a marked difference between the employment of women in the fully licensed houses in London and elsewhere. According to the Licensed Victualler's trade association in Portsmouth, there were only barmaids in 10% of the houses, whereas in Plymouth there were 90 barmaids in 600 houses. In Glasgow, the secretary of the trade association demonstrated that there were 331 women working in some 27 public houses, restaurants and hotels that served alcohol; this included waitresses. However, in Edinburgh Orme found that officials stated that very few women were employed in the trade, and that there was a very 'strong prejudice against what they described as "the London barmaid"'. If women were working in such places in the city, they could only be found in hotels, restaurants, and railway bars. Similarly in the north of England, it was against standard practice to employ barmaids in the so-called 'rough houses'. Orme was told that their presence would not be liked by customers. She didn't even find female relatives of the proprietors working in these public bars.

The situation in London was certainly different. Here, she identified that the largest public houses had several bars for different classes of customers, with the 'third class' of bar being staffed 'entirely by men'. Barmaids, and the wife of the proprietor or manager, she tells us, worked in the second-class bar or in the saloon. She noted that daughters were employed, under the supervision of their fathers and mothers. Often in Orme's study the public houses were owned by a man and his family, including his wife and daughters who worked under him. This is a common theme. Most of the barmaids Orme interviewed were relatives of publicans, who might not only have worked at their own family's pub, but found work elsewhere as well. Of all the barmaids she interviewed, 20 gave her some personal history. Of these 20 women, six were the daughters of publicans, five of whom came to London for work after the death of their fathers. A further two were wives of publicans, with one who took over after her husband's death and another who went on to work as a barmaid at a railway refreshment bar. A further three were related to publicans in some way, but not immediate family as such; she said in total there were 16 who were connected by relationship, marriage, or friendship with publicans.

One of Orme's witnesses, described only as a man who is 'connected with the trade,' argued that the public houses hired barmaids because they were cheaper, but they would hire a barman if they could afford to do so. Another witness, a publican, contended that he preferred to hire barmaids because they could better handle customers 'without a quarrel'. But he also believed that barmaids were 'useless in the roughest bars,' a sentiment we saw earlier. In contrast, another publican stated that he employed barmaids in any of the neighbourhoods, and that even though the customers were of a 'rough class,' they were well behaved.

As we saw in the earlier bylaws from Chester, there were bills put forth trying to remove or tightly control women who worked in these public drinking establishments. In 1906 one such bill was even called a Bill to Restrict Barmaids, which was defeated in the end. Nevertheless, the sentiment that women should not be working in pubs, or should be greatly restricted when doing so, was widely held. Returning to Orme's interviews, the barmaids were aware that there was a prejudice against them. One such barmaid got her friend a job working behind the bar in a large hotel. Apparently this infuriated her friend's parents and caused some serious problems. Another woman stated that 'she thought it was sure to be bad for any woman who tried it' when asked about working as a barmaid.

Many of the barmaids talked about the very long hours they were obligated to work. One spoke of only having five- or ten-minute breaks for food. Orme reasoned that they could not have taken their meals sitting down, and many of them were tired from standing all day. All the London barmaids did report that they had a period in the afternoon for rest, but how long this was varied greatly. She found one woman who had to work a total of 108 hours a week. Another worked 105 hours a week for five shillings. And though not all worked to such extremes, many reported working in excess of 80 hours.

But what could be done to improve their situation? Orme argued that it would have been difficult to create any kind of barmaid trade organisation because they were so isolated, though she mentions Hartley House, where a guild of barmaids was trying to take off. Several other barmaids told her that they would have liked to join some form of guild or society that would help them in cases of wrongful dismissal or when an employer refused a reference.

However, having to work long hours for low pay was not the only problem barmaids faced; they had to deal with harassment from customers and even from other staff. Historian Barbara Gleiss had this to say about how men viewed barmaids in this period: 'the barmaids were an ideal construction of male fantasies – maternal as well as sexual'. This sounds very similar to the experiences of female alehouse workers centuries before. And like those alehouse counterparts in previous eras, barmaids also faced exploitation and abuse. Sexual harassment, propositioning, and assault were rife: 18th- and 19th-century barmaids were often put in the untenable position of having to tolerate customer's advances or face losing their jobs – or worse. The *Derby Mercury* reported on 11 May 1732 that in Dover a 'merry dispoiled man was toying innocently with the servant maid' from the local public house. However, it is very clear it was more like he was harassing the poor woman, as she apparently responded by punching him the chest so hard that he spat up blood and later died.

The newspapers of the time are full of cases of barmaids being attacked. On 20 December 1862, Jane Black, a barmaid at the Swan-with-Two-Necks, was attacked by John Martin, a stonemason. He told her that he had some information to relay to her, and when she accompanied him to the kitchen he dragged her into the garden. Black fought off her attacker for half an hour before she was eventually able to escape and get help. In another case, in 1905, a barmaid was attacked right after opening the Duke's Head Inn in Somerieyton. A man came in and asked for a beer, and when she went to serve him, he drew a knife and slashed at her face and throat. The woman sustained severe injuries including a punctured lung and amputated finger. Her assailant tried to drown himself but was stopped before he could finish the job.

As well as sexual harassment and abuse, there was an additional layer of racism or fetishisation for women of colour who worked in public houses. Caroline Bressey, an expert on Black women in the Victorian period, found that some 19th-century adverts for barmaids specifically asked for Black women. In her article 'Geographies of Belonging: white women and black history', she cited four examples in 19th-century newspapers. Bressey contended that these examples can help us to ask questions about what kind of relationships white women and Black women had at work. (It should also be noted that white women, as Bressey argues, contributed to the creation and maintenance of such discrimination).

When trawling through the newspaper archives, I was able to locate several more in addition to the ones Bressey specifically mentions. The *Liverpool Daily Post* of 11 May 1864 featured a wanted advert for a woman of colour for a vault in Sheffield. *The Era* on 20 June 1880 contained a particularly exploitive advert for 'a Good ATTRACTION, for a bar'. The *Liverpool Mercury* on 23 March 1875 ran an advert for a Chinese or Black barmaid for Castle Music Hall, Nuneaton. *The Stage*, on 6 April 1899, featured an advert for a woman barmaid of colour for the Mountain Daisy Hotel, c/o Mr Brownhill. Such practice carried on into the early years of the

20th century. A wanted ad in the *Yorkshire Post and Leeds Intelligencer* from 23 September 1910 requests a Japanese or Black barmaid who 'must have good character; experience unnecessary'. And on it goes.

*   *   *

'So I got my first beer job working behind the bar as a server in the Belmont Social Club in County Durham in 1998,' Jules Gray told me. Now the owner and operator of Hop Hideout, Gray worked for years in pubs pulling pints. She fondly recalled stories of her time working as a bartender, especially at a place called Corporation Nightclub, a rock venue that brought in acts like Slash: 'obviously he is a massive rock star and you wouldn't expect him in a club in Sheffield. It was one of his later bands. Terrible beer, I definitely remember that about it.'

Corporation Nightclub was not Gray's only work experience pulling pints. Over the years, she worked in multiple venues, including some places that still had men-only bars. 'When I worked there I was a bit like, this is a bit rubbish. The men have got their own bar and it's got the snooker table and all of the TVs in it.' Looking back, she noted it could be quite a weird experience because there were times when she would be the only woman 'in a room full of men'.

Unfortunately, many women who work in pubs still find themselves working long, unsociable hours for not enough pay. Though not as extreme as our 19th-century women working 105 hours a week, Gray told me that sometimes her shifts would start at eight or nine at night and go on until seven or eight in the morning, after they were done cleaning. In one of her jobs, she would finish work and have to get home in the pitch black. At the time, she says, no one really considered the implications. 'I definitely think back then, people never used to think about, oh, you're a woman, a young woman on your own, leaving work at half 11, midnight, how are you going to get home? Are you okay?'

And just like our barmaids from centuries past, Gray experienced leering customers and creepy management. Sadly, though, her experiences aren't unique. 'I even had a guy put a five pound note down my top as a tip,' Sarah Sinclair, marketing and event manager at Moonwake Beer Company, told me about her experiences working in pubs. Sinclair continued, 'but he was one of the locals so my boss told me to brush it off, basically.' She spoke about the sort of everyday harassment she was expected to endure without answer; continuous comments that you were meant to let wash over you.

Sarah Sinclair, Marketing and Events Manager at Moonwake, and Women in Beer member.

Doreen Joy Barber of Five Points Brewing Company also spent some time behind the bar, and, like Sinclair, she ran into harassment from customers. She recounted a story with a guy who would simply not leave her alone as she was pouring shots for his group, badgering her for her phone number or personal details. She told me that, in general, people were fine, but added 'you can't really tell from interacting with people one or two times whether or not they're going to try and follow you home after work'.

So, it seems we aren't so far from those 19th-century stories of female bar workers being harassed. Of the women I interviewed who had worked in pubs, all of them had some story to tell of sexism or harassment. These sinister echoes of the past were clearly apparent in all of their stories. And it's not always overt abuse. Sometimes this sexism manifests itself in dismissal of their expertise. Sinclair told me that sometimes customers would be contemptuous of her expertise about the beers she was pouring. Gray recounted times when people would ignore her impressive beer knowledge, even now that she owns the place. After falling in love with craft beer, Amélie Tassin of Tipple Marketing and Women in Beer opened a beer bottle shop in Paris with her ex-husband. Tassin worked primarily in marketing, social media and finance in the shop, and after their split decided she wanted to continue to work in beer. But when she worked at the bottle shop she sometimes found herself on the receiving end of sexist behaviour from customers. 'I've experienced sexism since I started working in the industry,' she told me. 'In the shop there were some customers who were asking for my ex-husband because they didn't want me to serve them.' Basically, she said, they didn't trust her recommendations about which beers to try, with some people even leaving the shop when he was not there, and only returning when he was working.

These stories are not isolated incidents, but mere glimpses of the broader picture. A brief web search will uncover any number of stories of harassment and abuse that women working in pubs have to experience. An article on *WalesOnline.co.uk* from 12 October 2022 featured the story of a barmaid whose landlord allegedly told her that she should 'expect to get touched'; that somehow sexual harassment was part of her job. Another article by Rebecca Brown on Lappthebrand.com seems to summarise the experiences of many women in its title: 'I've Never Known Sexual Harassment Like When I Was a Barmaid'. Beer writer and founder of the South Asian Beer Club, Ruvani de Silva wrote an article for *Good Beer Hunting* in which she interviewed the Brown Gradient Beer Wenches about their experience as servers in bars. The results were appalling and de Silva, referring to this article, noted in our interview that some of the worst harassment didn't even appear in print. 'How is this 2022 and this is still happening?' she asks.

And as we saw in previous centuries, classism, xenophobia, racism, and many other prejudices, add another layer of bigotry to the experiences of women who work in pubs. Racism, for example, works in tandem with sexism to further harm women of colour who work in these spaces. In April 2023, an Essex landlady's premises were raided for the racist dolls that she insisted on displaying in her pub. In response to this event, de Silva wrote a post on her website, 'The Sound of Silence: Burnout and Allyship in Beer DEI', in which she noted that many people in the beer world were largely silent about this event. Importantly, she stated, unlike her white counterparts, 'as a brown woman, I don't have the luxury of ignoring situations like this. I can't let burnout and exhaustion make me immune to instances of racism.' And it is exhausting, she wrote, telling readers that people of colour 'didn't make the mess but we are expected to clean it up. And because we have no other choice, we often just end up doing it, taking on the extra work.' In short, de Silva said that every time something like this occurs and people dismiss it as not a big deal, 'I am receiving another message that people like me are not welcome in pubs. It's that simple.'

'TIL DEATH DO US PART

The whole thing, she told me, happened by accident. Nidhi Sharma is currently the brewer at Meantime Brewing Company, and she entered the trade in a very different way to most of the women I interviewed. Instead of the beer itself, it started with the brewing process. Sharma was working as an engineer when she met her now husband. He had moved to India from the UK to start India's first craft brewery. She told me that she would pop into the brewery from time to time to observe the goings-on and instantly fell in love: 'Brewing was the reason I got into beer instead of the other way round. It truly does make me feel like an Indian goddess with multiple arms.'

I don't think I've heard a more beautifully evocative description of brewing; an empowering portrayal of a goddess using her many hands to mash in, sparge, and watch the hops boil, all while monitoring the fermenting brews in other vats. This powerful love for the craft fuelled Sharma's desire to learn to brew. But, she adds, the 'mild subversion of choosing brewing as a career as opposed to what people imagine when they think of Indians, especially Indian women, also influenced my decision massively.' She went on to study at the Institute of Brewing and Distilling, gaining multiple diplomas in brewing over the years. 'I have grown up with the stereotypical Indian mother forcing her kids to always focus on their studies because that is the only way to make something of yourself, according to her.' And so, as she puts it, her inner nerd was excited about the prospect of getting the diplomas and learning more in a professional setting. Six years later, Sharma is still brewing, though on a much larger scale than she had perhaps first envisioned.

Like Helena Adedipe of Eko Brewery, Sharma also brings childhood influences to her brews. 'I know this will sound clichéd, but smells and taste based on memories of growing up in India. Mum's cooking, village farms, fresh Indian summer fruits and spices that you can't buy in the UK. Mangos.' She recalls all of these memories when building her current recipes. However, unlike many of the other women I spoke with, Sharma comes from a family of teetotallers. 'I have been brewing for over six years now and I am still afraid to tell them I am a brewer. My mother would probably skin me alive if she knew that not only I brew but drink the fruits of my labour too.'

Sharma and her husband share a passion for brewing, something that we have seen with other couples throughout the centuries. Women worked alongside their husbands in breweries from the earliest periods we have covered in this book. In the early days, men probably weren't the ones doing the actual brewing; that task fell to their wives who had learned to brew previously. Over time, men came to the forefront of brewing, often supported behind the scenes by their wives. Or perhaps, as we saw with Sharma, it was their husbands who introduced them to the trade.

Over the centuries women and men continued to operate breweries together as spouses, from small local concerns to large industrial plants. But whatever the size and scale of the operation, we can still find women, not as workers but as owners. Because death comes for us all, and usually for men first. After their husband's demise, women often gained ownership of the brewery through their inheritance. As the saying goes, 'til death do us part and then my brewery will be all yours'. Or something like that.

* * *

Near Halifax in West Yorkshire lies a very famous estate. Like many rural manors, it boasts extensive property, gardens, and even has a gothic tower. However, it is Shibden Hall's most famous resident, Anne Lister, who makes this place unique. You might know her better by the eponymous BBC show, 'Gentleman Jack'.

The derisive epithet 'Gentleman Jack' was given to Lister by her neighbours; a dig at her lesbianism and her behaviour, which they judged harshly. This didn't seem to faze her and she continued to live her life as she chose. Lister is often described as the first modern lesbian, and her diaries, which were encrypted and only recently translated by scholars, reveal the details of her many loves, including a possible brief flirtation with Mary Vallance, the daughter of a Kent brewing family.

But Lister's brewing connections don't stop there. Shibden Hall, where she lived with her wife, Ann Walker, boasted its own brewhouse on the premises, though it was built long before Lister called it home in the 19th century. She also owned at least one inn. Her diary contained insights into her commercial dealings, including one with a man called Thomas Pearson who, at the end of his lease of Stump Cross Inn, had left behind several brewing pots and pans that the new tenant was not going to use. Ann Walker also came into inn ownership through inheritance, gaining Shibden Mill Inn from her father. Lister's and Walker's relationship to brewing and beer was as part of the landlord – or landlady – class. They owned the spaces in which other people brewed or sold ale. And like many other women, the way they gained control of those places was through a family death.

Centuries earlier, the *Calendar of Wills Proved and Enrolled in the Court of Husting, London* contained examples of entire breweries left by husband to wife. In a will dated to 12 September 1410, John Wolfey, a carpenter in London, left his wife, Agnes, his brewery called 'le Cok on the Hoop'. He also wanted his other brewery, 'le Hert on the Hoop,' and its vessels to be sold and 20 marks sterling of the proceeds given to her. Similarly, in 1388 William Power, a skinner, left to his daughter Emma, and her husband, Thomas Provendre, a brewery called 'Lez thre Nonnes'. In 1390, William Yvory, a butcher, left a brewery to his wife, Johanna. John Oreleaux left his brewery 'La Bel on the Hop' [sic] to his trustees, but only after the death of his wife, Katherine. Robert Nicol, of unknown occupation, left his wife, Alice, a brewery called 'le Pecok on the Houp' in 1378. In 1414, Stephen Toppesfield, a cordwainer, left his wife, Agnes, a brewery called 'le Cok on the Hoop'. A break from tradition sees Richard Groom, a curreour, leaving his daughter, Juliana, and not his wife Emma, his brewery in the parish of St Botolph in 1377.

You're probably asking yourself why is everything 'on the hoop'? Well, like alestakes, hoops from barrels could be displayed outside alehouses with various animals or symbols inside them to let people know that this was a place that sold, and likely brewed, ale. According to Mia Ball, these hoops probably originated from brewers using them as a way to frame their sign. So these are places that not only brewed but also sold ale on the premises, which makes sense given the medieval context. However, in general – with a few exceptions – the men who owned the breweries listed here were not brewers by occupation. They are carpenters, butchers, skinners and the like; middling sorts of people who might have sought ways to make some extra income outside of their regular jobs. The brewery would likely have been a side business run by their wives, alongside their husbands or on their own. After their husbands died, the wives carried on with the business because it was a viable way for them to earn an income (not to mention the fact that they were also very skilled at it).

In the 17th century brewers continued to leave their breweries to their wives. Though whether their wives were directly involved in brewing itself or helped them run the day-to-day operations is a different matter. In Llandaff in Wales, a 1666 will from Edward Williams, a brewer, stated that he left to his wife, Jane, all that belonged to his brewhouse, as well as his acres of barley and oats. Given the location and time period, it is most likely that his wife was brewing with him and continued after his death. However, as brewing became more commercialised into the 18th century, and, more importantly, profitable, things began to change for women in the trade, as we have seen. Men took over the brewing of beer and ale, and women took a step back, serving it or selling it, or helping their husbands with the administration of these larger breweries. I think we can say, however, that if men are continuing to leave their breweries to their wives, these women are certainly still brewing, or at the very least are knowledgeable about the brewing process.

One of my favourite examples of evidence of women brewing in the 17th and 18th centuries is brewer's marks. Like the name suggests, brewers marked their beer for sale with symbols specific to them. These could be quite simple or more complicated designs of interwoven lines and shapes. According to Robert Fitch, who studied these symbols in early modern Norwich, brewers registered these marks after they were licensed, and the people who later took over their business – for example, after their death – often used the same designs. Fitch was able to identify some 50 separate brewer's marks dating to between 1606 and 1725. I was able to locate two women who were brewing in this area using these marks. The first was Mary Marker, who brewed alongside what appears to be her husband, Thomas Marker. In 1713 they used a symbol Fitch identified originally with Clement Shepard in 1645. The second was Judeth Peckover, who, in 1657, was brewing on her own using a symbol that was apparently created by John Sporle around 1616. She could have bought it outright, though it's more likely that she inherited the brewery from a family member. Peckover was one of a declining number of single women who continued to brew in the 17th century, though single women did not entirely disappear from the trade.

Elizabeth Pease was a single woman and professional brewer for Temple Newsam in Leeds for some 30 years in the 1700s. She made ale, strong beer, table beer and small beer. From their online exhibition, 'Beer! A History of Brewing and Drinking', we learn that her work for Temple Newsam was seasonal, so it is assumed that she was of modest means. As we have seen, those on lower incomes continued to brew for centuries out of economic necessity. The letters of Caroline Frances Cornwallis, who lived from 1786 to 1858, hint at such an arrangement. Writing to Miss Frere on 23 June 1830, Cornwallis tells her that the removing of the excise duty of beer must be helpful to the 'poorer sorts': 'Those who still have their brewing utensils are proposing to brew and sell to their neighbours who have not, and thus, if the great brewer should be a little the sufferers, a much larger portion of the community will be the gainers.' So essentially, the change in brewing regulations helped those on lower incomes, to the detriment of the bigger breweries. This certainly may have benefitted women who brewed.

Sources from 18th-century Scotland reveal that women were still brewing on their own, without any sign of their husbands as business partners, though whether they were single women or widows is a matter of some debate. The John Gray Centre has a fascinating archive collection of brewing records. Included amongst those is a 1751 account of impost (a local tax) which listed all those who were brewing in Dunbar. Of these 22 brewers, five were women: Isobell Christy, Elizabeth Skirven, Jean Purvess, Robina Young, and Jean Gibb. Let's compare them to the 17 male brewers, or men who were brewing with their wives as a couple. Based on this impost, no women brewed strong ale; they only brewed what was termed 'twopenny ale'. Only two men brewed strong ale. The largest brewers in terms of output were Mart Sibbald, who brewed just over 17 barrels of twopenny ale, followed by Christopher James with 14 barrels, William Vaillie with 10, Elizabeth Skirven with 9¾, James Smith with 7½, Jean Gibb with just over six barrels, and Isobell Christy with six. This shows that of the five women brewing in the town, three were among the six largest. So, women's brewing operations on their own were not necessarily small scale or paid less than their male counterparts. At least in Dunbar.

Women Owning Breweries

At the end of the 18th century Britain's urban landscape underwent a massive transformation as the Industrial Revolution took hold. Factory chimneys belched clouds of black smoke into the skies above the hordes of workers below. The cacophony of the new steam engines and overcrowded streets created a soundtrack for the new face of commerce. It was progress, many claimed; a new era ushering in improved technologies and heretofore unimaginable capabilities in the brewing world.

Such dramatic and far-reaching changes did not result in a beer trade devoid of female involvement. Women were still very much a part of the brewing industry, and in fact, were sometimes in charge. Scholars like Martyn Cornell and Ron Pattinson, and many others who fill the pages of *Brewery History*, the Journal for the Brewery History Society, have carried out fascinating research on UK breweries in the 18th, 19th and 20th centuries. In various articles and books you can find detailed descriptions of breweries and their former owners, some of whom were widows who took over the reins through inheritance, just as they had in previous centuries.

In the wake of her husband's death, Mrs Burgham took over the running of Redbrook Brewery. Perhaps nervous that her customers might not have as much faith in her as they had in her spouse, she took out an advert in the *Monmouthshire Beacon* on 27 November 1869 in which she reassured readers that the brewery would continue trading as usual and hoped they would bestow their patronage upon her establishment in the coming years. Warn & Sons' Barton Brewery in Tetbury was once owned and operated by Mary Warn, wife of John Warn the previous owner, who took over after the death of her husband. In the 1851 census, she was trading as a widow and listed as a brewer, as well as a wine and spirit merchant.

The newspapers are filled with stories of female brewery owners, most taking control after the death of their husbands. And these were not limited to small local places. Some of these operations could be sizeable, with multiple pubs and beerhouses under their purview.

Ann Gundry, owner and operator of Gundry and Co, was particularly popular with her patrons. Like Mary Warn and Mrs Burgham, she ran the brewery alone after the death of her husband, Thomas. And she wasn't just in charge of the day-to-day operations, she was also the head brewer. But what made her such a local legend, we are told by the *Reading Book of Days*, is that when the price of beer increased by a penny she absorbed this extra cost. Gundry and Co was sold at auction in 1940. At the time of the sale, they had nine licensed pubs, 16 beerhouses and four off-licenses, in addition to the actual brewery.

Gundry was listed in *The Directory of Wholesale Brewers in the United Kingdom* from the early years of the 20th century alongside at least three other breweries owned by women: Miss E. Amey, Borough Brewery, Petersfield; Mrs F. Farey, Girton Brewery, Gorton, Cambridgeshire; and Mrs M. Hinde, National Brewery, Durham, Darlington and Eastbourne, who was, incidentally, also a member of the Brewers' Society.

As was so often the case, these latter three women assumed control through inheritance. Miss E. Amey, or Elizabeth Amey, at one time ran the Borough Brewery in Petersfield, Hampshire, which was founded by her father, Thomas Amey, in 1875. According to the *Brewery History* article by Nicholas Redman, Elizabeth took over the business in 1898. They apparently had their own railway siding and were able to supply beer as far afield as the Hole in the Wall, their pub near Waterloo Station. They brewed a variety of beers including a mild, a strong mild, a light bitter, a stout, an oatmeal stout, double stout and pale ale, among many others. Tracking down Mrs F. Farey of Girton Brewery was much more difficult, but Mrs M. Hinde of the National Brewery proved easier. Brian Robert Bennison in his PhD thesis talked in some depth about the history of the National Brewery, which was apparently quite successful in the latter half of the 19th century. Mrs Hinde certainly ran it for a time in the early years of the 20th century before it passed on within the family. Women-run breweries weren't outside the norm in the 19th and 20th centuries. In 1877 Joseph Benskin of Benskin's Brewery in Watford died, leaving it to be run by his wife, Maria. According to the historian Martyn Cornell, when Maria was installed as owner, all three of the big breweries in Watford – Healey's, Sedgewick's, and Benskin's – had women running the show.

Women who owned breweries weren't always the ones doing the actual brewing. In many larger operations these female owners managed the brewery operations but employed professional brewers to make their product and teams of people to run the day-to-day business. One of those bigger breweries was W.A. Falconer and Co, Ltd, who in 1893, according to *The Brewer's Guardian*, was registered with a capital of £50,000 in £5 shares. This was to raise enough money to pay brewers, maltsters, and other professionals, and was agreed upon between Mr T.D. Fenwick and Mrs

D. A. Falconer, who was the part-owner. St Austell brewery in Cornwall had Hester Parnall as chairperson from 1916 to 1939. She was one of several female heads, as described in Roger Protz's excellent *The Family Brewers of Britain: A Celebration of British Brewing Heritage* (CAMRA Books, 2020).

As brewing became increasingly commercialised after the Industrial Revolution, breweries grew in size, both in terms of output and reach. As a result of this, many breweries folded, or were taken over, leading to even larger enterprises. Smaller breweries had to shut down as they could no longer compete with these new industrial giants with more capital, more investment opportunities, and better networks.

We saw in Chapter One that expanding medieval breweries needed more capital and more workers to keep up with the increased demand. This became difficult for women in the trade as they did not command the same managerial authority as men during this period. By contrast, female brewery owners in the 19th and 20th centuries, like their male counterparts, could become part of a wealthy class of people who made their money employing others to do the brewing work for them. They were able to command authority, thanks to their wealth or social status. And so, when women inherited large breweries from their spouses, they were able to assume control. That is not to say that their new position was not challenged or thwarted because of their gender, but for those women of the privileged class who owned large industrial breweries, wealth and social position could have a substantial impact on how they were treated and perceived.

Not everyone who owned shares in a brewery was part of the small, wealthy elite, however. The *Mid Sussex Times* of 3 March 1908 reported a speech in the House of Commons by one Lt Col Rawson. He specifically criticised a Licensing Bill of that same year which set out to control public houses by a number of measures including banning the employment of women and reducing Sunday opening hours, arguing that 25% of shareholders in brewing were women and small holders who had their entire life savings invested into these stocks. This new Bill would 'wipe out three-quarters of the value', and they would lose their entire savings, which, he argued, would be unjust. This Licensing Bill would come up later in the context of women's suffrage, when Mr Malcolm Mitchell, the Honorary Secretary of the Men's League for Women's Suffrage, made the argument in October 1910 that women should have the right to vote because they owned shares in breweries:

Some time ago brewery shareholders were said to be threatened by what was known as the Licensing Bill. They had the power to work against this through their representatives in Parliament, No doubt there were some women who had brewery shares. Can it be suggested that their interests did not require protection?

Women Working in Breweries

It is clear that women did not stop owning breweries, or have shares in them, during the 20th century. They were also still working hands-on in breweries, albeit in significantly smaller numbers. But while it is true that female workers did leave the commercial brewing industry in the face of increasing industrialisation, they didn't leave entirely.

Women were employed at Bass and Co in the catering department at least as far back as 1890, and likely earlier. An advert in the *Falkirk Herald* of 14 April 1894 asked for 'One or two respectable women' to apply to Mr Henderson at The Brewery. The *Dundee Advertiser* reported on 9 March 1865 that two women employed at the Falkirk Brewery went to prison for some 20 days for apparently 'stealing a considerable quantity of bitter beer from the export packing room'. Not everyone was keen on the idea of having women work in breweries. The *Edinburgh Evening News* ran an article on 28 November 1899 entitled 'A Tory Candidate and Female Brewery Workers'. Here, readers are told that Mr Younger, of Younger's brewery, held a meeting in Alloa, Scotland. Apparently, someone asked him if his first act would be to create a bill banning women from working in breweries. He replied, 'he should be very sorry to interfere with any woman doing work which she was competent to perform, but if he did introduce a measure such as had been suggested it would certainly not affect him, for they did not employ women in their brewery.' This statement was met with laughter and cheers. I think we can venture that his line of thinking wasn't particularly unpopular.

The first *Census of Production in the United Kingdom* took place in 1908. It recorded data on where people were working at the time. The category we should concern ourselves with is 'brewing, distilling, bottling, aerated waters'. We are told that 697 girls reported working in bottling lines and 3,148 women. This compares to 3,115 boys and 9,793 men. While we can see that men were certainly in the majority, the numbers of women and girls employed in these positions were not insignificant.

Women would have a strong presence in at least the bottling lines in the early years of the 20th century. But employing women in breweries was not without controversy. One reason that women were still employed in the brewery trade is that they could be paid less, and were, therefore, sometimes preferred to their male counterparts, which, understandably, did not go down too well. According to the *Manchester Evening News*, in an article dating to 20 March 1907, Messrs Allsopp brewery decided to switch from male clerks to female ones, 'and thus save half the amount spent in wages without impairing the efficiency of the service'. This proved unpopular in Burton upon Trent, where the wives of the male clerks decided to apply for their husbands' positions 'on the ground that they will now have to assume the position of breadwinners'. Here we can see that women did replace men in brewery work because they were cheaper. What is also clear is that women workers were just as efficient, despite being paid less to do the same job.

When women did work outside of the home they were often barred from, or underrepresented in, those very organisations that would have helped improve their pay and conditions; i.e., trade unions. They weren't always excluded, though, and there are examples of unions helping female brewery workers secure better wages. The *Berwick Advertiser*, on 2 April 1920, discussed the formation of a new local branch of the National Union of General Workers. A Mr McMann gave a talk on organising the workers in which he told attendees that the union was able to secure women brewery workers a standardised wage. A further case, from the *Burton Observer and Chronicle* on 24 January 1946, detailed a new brewery workers' agreement between the Burton branch of the Transport and General Workers' Union and the Brewers' Committee. According to this agreement, women brewery workers were to get three-quarters of the wages of men, and women, girls and youths that worked in bottling were to get 'proportionate advances of the men's rate'.

Unions continue to play an important role in the brewing industry, according to many of my interviewees. When I asked Amélie Tassin, of Tipple Marketing and Women in Beer, how we can support workers' rights, she immediately answered, 'Well let them join a union. I would say it's the main thing.'

The First World War

The First World War saw women returning to work in breweries in large numbers. Many men had gone to fight overseas, leaving behind a large gap in the labour market. Women were once again doing male-dominated jobs such as brewing, malting, and coopering. During this period the share of women as a percentage of the overall workforce (excluding domestic service) rose sharply from 23.6% in 1914 to between 37.7 and 46.7% in 1918. In 6 June 1916 the *Burton Observer and Chronicle* stated that, according to *The Times*, in July 1914 there were a total of 170,000 women employed in the manufacture of drink, food and tobacco, compared to 350,000 men. The same article reported that about one woman was employed for every eleven men in breweries, and that around 10,000 women had recently joined the trade. The article went on to say that most women were employed in bottling – washing, sorting, filing and labelling – 'and other similar tasks for which special strength or much training are not required'.

As in previous decades, women were certainly present in overwhelming numbers on bottling lines during the First World War. An advert in the *Aberdeen Evening Express* of 22 April 1914 from Devanha Brewery Ltd of Aberdeen wanted women for bottle washing, for example. But women were now entering other parts of the brewery. Returning to the article in the 8 June 1916 *Burton Observer and Chronicle*, the writer lists other jobs that women are doing, such as filling and washing casks. Further, 'gradually they are penetrating into actual brewing itself', with the writer stating that, 'women are now used in all parts of the brewery except where the work is too heavy'. The 'Ladies Column' in the *Hendon & Finchley Times* from 7 April 1916 echoed these sentiments. When discussing women in work uniforms, and specifically those who worked at breweries, the author said, 'I know of at least one brewery where the places of men have been filled by uniformed women; so that in every class of society the uniform has usurped the ordinary dress of women to an extraordinary extent.'

There is plenty of evidence to back up these statements. *The Employment of Women in Britain 1914-1918*, part of the Imperial War Museum Photograph Archive Collection, is an excellent source of images of women working in breweries. One from Watney, Combe, Reid and Co Ltd, in London, shows a woman using a large funnel to add hops to a cask of beer, while others are of women hard at work making barrels in their cooperage. Amongst these photos women are seen in a variety of roles, cleaning out casks, or even rolling them out, while working in the cellar. There's an image of two women with big shovels moving wet hops onto driers. In another, a woman fixes the main pipe in the refrigerating room. There is also a photo of the 140 women who were working in this brewery. Elsewhere, in Staffordshire, we see many of the same types of photographs: women rolling out massive casks of beer into a storage house; or posing for a photograph outside the brewery. The same can be seen in Cheshire, where again women are photographed rolling casks of beer, labelling bottles of lager, dry hopping casks, filling barrels of beer, and working the bottling line.

Women worked in all parts of the brewery during the First World War, and fears were growing, especially among the male population, that they would refuse to leave their positions once the men returned from war. There were also concerns that they would demand higher pay. But though women did demand higher wages, the 1917 *Report of the War Cabinet Committee of Women in Industry* argued that they were not as productive as men, and, therefore, were not entitled to equal pay.

After the end of the war, and the return of those men who survived, women would not continue to work in such large numbers in breweries. They didn't disappear entirely, however. In 2015 the John Gray Centre held an exhibition called 'Drink, Public Houses, Brewing, Distilleries and Temperance', part of which included photographs of workers from the Belhaven Brewery in Dunbar. In one photo from 1928, four women and two girls are seen alongside two boys and 11 men.

The Second World War and Latter Part of the 20th Century

By the middle of the 20th century, women could be found in a variety of positions at many breweries throughout England, Scotland and Wales. They worked as clerks and secretaries, and ran the catering departments. They could even be found working as lab technicians, analysing yeast cultures; the National Brewery Centre Archives has several pictures from Bass Holdings Ltd of women employed in the labs. And in the 1960s women were employed in their tailoring and clog-making department.

As in the decades previously, women worked mainly on the bottling lines. Aitken & Co in Falkirk had an extensive bottling hall at the time of its launch in 1938. Pulling the lever to start the new machinery was Miss

Elizabeth Aitken, a shareholder and descendant of the Aitken family. She presented a bouquet of flowers to Miss Lizzie Fallon, the longest-serving woman at the brewery. Images from the Aitken brewery bottling line prominently feature women throughout the 20th century, and we know that women worked on bottling lines in many breweries, based on photographic evidence and also from the slew of newspaper adverts calling for women workers. Adverts like the one that appeared in the *Evening Despatch* on 20 December 1941, which stated that the Mitchells & Butlers' Cape Hill Brewery in Birmingham had part-time vacancies for women in brewery work, on the bottling line or elsewhere. During the Second World War women worked at the bottling line at Wards of Sheffield, and John Joule and Sons Ltd from Staffordshire had women overseeing their bottling machines in the 1950s.

Paying women less than men, even for the same work, lasted well into the latter part of the 20th century. The *Liverpool Echo* reported on 13 December 1962 that the Manchester Brewers' Society and the Transport and General Workers' Union opted to give weekly pay raises of 10s and 6d for men and 8s and 9d for women. Of course, women didn't always accept such unfair treatment. The *Coventry Evening Telegraph* told readers on 2 June 1960 that 1,000 women walked out of Carlsberg and Tuborg, Denmark's largest breweries, because only men had been granted a raise. Some women took a similar approach in the UK. The *Sunday Sun* of 23 January 1966 wrote that in Newcastle, 'Women May Join Brewery Strike'. This was in reference to the strike by the Transport and General Workers' Union draymen of Vaux Brewery after many were laid off. Not every woman was pro-union, of course. Referring to the same strike in Newcastle, the *Newcastle Journal* of 25 January 1966 published a story entitled 'Mother Tells Vaux Chairman: I Will Drive Beer Truck', in which Mrs Joan Rough decided to protest against the strike by offering to drive the beer trucks for free, even though she had never driven a truck before. While it doesn't appear she was taken up on her offer, Rough did get what she wanted in the end, as the strike had collapsed by the end of January due to a lack of support.

However, there are many positive stories involving brewery unions in the latter half of the 20th century. *Brewing Stories: An Oral History of 3 London Breweries*, a project run by the educational charity digital:works, is a fantastic resource for first-hand accounts from brewery workers during this period. It is supported by Fuller's brewery, Chiswick Archives, Richmond Local Studies Centre, and Wandsworth Heritage Service, and funded in part by the Heritage Lottery Fund and Unite Union. As part of this oral history project, the interviewers spoke with people who worked at three West London Breweries: Griffin Brewery (Fuller's) in Chiswick, the Ram Brewery (Young's) in Wandsworth, and the Stag Brewery (Watney's) in Mortlake.

Amongst these interviews are those with several women, including Denise Annon, who worked as a bottling line operative for over 20 years at Young's Brewery in Wandsworth. She got the job after her stepfather, a foreman at the brewery, put her forward. Annon was a representative for the Transport and General Workers' Union, and was a leader in female workers' rights, fighting for, and succeeding in winning, equal pay for women doing the same job as men. During her time on the bottling line, she told interviewers that most of the workforce there were women, much like they had been historically. She described the brewery like a multicultural family, full of 'tough and mouthy' women who would bicker but also rally round when people needed them. She also said that women worked in sales, admin, and in the canteen, but that apart from the bottling line there were no women working in production. In fact, Young's did not employ their first female brewer until after Annon left in 1997.

This same series of interviews included Sila Singh, an accountant at Fuller's. She started working there in 1986 as a 'post room girl'. She was the youngest person on the staff and was 'mothered' by the other women who worked there. She described Fuller's staff as being incredibly diverse, coming from a variety of backgrounds. From her interview, she spoke highly of working at Fuller's, telling interviewers that the company paid for her to do evening classes in finance and business, allowing her to eventually move to the finance department. Another interviewee from *Brewing Stories* was Maureen Barney who worked as a payroll clerk at Fuller's at the Griffin Brewery from 1973 to 1978 and 1986 to 1996. Charlotte Donohoe was a switchboard operator there from 1975 and Val Hobson started in 1978 as an IT worker, witnessing the growth of the IT department from only two people and 'big, old machines' to 14 members of staff with PCs many years later.

As we have seen in this chapter, women did not stop working entirely at large, industrial breweries, though their numbers certainly dwindled during the late 19th and 20th centuries. At times of need, they re-entered the trade, for instance during the First World War when they had to take over men's positions. Some women remained in these positions after the war, particularly in bottling lines, in the canteens, in finance, or in the labs, and continued to work in these roles for decades. This expanded over the years as many women re-entered the world of brewing the beer itself, taking on roles as head or assistant brewer (as we have seen in the interviews of women throughout this book). The number of women brewers in the UK is still significantly lower than their male counterparts, but hopefully more will continue to enter the field in the years to come.

21st-Century Women Brewers

It was the wedding that really started it all. At least, that is what Lucy and Lizzie Stevens, owners of Edinburgh's Closet Brewing, tell me. They are aptly named, in part due to their small size, but also because, in Lucy's own words, 'I was also in the closet at the time, so it's a bit of a double entendre'. Influenced by women like Lily Waite of Queer Brewing Project, Lucy Stevens created numerous beers, while Lizzie would check in and observe the proceedings. In 2019, when they began looking for wedding venues, they found that most places didn't have great options for beer, so Lucy Stevens came up with the idea of making their own. Lizzie figured that if they were going to make something special for the wedding, she also wanted to create a beer she would like, and that's when she began to take a more hands-on approach to the whole thing. As she says, 'It stopped being just Lucy brewing in a plastic bucket in our cupboard and became something that we wanted to share more broadly with other people.' The beer they brewed for their wedding was called Let's Get Married, a raspberry and strawberry Berliner Weisse. Now, they now operate a small professional brewery, creating artisan beers for their increasing fan base in Edinburgh. As Lizzie Stevens told me, 'Lucy believes that there's a beer out there for everyone. And I'm fairly certain she wants to be the person to make all of them.'

In fact, their motto is 'drink good beer with good people', echoing Eliza Smith's 18th-century life lesson of good food deserving good beer. Brewing is Lucy Steven's creative outlet, and she likes to make a little bit of everything, sampling different styles and adding local ingredients. To that end, they recently collaborated with the aptly named Sea Buckthorn Scotland, a small local business located just up the road from them. As Lizzie Stevens puts it, 'sea buckthorn, I feel it's having a bit of a moment right now, which is possibly the most hipster thing I've ever said'.

Lizzie and Lucy Stevens, co-founders and co-owners of Closet Brewing.

Unlike married couple Anne Lister and Ann Walker of Shibden Hall, who were landladies of brewing inns, Lizzie and Lucy Stevens are hands on. They told me that they don't really see any profit, just making enough to cover their costs, so it is very much a labour of love. They only got licensed so they could share their beer with other people, but working together is a lovely bonus. Lucy Stevens said, 'I think one thing that makes it very easy to do is that we both have our own areas of expertise. So I know a lot about the brewing side and Lizzie is more about marketing.' Something that Lizzie Stevens echoed, saying that she feels you can be honest with a spouse in a way that you perhaps can't with a co-worker. She added, 'brewing together is just a genuinely enjoyable experience. We don't have to answer to anyone other than each other, which gives us a lot of room to have fun with it.'

Speaking of working alongside your spouse, the same is true for Drop Bear Beer Company, started by Joelle Drummond and Sarah McNena in 2019. The couple were big foodies, Drummond told me, and also huge craft beer lovers. But when McNena took a break from drinking alcohol, which Drummond soon followed, they found it difficult to find good alcohol-free beer when out for drinks with friends. They missed the 'experience of craft beer, the quirkiness of it', so they wondered if this was something they could do themselves. They quickly realised that alcohol-free beer was a market with huge potential, growing at a staggering rate in the last few years: 'We like to say we started with a saucepan and it escalated.' A nod perhaps, to the many homebrewing women we have met throughout this book. They wanted their beers to be accessible to as many people as possible, so they opted to make their alcohol-free beers gluten-free and vegan. 'People were crying out for a product that ticked those boxes, so we decided to create it for them.'

McNena had experience of homebrewing, but alcohol-free beer was a whole other kettle of fish. Drummond told me that they raided their local library for all the books they could find on brewing, scouring the internet for more resources, and even turning to YouTube videos to help them learn more about making alcohol-free brews. 'We certainly have horror stories from the early days,' she says. But they persevered. Drummond told me it was 'extremely hard and extremely taxing', noting that people sometimes viewed their brewery as a hobby investment compared to their male counterparts who were taken more seriously. However, she said:

> At the end of the day, the numbers don't lie. We always went back to our financials, our growth, the market, and we just got louder. People don't like it when you get louder and they try to shut you down. I'm sorry, but we're not that type of people. So if you shut us down, we're going to be ten times louder.

Their strategy worked. Eventually they piqued the interest of a billionaire investor, 'who came in and basically changed everything for us'. But their success has not affected their core values. If anything, it has given them a larger platform from which to practise them. Drop Bear Beer Company was shortlisted for the Startups Diversity and Inclusion Awards. Drummond told me that she thinks that 'the industry benefits from more diversity'. This approach is carried into their recruiting. They want to ensure that 'any type of person feels like they can apply and be treated with respect and dignity'. Further, they are a Living Wage Employer, which they describe as doing the 'absolute minimum, to be honest', stating that they couldn't 'in good conscience not pay someone a living wage'. It is important to them that their team be 'happy and healthy and to want to stay with us a long time'. Drummond also noted that brewers themselves have always been very inclusive and accepting, in their experience, but that more representation of people from diverse backgrounds is needed. 'We need women, people of colour, and the LGBTQ+ community to feel safe, welcome and encouraged to join our amazing industry,' she says.

This is something that is very close to her heart. She told me that, when growing up, 'I never came out. I was outed.' She spent much of her childhood severely bullied because of it, and this has followed her into adulthood. She and her wife were the victims of a hate crime in 2022, 'while we were doing our job, just doing our job. But people didn't like what we

Joelle Drummond, co-founding director and Director of Sales and Marketing at Drop Bear Beer Company.

were doing, so they decided to target us personally based on our sexuality, which is completely irrelevant.'

This has served as a wake-up call. 'We need to stand tall and show that we're here, we're present, and we want people to feel safe at Drop Bear and see it almost as a haven,' she tells me. Drummond and McNena have talked at length about the importance of representation and having role models to look up to. She says that people come up to her and her wife and say things like, 'it's just so nice to see different types of businesswomen out there, and I feel like I can go out there and do something now'. In this vein, Drop Bear Beer Company are also a B Corp, currently paired with the charity Galop, an organisation that works with LGBTQ+ people who have survived hate crimes, abuse, or any kind of violence in the UK. Drummond told me that they want to be 'really eco-friendly and charity driven', but also 'a super badass craft beer brand'.

Lizzie Stevens from the Closet Brewing told me that 'as two queer women, spaces typically dominated by men like the beer industry aren't always welcoming'. But in contrast to what you might expect, they found that the beer community in Edinburgh has been very supportive. When they started brewing they had support from women's communities like Women in Beer, and other groups for LGBTQ+ people in the area, all of whom helped them set up their business and navigate getting their licences. Lucy Stevens told me that they count themselves lucky to live in such a 'progressive city'.

> When I came out, I had a lot of anxiety about going along to the homebrew club that I'd been part of and openly presenting as trans, and how I was going to manage that change. I went along, and I was kind of like, okay, I go by Lucy now, and one of the guys at the homebrew club was like "Great! What pronouns do you use? What beer have you brought with you today?"

Both Lizzie and Lucy Stevens acknowledge that their story is not necessarily the norm. Lizzie said, 'we know a lot of people who faced quite significant difficulties in the industry'. However, she told me that because of their 'really enjoyable and really positive' experiences, it demonstrates that 'the space is there. But you get there by being supported by wonderful people.'

That support can come in the form of those beer groups that the Stevens mentioned. This is where many women working in beer might find a strong network to help them in their careers. Like their historical

Nix Prabhu, founder of Glasladies Beer Society, activist for women and non-binary people in the beer industry, expert in Canadian beer history and tour guide.

counterparts, women in the industry have sometimes found the road to success paved with difficulty. Nix Prabhu of GlasLadies Beer Society put it bluntly, 'I would start off by saying there are nothing but challenges to being a woman in this industry.' Prabhu told me she believes that women have definitely made inroads in the industry recently, adding, 'it's not the same as it was five, ten, fifty years ago'. However, she stressed that 'progress has been painfully slow ... and completely fraught with difficulties,' adding, 'we must work twice or three times as hard just to get recognised as serious contenders in the industry, or even a viable consumer base.'

When Nidhi Sharma of Meantime Brewing Company got her start in India, she says, 'I had to be sheepish around the place. Because I knew I wasn't welcome.' She recalled that in India all alcohol producers are required to have a government official onsite and the one at her brewery was a massive misogynist:

He'd comment on what I wore to work, how I spoke to the guys at work. In fact, there was a female food inspector who came to site once and said she could shut the brewery down for having a woman on the production floor because women should only be in the lab.

In spite of all this, the owner of the brewery where she was employed worked tirelessly with her to support her career and education. Upon moving to the UK, she discovered that things were very different within the industry, finding it more respectful. But dealing with outside workers can still bring her face to face with sexism. Referring to contractors coming to work on equipment, she told me, 'They almost always assume that I am a nobody and ask me if they can talk to a man instead because how could I possibly understand the workings of a centrifuge being a woman.' This attitude even extends to visitors to the brewery. She told me, 'I have been mistaken for a cleaning lady in the brewery by visitors.' She finds that

Nidhi Sharma, current Brewing Team Leader at Meantime Brewing Company. Sharma has extensive brewing expertise and has previously worked in other breweries like The Kernel.

within the craft beer community in the UK 'we're all slightly safe 'til we must deal with everyday people who still don't understand my choice of career and will mock it, too'.

This marked difference between the treatment received from people inside the brewing industry and the general public is something that many of the women I interviewed spoke of. Almost all of them had stories of prejudice coming from people outside of the brewing world. Helena Adedipe of Eko Brewery was at a beer festival representing her brewery and explaining to a male customer that a pilsner was a type of lager. He completely disregarded her expertise and insisted they were completely different drinks. Adedipe said that people need to be actively working towards change, and that institutionalised racism and sexism need to be called out. She says: 'Rome wasn't built in a day. But definitely, there's a long way to go. I think that's one thing maybe craft beer gets really uppity about and pat ourselves on the back. We think we're so much more different than other industries, but we're really not.'

All the women I spoke to had clear directions on how to change this. Amélie Tassin of Women in Beer says that the industry itself needs 'to grow up a bit', and that transparent and highly visible policies need to be put in place to ensure that it does. In a similar vein, writer Ruvani de Silva told me that it's important to create and maintain structures within the industry that support 'equity and accountability'. But there is still a long way to go, and people from historically marginalised groups still do not have enough positions of power to enact that change. This was echoed by Emma Inch of *Fermentation Beer and Brewing Radio*, who told me it's not just about hiring people, it's also about giving them a voice. Marginalised people need to have a platform and positions of power.

Inch also spoke of the difficulties of being a parent while working in the beer industry due to the late hours and strong drinking culture. This, she believes, might be a reason more single parents aren't able to join. In Chapter One we saw the challenges in balancing childcare and work during the pandemic, but this extends to non-lockdown times as well. One key factor that was brought up in many of the interviews I conducted was a need for a transparent and robust maternity policy. Joanne Love and Tori Powell, hosts of *A Woman's Brew*, stressed that these policies should be clearly outlined to all potential employees during the interview process. And though this doesn't only impact women, it is certainly something that is a potentially large obstacle for those who have or want to have children.

Brave Noise

The women I have spoken to are hopeful for the future. This hope is fuelled by the increased visibility of efforts of people around the world to make the beer industry a more diverse and inclusive place. Some of these are grass-roots initiatives to help their local communities. Others have a wider scope, designed to create change in the broader world. In South Africa, Apiwe Nxusani-Mawela of Tolokazi Beer Company started Brew4Change, a non-profit organisation that runs programmes designed to 'highlight issues of diversity and transformation in the industry,' while also providing a youth outreach programme for potential jobs in brewing. On a more international level, one organisation in particular came up frequently, spoken of with optimism for a better beer industry. And that was Brave Noise.

A bit of background if you aren't familiar. In 2021 an Instagram post by Brienne Allan kicked off a wave of reckoning for the beer industry. In her post, she asked other people to share their experiences of racism, sexism, prejudice, harassment and exploitation. She was quickly inundated with replies from people all over the world detailing their stories of abuse. From bartenders to brewers, people from around the globe wrote in with their stories. But this was not the end. In fact, later Allan teamed up with Ash Eliot from Women of the Bevolution to build something to help bring an end to this discrimination. Thus Brave Noise was created.

I spoke with Eliot about her experiences creating Women of the Bevolution and working with Allan to start Brave Noise. She told me that the beer industry is not set up to help or support women, never mind enable them to thrive, and that even getting in the door can be a challenge. Importantly, she said that even with all the talent and motivation to work, 'if the environment is filled with microaggressions and inappropriate behaviour that becomes mentally draining, causing all sorts of health problems, and it makes it extremely difficult to do their job well'. To draw attention to these important issues, Eliot and Allan collaborated to turn the latter's Brave Noise Pale Ale into a global beer initiative to create a 'safe and discrimination-free beer industry'. The beer is brewed all over the world, and its goals, Eliot told me, are:

> to honour those who have shared their stories and request action by asking breweries to be transparent with their policies/value, commit to the long-term work and brew the Brave Noise Pale Ale with the majority of proceeds supporting a charity or advocacy group dedicated to creating safe and inclusive spaces.

Ash Eliot, freelance professional in marketing, PR, and sales, founder of
Women of the Bevolution and co-founder of Brave Noise.

Breweries can put their own spin on Allan's recipe if they so choose.
There are currently some 20 breweries in the UK that have participated
in making it. Their work doesn't end there, of course. Eliot's organisation,
Women of the Bevolution, created the *BIPOC Female and Non-Binary Creators
in Brewing Grant*. And, in concert with Beer Kulture, the *Beer Kulture Women of
the Bevolution Creator Launchpad Grant*. Both of these are designed to support
women of colour carve out their own niche in the beer world. Importantly,
these grants acknowledge the critical role that women who may not work
in breweries, or desire to start their own brewery, play in the brewing
industry. The beer world is not limited to those who brew, as we have seen,
but it's also not limited to those who work in breweries. In our final chapter,
we will take a look at all those women who contribute to the very existence
of beer as we know it from outside the walls of the breweries themselves.

BEYOND BREWERIES

Well, it turns out horrendous mother-in-laws aren't anything new. On 14 September 1608, Lettice Kynnersley wrote to her brother, Walter Bagot, begging for his help. Her husband was a vile man with a particular penchant for cruelty who had deliberately set her up to fail. In her letter, she told her brother that she had beseeched her husband for malt so she could brew. But he refused. He would neither get her malt nor would he give her money to get it herself. She attempted to mitigate this by borrowing from her neighbours, but that amount would only go so far, as she relayed to her sibling. And yet, her unbearable husband blamed her for all this. As a result, she was removed from her position in charge of the household, her servants were sent away, and she was told to keep to her room. But it gets worse. She told her brother that her husband wouldn't be so bad if it weren't for her awful mother-in-law. Apparently, this wicked woman had her servant standing at Lettice's door to spy and report back to her. She begged her brother to write, or get their brother Anthony to write to her husband to help her sort this out so that she could have care of her children 'and somewhat maintain them. And myself. I would desire no more.' She wrote that she feared her mother-in-law would have oversight of the entire household and 'then shall not I be able to stay'. Poor Lettice. I think some people could relate to her letter, at least a little bit, and we have all heard stories similar to hers, either from family, friends or the good old-fashioned internet.

Women and Malting

As well as evoking sympathy, Lettice's letter introduces us to the link between women who brewed and women who malted. We can see that malt was as important to the maintenance of the household as it was the key component for brewing. I don't think I need to stress how important ale, and later beer, were to the running of the country. From individual families to entire army battalions, England, Scotland and Wales ran on the stuff. The lines between maltsters and brewers could also be quite blurry. Many women who malted also knew how to brew, at least in the medieval period. Of course, not all women who brewed also malted and vice versa. Unfortunately for Lettice, this seems to have been beyond her ken.

Women certainly dominated the malting industry in the early days. As with brewing women, in many places the legal codes referred only to women making malt. In medieval Scotland, for example, women seem to be both the primary maltsters and brewers. The 1249 *Statuta Gilde*, or the *laws of the gilde of Scotland*, offered the following, 'that no woman buy in the market oats to make malt for sale more than one chalder, and if she buy more, she shall forfeit all that she buys'. Women throughout the medieval period made their own malt for commercial sale, and many made it for their own ales, as Judith Bennett contended, at least in the earlier part of the period. This practice was not always popular, however. In London in 1317 there was an effort to block brewers from making their own malt, likely due to famine conditions.

Moving forward in time, during the early modern period, malting remained an important part of the household economy. Gervase Markham's 17th-century book, *The English Huswife*, instructed his female audience that malting was part and parcel of being a good housewife. He waxed poetical about this, telling his audience that it is 'an excellent merchandise,' and so vital that entire counties and towns were supported by the buying and selling of it. We are told that the housewife should be well practised and experienced in the art of making malt, not only for the use of the family but also for profit. And, Markham contended, while there were some good men who made malt, 'it is properlie the worke and care for the woman, for it is house-worke and done altogether within dores'. So, there you have it; it's an inside job, only for the ladies.

Markham insinuated that the housewife might be hard pressed to do this work all on her own. After all, though it is inside work, it is still hard work. For this, he believed they should turn to their maidservants. Jane Whittle's study, 'Housewives and Servants in Rural England, 1440–1650: Evidence of Women's Work from Probate Documents', found that 'malt maker' was considered a specialist duty for female servants, and something readily sought after. For example, she found a man called Robert Loder who employed women on his property to make malt to sell. Brewing and malting could be distinct skills. John Bickerdyke, in his 19th-century *Curiosities of Ale and Beer*, discovered that in 1610 the Justices of Rutland, in settling the rate of domestic servants' wages, adjudged that the very best women were those who could bake, brew, and make malt, and therefore should be paid a sum of 24s 8d per year. Women who could brew but not make malt were to receive 23s and 4d.

Women continued to make malt through the 17th century. Returning once again to the *Intoxicants and Early Modernity* database, in 1601 Elizabeth Helin testified that Alice Johnson made malt that she sold. Further, we learn that Helin herself purchased her malt, which she then used to brew. This was a bit of a scandal because Helin was not legally allowed to brew for sale and yet, 'she keeps a victualling house and makes pies of flesh and fish'. Once more we are back to ignoring regulations.

Later in this century, the *Household Account Book of Sarah Fell of Swarthmoor Hall* provides genuine insight into the inner workings of a family estate that thrived on making malt. Something that they were particularly successful at doing. How they sold their malt, who they sold it to, and who helped them, is all revealed in the *Account Book*. For example, in September 1673 they paid Mathew Gardner for looking after their marshgrainge malt (likely so named after Marsh Grange, a property owned by one of her sisters, Mary Fell, the wife of Thomas Lower). Gardner appeared to be someone in their employ as he regularly helped them with their malting business. Sarah Fell also recorded that Gardner helped sell it alongside herself, and possibly on his own at times. While Gardner helped them out, it was the women of the house who were in charge of the malting process and the business. Her mother's malt was particularly sought after and she frequently sold it to other women in the area. The *Account Book* offers us details of these transactions. On 13 November 1673 they sold her mother's malt to Margaret Woodburne, on 27 November to Ann Chanelhouse, and on 11 December to Joyce Benson, and so on. Details of selling her mother's malt are repeated over and over again, and it is most often sold to other women. Of course, it wasn't just their mother's malt that was sold to women. For instance,

Thomas Taylor's wife bought their marshgrainge wheat, Washing's wife bought six barrels of their marshgrainge old malt, Becke's wife bought three barrels of the same, and Alis Prissoe bought three barrels of malt.

This is not the first time I have brought up the Fells' accounts. You may recall me talking about them in terms of women brewing ale in the households. Well, here they are again with evidence of malting. In fact, their malting business and their female neighbour's brewing nicely demonstrate what a small farm economy might have looked like in the 17th century. The Fells make the malt, sell it to their neighbours, the Greaves', whose wife brews the ale and sells it back to them, thus making this a largely female-led economic practice. And though it is clear that the Fells had the help of several men on their payroll, and that Greaves' wife conducted her business alongside her husband, it does seem that the brewing and malting for this small sector was at least to some degree female led.

The role of women in the malting industry did not end during the 18th and 19th centuries and the rise of industrial brewing, but it certainly became less significant. As was the case with brewing, over the course of these centuries women would be less and less involved in the commercial creation and sale of malt. The *Universal British Directory 1793–1798* records at least one woman in Carmarthen in Wales who made her living as a maltster. Other women who worked as maltsters are also present throughout the UK. In Hampshire, Mary Neale was listed as a maltster in Andover, and in Droxford, Joanah Cammis filled the same role. In Henry Stropes' *Malt and Malting, an Historical, Scientific, and Practical Treatsie,* he presented the number of maltsters from the 1881 Census of England, Wales, and Scotland. England and Wales had 44 boys employed in the trade, 484 teenagers and young adults, 1,182 men under the age of 25, 4,671 under age 45, and 2,553 under age 65, with 539 older than 65. Compared to women in the trade, where we find no girls, only two teenagers or young adults, three women under the age of 25, 11 under the age of 45, 29 under the age of 65, and 13 over 65, this represents a stark difference between the two genders. It also tells us that women were still participating in the industry, albeit in a very limited capacity. In contrast, this same census recorded precisely zero women in the malting industry in Scotland. The data isn't perfect, but it does show the marked shift.

The 20th century brought with it the two world wars, and as we saw in brewing, women stepped up to fill the malting roles in the absence of men. On 8 June 1916 the *Burton Observer and Chronicle* reported that 'one hears experiments being made elsewhere of women maltsters, and even of women who are doing cooper's work, but these things are not common, and coopering, in particular, a trade not easily learnt.' But the rumours were true, and perhaps more widespread than the *Burton Observer* reporter may have known. On 14 October 1916 the *Birmingham Daily Gazette* told readers that the Home Office sent a letter to the clerk of the Burton-on-Trent Military Tribunal stating that women were permitted to work in the maltings on Sundays. Though apparently for 'not more than seven hours between 6 a.m. and 6 p.m., the total weekly hours not to exceed 60'. This was apparently to release male maltsters for military duty.

In fact, women were settling nicely into the trade of malting during the First World War. The *Yorkshire Evening Post* of 19 May 1917 ran 'A New Demand for the Munitions, Ale', stating that 'one of the new occupations for women is malting'. The reporter went on to say that malting was a very physically demanding job, 'but some parts of it can well be done by females', and that, 'so far, the women engaged on the work have done quite satisfactorily.' Women maltsters didn't just exist in England during the war. For example, *The Scotsman* advertised for a foreman maltster on 23 November 1917, and one of the key roles was to train and 'control' women maltsters.

We saw in the previous chapter that women did enter the malting and brewing industries in some numbers during the First World War. On 11 July 1916 the *Westminster Gazette* carried a feature entitled 'Women and the War', in which it published official figures related to women working in the food trade. It reported that some 20,000 women joined the brewing trade since the previous April, 'and more than doubled the number of women employed in the trade at the end of July 1914'. Readers were informed that 'many of these additional female workers, of course, are filling the places of men withdrawn for military service; but it would be rash to assume that the full complement of 10,000 may be placed in the category of substitutes for enlisted men.' From the breakdown of figures in the brewing category there were an estimated 10,000 women employed in July 1914, rising to 20,200 in April 1916. This figure also included malting women. The *Westminster Gazette* noted that, as we saw previously, many of these women were employed in the filling operations such as bottling, kegging, etc. And though not every employer was particularly thrilled about the prospect of hiring women, many embraced the change and were 'almost enthusiastic in their praise of the women who have taken over the duties of enlisted men'. We are told that one brewery had begun to use women maltsters:

'women are faced with a severe test as to their adaptability; but even here they are improving with practice, and many be expected to "make good" if the employers will give them a fair chance to acquire the necessary skill through training.'

Many women seemed to enjoy their new roles in the malting trade and fondly recalled it in years to come. The *Newark Advertiser* from 17 February 1968 tracked down two sisters who had worked in the Newark malting kilns and were now in their 70s. Reminiscing warmly about the smell of barley, one sister recalled how much she enjoyed the work.

It wasn't all positive for women working in the maltings, however. On 5 March 1917 the *Sheffield Independent* ran an article entitled 'Brewery Women Under Notice'. As the heading suggests, it was reported that all the women engaged in the Burton maltings were under notice, and that several hundred would be affected. The newspaper reported that by the following week malt manufacture in Burton would end under the Food Controllers Order. This was not an issue for the skilled workmen, who were to be retained in other brewery occupations, but the women were to be let go.

Women were often given the short end of the stick in industrial maltings and breweries. They weren't paid the same as men, even though the job came with the same level of difficulty. On 25 October 1915 the *Burton Daily Mail* reported that the Burton Workers' Union was attempting to organise local female workers by asking their members to encourage their daughters who were employed in local factories to join up. The article noted that female maltsters' wages had gone up by 3 or 4s a week that year, which they attributed in part to the shortage of men, but also 'the improvement was largely due to organisation'.

Wages for women in the malting industry didn't necessarily improve as the century wore on. On 18 December 1941 the *Burton Observer and Chronicle* ran an article entitled 'Burton Brewery Workers' Wages', which detailed the increase in workers' wages starting in the following month (January 1942). This was their third raise since the outbreak of war, but what is important for us is the marked difference in the increase for women and men. The report showed that women and girls were employed in the bottling stores, and women were also employed in the breweries themselves, as evidenced by the different rates of pay. However, 'women in breweries', as they were categorised in the article, were only paid '75 per cent of the basic rate for men, and 75 per cent of the [...] war bonus.' The same went for 'women maltsters', who were paid 75% of the basic men's rate in addition to 75% of the war bonus. Interestingly, girls aged 14 employed in the bottling stores and boys aged 14 employed in the brewery were paid the same, 17s and 6d a week, but once they reached 15 this changed, with boys being paid 22s and girls 20s. So, somewhere between the ages of 14 and 15 girls begin to be viewed as less competent, at least according to this brewery. This discrepancy in rates of pay doesn't take into consideration that working in malting could be dangerous, regardless of gender. In one instance, the *Burton Observer and Chronicle* reported on 11 January 1919 that a Nellie Woodhund had a serious accident at Messrs Ind, Coope, and Co's maltings, where she was employed as a maltster. Apparently, she fell from a very high ladder and severely injured her head and back.

As we have seen previously, women left the brewing industries after the end of the First World War, but this wasn't the end for women in malt. In the late 19th century, what is now Crisp Malt once had a woman at the helm. Betty Wharton covered this in *The Smiths of Ryburgh*. Like some of our female brewery owners we have discussed, Anne Smith inherited the business after her husband, Frederick, and his brother, George, both died. And women are still working at Crisp Maltings today. Women like Hannah Beer, the quality and improvement manager, and Jodie Harvey, the marketing manager. In the late 20th and early 21st centuries women have re-emerged in pivotal roles in the malting community throughout the UK and beyond. Another example can be found at Crafty Maltsters of Fife, Scotland, a family business run by Alison Milne, her husband, Daniel, and Daniel's father, Norman.

Malt has always been a key ingredient in brewing since long before the period discussed in this book. But in the wake of the Black Death, we learned of that other component, one that caused quite a stir in the brewing trade in medieval England.

Women and Hops

In the 18th century Eliza Berkeley compiled and edited a collection of writings from her son, George, in a text called *Poems*. In between George's litany of verses dedicated to death, his various lady loves, cupid, and the wind itself, she took some time to have a bit of a rant about all those things that ruin a beer. In particular, she had some strong opinions on hops. Eliza Berkeley was, to put it mildly, not a fan. She regaled readers about her friend the countess. She described a scenario in which the countess' butler came and whispered to her that she must come and weigh the hops, otherwise they cannot brew the beer and it will all be spoiled. Berkeley dually informed her audience that her friend did 'her duty as housekeeper' to carry out this task. However, she then began her tirade against the hop: 'Beer is generally spoiled by hops; and the Editor has been repeatedly told, that there is still an act of Queen Elizabeth unrepealed, forbidding the planting or cultivating that pernicious weed called hop.'

The myth that any English monarch banned hops outright is more 'pernicious' than the flower itself. But Eliza as the Editor isn't quite finished her anti-hop diatribe. She goes on to wax poetical about the 'wholesomeness of aged hard beer'. She told readers of a Mrs Tucker, whose father was the headmaster of the King's School when a fever broke out amongst the male attendees during the summer months, but her father was able to ward of the disease because he had them all drinking 'very hard home-brewed beer'. She further exclaimed that 'all the world have of late found out the virtues of beer without hops', and that new or sweet-wort is particularly excellent for children with worms and scurvy. Finally, she ends with this gem, 'when the poison of the strong rank weed, hop, is gone off, it is aqua vitae to many, to the Editor, even when almost vinegar; but a table spoonful of stale brewer's beer is almost death to her. Qu. Why is this?'

She certainly had strong feelings on the matter, but luckily for us, her opinions were not widely held, for hops would eventually dominate the British beer scene.

Hop Picking

During the 16th and 17th centuries hops were cultivated throughout the United Kingdom. Hop picking was done by local people, either servants who lived close to the property or temporary workers from the area. And many of these pickers were women. Pamela Sharpe's study 'The Female Labour Market in English Agriculture during the Industrial Revolution: expansion or contraction?' considered the intersections of hops and women's work, specifically in Essex. She found that during the 16th and 17th centuries hops were grown in nearly in every parish in the county and that growing, tending, and harvesting the plants was women's work. This was a critical source of paid labour for women between March and September.

In Ruth Facer's *Mary Bacon's World: A Farmers Wife in Eighteenth-Century Hampshire*, we learn all about hop farming from Bacon's 18th-century perspective. Like many of the women we explored in the housewives chapter,

Bacon wrote instructions for maintaining a household and recipes for creating various kinds of foods and medicines. Mary married William Bacon in 1765, and they had a farm with land that was particularly suited to growing hops. This is not the only Mary Bacon associated with hops. Another one appeared in a port book, which is a text that registers the customs duties people paid on items that had been imported or exported on ships through the ports of the England. From this source, we discover that a vessel called the *Baachelor*, which made berth at Great Yarmouth in Norfolk, carried a consignment of two-hundredweight of hops returned with a trader called Mary Bacon of England.

The work of hop picking captured the imagination of artists throughout this period and hop-picking women are depicted in many paintings and drawings. George Smith (1714–1776) painted the aptly titled 'Hop-Picking,' which is now held by the Maidstone Museum and Bentlif Art Gallery. It depicts several women of various ages clearly engaged in the process of picking the hops from the vines, while a man carries over to them yet more hops to be plucked. This is just one example of many such works to feature women growing and harvesting hops.

'Hop Picking', George Smith 1714–1776, mid-18th century, oil on canvas.

Thales Fielding, 1739–1837, 'Hop Picking', 1832.

Women continued to pick hops throughout the 19th century, generally alongside their families. They came from all over the country, travelling to the hop fields of Kent during the harvest season. In the 1870s there were even trains called Hop Pickers' Specials run by Southeastern Railway, delivering families from London to their hop-picking destination. On 8 October 1874 a feature in the *Pall Mall Gazette* entitled 'Rural Hop Pickers', told readers that there were lots of people from East London

> who troop along the southern roads on the eve of the hopping season, when they cannot muster the third class railway fares, limping painfully under heavy bundles, or trailing wearily behind the hand-barrows that carry their children and simply camping equipage, who either have to huddle themselves together promiscuously in the public sheds we have heard so much of, or make the best of our broken weather among the hedgerows.

The article noted that locals also pick hops, 'to the last capable child, before applications from strangers are listened to'. These locals, the paper tells us, have very little income, and live in houses that threaten to come down around their ears.

As we might have guessed, living conditions for the pickers were not particularly good. In fact, during the Victorian era they were downright awful in most cases, with poor sanitation and rampant disease. There wasn't any permanent housing and workers would have to stay in whatever was available, including barns and tents. This would not be ideal during wet summers, with lots of people jammed into cramped, soaked, small spaces. We can get an idea of what things might have been like from the *Illustrated London News*. An article from 11 September 1897 includes a drawing of two women huddled together in a downpour. The older one holds an umbrella that affords her some shelter from the torrential rain while her younger companion is getting absolutely drenched. Both look utterly miserable, and it is clear that this kind of work could be hard, wet, and altogether unpleasant.

It wasn't just the rain that made life hard for hop pickers; there was also the accompanying disease and death. In September 1849 cholera broke out in East Farleigh hop farm, killing 43 pickers. In 1898 Father Richard Wilson founded the Little Hoppers Hospital, where he employed women to help nurse sick hop workers. The hospital ran for some 60 years before closing. These abysmal conditions led to the formation of the Society for Employment and Improved Lodgings for Hop Pickers in 1866, which was led by women and campaigned for better working conditions. They specifically advocated for better accommodation, leading to the creation of Hopper Huts. An article in the *Canterbury Journal, Kentish Times and Farmers' Gazette* on 21 September 1872 told readers that women were at the forefront of recent hop-picker strikes demanding better and more transparent rates of pay. The article went on that that these 'weaker vessels' were 'inspired by the spirit of the times', and so were attempting to 'so firmly try to shake down the barriers of custom'.

The conditions on hop farms eventually improved in the 20th century. An article in the *Belfast Telegraph* from 25 August 1937 described farms that had a nurse to attend to the hoppers and hospitals set up to deal with minor complaints and injuries. The newspaper told its readers that 'society women and London business girls' would volunteer at these hospitals to look after the hop pickers. One of those 'society women' was, in fact, Miss Diana Churchill, daughter of Winston.

On Saturday, 8 September 1951, the *Kington Times* reported on hop picking at Kyrewood Farm in Tenbury, Worcestershire, where 230 people came from Manchester, Wolverhampton, Dawley and Ellesmore Port to pick hops for three weeks. Mrs Fanny Overton from Dawley, Salop, now aged 56, had been picking hops at Kyrewood Farm since she was eight years old. She was also carrying on a family tradition as charge-hand of the hop fields, just like her mother and grandmother had been before her. She spoke in depth about the differences between current hop-picking conditions and those just a half a century previously, noting that there were now 'properly built barracks, field kitchens, and daily visits by the district nurse. Things have certainly changed for the better.' Overton enjoyed her time picking, telling interviewers, 'it has always been a good holiday – far better than going to Blackpool.' She went on to say that the educational authorities now frowned upon pulling children out of school to go hop picking, but that she disagreed. 'I am certain that being in the open air does them the world of good.' Not all hop farms were family friendly, however. An advert in the *Herne Bay Press* on 6 May 1966 asked for women for training hops, with no or very few small children, to apply to J. E. Batchlor, Ford Manor Farm.

Hop picking often attracted people from urban environments. They travelled on the special trains out to farms in Kent and other south-eastern counties for a working holiday in the countryside, and an escape from their city life. The majority came from working-class or lower income households. An article in the *Tonbridge Free Press* on 27 August 1943 reported on this 'Annual Hop Invasion'. We are told that 'Once again the indefatigable Cockney proves that neither the war nor anything else will be allowed to interfere with his annual "hopping holiday".' Referring to the annual picking season as a hop 'invasion' would become a favourite headline of local newspapers.

Hop pickers represented a variety of religious affiliations, backgrounds, and ethnic groups. One photograph from 1933 is of a Franciscan Friar nailing up a flyer which was addressed to 'Catholic Hop Pickers', with details to be given on 'Sunday Next Holy Mass'. Other images from Paddock Wood in Kent show young girls and boys walking with a friar and a nun. Hop picking was a popular job for Traveller and Romani people, especially in Kent. In the 19th century, people from Traveller and Romani backgrounds would have been involved in every stage of the hop growing, and entire families would come together to the harvest. On 16 September 1939 the *Evesham Standard & West Midland Observer* published an article called 'War Time in the Hopyards' written by a woman signed only as J.K., possibly making her one of the earliest female proto-beer-writers. J.K. interviewed some of the Traveller and Romani women working on the farm. One woman was there with her family, as her husband and brothers were preparing to go off to war. She was picking alongside her mother, who J.K. referred to as an 'expert in her movements'. The writer found many children employed in the same task, writing, 'they pick hops as industriously as their parents, their little tongues as busy at their fingers, their little bright eyes never missing a single hop'.

Pearly Butler and her daughter, Rosie, were busy picking hops at Claston Farm in Dormington, Herefordshire. Butler and her family travelled there to pick hops in what would be the last year the hop harvest would be done by hand. Rosie is maybe four or five years old, and when not playing she is working alongside her mother, helping her with the hop harvest. Similar to those in J.K's article, the Butlers were from a Romani family, travelling to work on the harvest. Photos of Rosie and Pearly Butler come from a collection called *Herefordshire Life through a Lens*, a social history of Herefordshire based on the photo archive of Derek Evans Studio. These photos illustrate a preponderance of women and children hop pickers well into the 20th century, and also demonstrate the vital role that Traveller and Romani women and children played in the hop harvest. The photos include a wide range of people who came to pick hops, many of them white working-class families from towns and cities.

A woman decorating a girl's hat with hops in a hop field during harvest.
Stipple engraving with etching by H. Bourne, *c.*1845, after W. Witherington.

The reason that there were so many female hop pickers could be because they were just better at the task. At least, that is what some people thought at the time. On 24 August 1932 the *Halifax Evening Courier* argued that women were first-rate pickers as it reported on the arrival of some 50,000 hop pickers in Kent on special 'hoppers trains', many from the East End of London. An official of the Kent Hop Fruit and Stock Farms stated:

> A woman gets on better at hop picking than a man. A man's fingers are often clumsy, and he worries over the work and does not get hold of the hops so neatly as a woman. Feminine fingers are more deft and quick, and children are also very good. They work with their parents and thoroughly enjoy it.

Payment was per basket so women could earn as much or more than men. The *Vote*, on 9 September 1921, found that the women at the harvest in west Kent vastly outnumbered the men: 'In many gardens women have been at work at 6 o'clock,' and that 'they have had to work to live' as many of their 'men in London have been unemployed and are sending no money, and the women have to rely on what they can earn.'

Eventually, the introduction of the mechanical hop-picking machine pushed hand-pickers out of business. An article in *The Sphere*, on 28 September 1957, entitled 'Mechanical Hop Picking', told readers that 'two hundred hand-pickers are replaced by a machine and twenty-one workers'. This decline in the need for hop pickers would disproportionately affect women, though women could still be employed to operate the machines. The *Sevenoaks Chronicle and Kentish Advertiser* featured an advert on 26 August 1955 for women to work with a hop-picking machine for Hadlow Place Farm, Golden Green, Tonbridge. But, as always, women were paid less. Another advert in the same paper, dated 27 July 1962, for Bourne Farm, Sandhurst, said that men and women were wanted for hop-picking machines, with men paid 4s 6d and women 3s 8d.

Women have not disappeared entirely from hop growing in the UK. Hand-picking hops on large farms may be a thing of the past, but local hop yards and breweries are bringing back the tradition – at least on a much smaller scale. At Sadeh Farm and Lone Goat Brewery, Talia Chain and her husband grow seven varieties of hops which they use in their beers. Their hop growing actually predates the farm. They first starting to cultivate the plant in their parents' gardens and in her sister's garden: 'we've put them all over the place'.

And, of course, women still work for hop yards, though perhaps no longer as manual pickers. Another one of the women I interviewed, Joanne Love, is an assistant events manager at BarthHaas X, the UK craft arm of BarthHaas, one of the largest hop growers and merchants in the world. Furthermore, beer lovers throughout the UK have gotten in on the act as a way to reconnect with the past or to feel more involved in the creation of their favourite drink. A project in 2014 brought back hop pickers old and new to the farms of Kent to relive the harvest days. Created by artist Kathrin Böhm, *Company: Movement, Deals and Drinks* sought to forge links between old hop pickers and craft beer geeks, with the aim of using locally grown hops to brew beers back in London.

Beer nerds seem to be particularly drawn to learning about long-standing traditions in beer and brewing. And, of course, there would be no beer industry without those who like to have a few pints. And so, we will finish the book with a brief look at the ever-evolving role of women who drink beer.

Women Drinking Beer

The Women's Section of the British Legion supported widows and families of ex-servicemen in the early 20th century. They hosted fundraisers and collected clothing donations. They even secured capital for training loans to give to women who found themselves as the main breadwinners while their husbands were off to war. But on 11 August 1936 they were off to do something completely different. They were going on a brewery tour.

The *Middlesex Gazette* gives us a rather blunt headline: 'Women Visit a Brewery: And Receive a Sample!' The exclamation point here is rather amusing. Drinking beer? At a brewery? Shocking. In any event, we are told that the committee of the Women's Section visited Watney, Combe and Reid at Mortlake for a two-and-a-half-hour brewery tour. They saw the cooperage, watched the bottles being filled, and finished with 'an acceptable tea, cigarettes and a sample of the works' beverage'. It sounds like a lovely day out. But they weren't quite the trendsetters in doing this. Almost 10 years earlier, the Edinburgh Women's Citizens Association visited the brewery of Messrs McEwan at Fountainbridge for their own tour.

Women supporting women and having some beer along the way isn't a thing of the past. In more recent times groups have sprung up with the express purpose of empowering women to do a bit more than tour a brewery as a rare consumer of the product. But while brewery tours are still key parts of what brings members of current women's beer groups together, these days there is more of a focus on education, on teaching members about the brewing process. They also teach their members how to judge and analyse beer, harking back perhaps to those days of aletasters travelling around the town and setting the assize, though beer judging generally happens at competitions these days.

Many women in the UK are taking up the mantle of beer education by taking on the role of beer group leader. Nix Prabhu, founder of Glasladies Beer Society, told me that their key aims were to 'engage, educate and empower'. This was echoed by Amélie Tassin, founder of Women in Beer, who told me that she 'wanted to create a safe space for women, either working in the industry, but also who just like beer and want to drink beer with like-minded people.' The aims of both groups clearly align, working to highlight the important role of women in the industry, both those who work in it and those who drink the final product. Strength in numbers, Tassin told me, can help women when they are at the pub feel more comfortable in their beer choices. This was something that Monica Mendoza, a member of Tassin's organisation Women in Beer, echoed. Mendonza is an avid beer lover, and told me that she sometimes finds reactions to this fact can be quite mixed, with some assuming that she doesn't know what she is ordering. 'It's quite normal to find that in some pubs sometimes when you

Monica Mendoza, craft beer aficionado and Women in Beer member.

go and order a strong imperial stout or something like that, they always say "do you know that is 14%".' Attending events with Women in Beer can help other female beer drinkers feel more confident in ordering their beverages of choice, even in the face of such responses.

But they also fill another important role, one that is more aligned to our medieval guilds; they support women who work within the industry. Importantly, they encourage women to join the brewing world through hosting festivals to showcase beers made by local women, while also offering advice and support to women getting their breweries off the ground. Prabhu told me, 'we really want to be a group that empowers other women, other non-binary people, to play a more active role in the industry. Whether it is being an active consumer or an agent for change.' Tassin and Women in Beer were instrumental in helping Closet Brewing navigate their journey from homebrewery into a professional one. And, in some ways like the women we discussed in Chapter Four, swapping recipes or collaborating on a brew, working to support breweries has inspired Tassin to start a mentorship programme for women to help launch them into the brewing world. Whether it's in these beer groups as mentors for new breweries, or as consumers who quite literally spend the money that keeps the breweries' lights on, craft beer in particular could not exist without the women who drink it.

Historically, women have always played a part in keeping breweries in business. To put it simply, as long as there has been beer, there have been women drinking it. And while I acknowledge that I can't do justice to the subject of women and drinking beer in just a few pages, I can at least deliver a crash course of the key ideas.

The idea that beer (and brewing) is associated with men came in three separate yet connected strands. The first is the masculinisation of brewing itself; men taking over the process of making beer. We have seen quite clearly that it was never the case that men took over entirely, but they did manage to claim ownership of most commercial breweries. They also dominated the workforce, with some notable exceptions, as we have seen.

The second, which we are about to start looking at now, is the masculinisation of drinking in public spaces. That is, the idea of the pub being a space for men to drink mostly amongst themselves. This one, again, is quite complicated. Over the centuries, many women stopped visiting public drinking spaces for various reasons, though it really – and I cannot stress this enough – depends on the context: namely location, time period, and even socio-economic status of the women themselves. This second strand is neatly intertwined with the third, the idea that drinking beer, regardless of where, is a man's activity. While quite closely related, they are separate notions.

*   *   *

From the medieval period through the early modern era beer consumption was something that traversed class, age, gender, religion, race, and ethnic barriers. In fact, until quite recently it was a normal, mundane thing to consume ale as part of your everyday diet. It was a means for many people to gain their nutrition. But there was certainly a difference between drinking at home with your family, or even while you worked, and drinking in public establishments designed and created for the express purpose of eating and drinking (or maybe even staying over).

We learned in chapter five that women often worked in or owned these sorts of places, alongside their husbands or even on their own. We also know that these spaces could be dangerous for women, not only physically, as they were at risk from assault, but also socially, as slander and defamation could destroy the careers of female staff or owners. Women could and absolutely did drink in alehouses and, later, pubs. In fact, women were a constant presence in these spaces for centuries. For women who frequented such places, the risks could be similar to those who worked there, especially if they didn't follow the socially prescribed rules. Michelle Sauer argued that these rules were clear: that they could not drink alone; that they should be with a group of women, or male relatives; and they were to be there only during the day and only for a little bit.

Over the course of the 17th and 18th centuries women would continue to drink in public, with the above caveats, and with a few new additions. Socio-economic status also played an important role in what kind of public drinking places a woman might attend. Many scholars have argued over the precise point in time when women supposedly left the pubs and alehouses in large numbers. Some contend that it was in the later 19th century, still others the early 20th. David Gutzke's book, *Women Drinking Out in Britain Since the Early Twentieth Century*, argued that the temperance movements were particularly interested in targeting women's drinking. This resulted in people from upper-working, middle, and upper classes removing themselves from 'licensed premises, turning instead to wine merchants, off-license shops, private clubs, or restaurants for wines and spirits'. By the

1850s, most were simply drinking at home, according to Gutzke. His study contended that there was a socio-economic element to those who drank outside of the home. While there was certainly a general trend of women leaving public drinking spaces, the reality is, as with brewing, there was never a time where women were gone entirely. And in some places women continued to drink in public, in not insignificant numbers.

Between 1886 and 1903 Charles Booth conducted *The Life and Labour of the People of London*, a series of surveys on how people went about their daily lives, including how they drank beer, and importantly, where they drank it. One of the researchers that he recruited was a man by the name of George Duckworth. He interviewed several members of the Women's University Settlement: namely, Miss Gow, Miss Sewell, Miss Kerby, and Miss Sheepshanks. All of these women stated emphatically that there was no shame felt in their area about entering a public house as a woman. In another interview, local Police Superintendent Furnett told Duckworth that he believed 'public houses are more attractive than they used to be and the ladies salon bars are to be seen everywhere'. He contended, 'Norms now speak of women in public houses as something shocking [...] the change of feeling in this matter has come about gradually in the last 10 to 15 years.'

However, this change was not universal. As noted by other interviewees Duckworth spoke with, it could be based on socio-economic status. At least in London. In one interview, an officer called Dybell stated that women from working-class backgrounds were going to pubs. In contrast, clerks' wives or artisans' wives sent their children to the beer house or public house to fetch beer. Even though generally frowned upon by police, the youngsters were often rewarded for their efforts with sweets from the landlord. Many of Duckworth's interviewees noted this class divide, with those from middle socio-economic groups being less likely to venture into pubs than their working-class peers. But this certainly wasn't always the case. According to another one of his interviews, this time with an officer called Flanagan, women of all different backgrounds drank alcohol in the Kings Arms public house, and 'no one seems in the least to mind being seen'. This is the same Kings Arms that Flanagan referred to as a 'cowshed par excellence of the district'. Thus, we are introduced to the 'cowshed', a somewhat derogatory name for a drinking space that catered to women. Discussing these 'cowsheds', beer historian Ron Pattinson noted the hypocrisy, snobbery and outright falsehoods that the upper classes demonstrated in their views of public drinking, which, he says, 'illustrates how much our view of Victorian society – seen through the eyes of the higher classes – is a distortion of the reality. The attitudes of the London poor seem remarkably modern, compared to the pompous, often hypocritical morality of their "betters".'

To be clear, though, as Pattinson mentions, drinking in a public house was also a very different experience, and depended on where you lived, your socio-economic status, or your ethnicity or religion.

*   *   *

During the First World War many women took over men's jobs, as we saw in the last chapter, but they also visited pubs in higher numbers than they had in previous decades. This included women from a middling economic status who had previously been mostly absent. Gutzke argued that this represented a shift in drinking habits for the first time in half a century.

In the post-war period drink sellers feared that women would once again be pushed out of pubs, so attempted to reform and refurbish them. At the forefront of this move was Sydney Neville, who helped introduce play areas for children, as well as food, entertainment and games, and alcohol-free drinks. These new changes would not necessarily encourage middle- and upper-class women to attend public houses in large numbers. Many continued to stay away, though again this really depended on the context. Neither did these proposed new features alter the fact that women who visited pubs on their own could be in danger. As we saw in previous centuries, women who entered these spaces alone threatened male norms and so some men thought they could harass and abuse them.

But despite all this, women still drank a whole lot of beer, as we can see from *The Pub and The People*, a Mass-Observation Study from 1938. As part of the study, the observers interviewed many pub landlords, bartenders, and others. In one interview, a pub landlord reported that most women drank stout, if they were drinking beer, and about 60% of those chose Guinness. They found that more 'respectable women' drank bottled beer, again mostly Guinness or stout, or, very rarely, mild. In a random count in May, 43% women were drinking beer or spirits, 57% bottled stout or Guinness. One older landlady, apparently aged 72, was 'emphatic that Guinness was good for women, and was supported by two other women,' which sounds like their marketing campaign was working well. Overall, the study found that women beer drinkers were driven more by taste and 'the externals', whereas men were motivated more by price.

What women did not drink was pints, lest they be judged as less womanly, less feminine. Pints were overwhelmingly viewed as something 'for men'. *The Pub and The People* cited Nicholson's *London Survey*, which argued that men drank pints 'because it is something to grip onto', and that 'it makes the beer last longer'. Which is, of course, ridiculous, and in contrast to what they found in their own investigation in Bolton. Instead, they concluded that men drank pints and gills (half pints) at the same rate on average. This perceived association of men with pints meant that women who drank them could be subjected to serious social scorn. In fact, there were clear consequences for women drinking pints. It was believed to be a transgression of womanhood. A woman who did drink pints is remembered with derision by other women, as reported by an observer for the study. The following paragraph was reproduced with permission of Curtis Brown, London, on behalf of the Trustees of the Mass-Observation Archive:

> Discussion about a lesbian woman. They concentrate *like hell* to try and remember her name … the following remarks were made about her: "She be dead and buried now", "The worst thing about her is neither woman nor man", "'er and Emily lived together", "She was rather on the vulgar side", "She was very dirty spoke though", "She'd stand up at the fire", "She'd rather have a pint than a gill".

This reinforces what we have seen, and such dislike and outright disgust of women drinking pints would continue over the course of the following decades.

It was in the second half of the 20th century that women began to enter the public house in greater numbers. Barbara Gleiss argued it was in the 1960s and 1970s. Fuelled by many factors, including advertisements aimed at women, and motivated by the feminist movement and university students, women attended more regularly and in increasing numbers. However, for many the long-standing social rules still applied; those words of warning that many women have heard from their mothers: don't go alone, don't stay too late, and don't drink too much.

The demographics of many pubs have changed over recent decades, with many becoming family friendly environments, or open to people of all genders without stigma. And as we saw in chapter five, pubs are becoming spaces for creating community and building friendships. But this isn't always the case. The notion of the pub being a space for men only still persists.

Earlier in the book, I introduced you to Dea Latis. In addition to all their work for women in beer, they are responsible for two studies: *The Gender Pint Gap* and *The Beer Agender*. From their findings, we can learn more about why women continue to be deterred from visiting pubs, and it sounds like an echo from the past. Annabel Smith, co-founder of Dea Latis, told me that some of the women who responded had the following to say: 'Pubs were described as "blokey, brown and boorish". This is only three years ago. A lot of women said they still didn't feel comfortable walking into a community pub on their own. Which, yeah, blew me away.'

So, many women still don't feel comfortable being in pubs alone or even walking into their local by themselves. This concept of the pub as a masculine space is pervasive. Not only the pub, but even beer itself. Amy Rankine, Women in Beer member, is also a doctoral researcher studying the intersections between beer and masculinity. In our interview, Rankine told me that beer is so strongly tied to masculinity because it is an accessible way to perform it. It serves as a ritual to cross the threshold between boyhood and manhood. Rankine found that the links between advertising and beer in the 1980s and 1990s represented a shift. She said:

> I think a lot of the issues that we have around women in brewing spaces are linked to the sexualisation of women within brewing advertising during the eighties and nineties, where there's the kind of capitalist ideal that if you go to a bar and if you buy beer, you will also get women.

One of her most interesting findings was that beer allowed men to behave in ways more commonly associated with femininity. They can talk about their emotions, or hug their friends, or kiss each other 'without any penalty' for doing so. Perhaps, she argued, this is why the pub was and is so guarded from women; because men can do all of these things in this 'highly masculinised space'. She continued, 'I think that's actually also why it's so difficult within our beer spaces to allow women [...] It threatens the escape.'

Jane Peyton of the School of Booze told me something similar: 'Beer has been assigned a gender and that gender is male. That is largely to do with the way beer is marketed in the UK. Marketed at men.' This was also reflected in Dea Latis' *The Gender Pint Gap* study in which 27% of women felt that beer was advertised to men and that turned them away. The Dea Latis studies also found that pint glasses themselves were 'still perceived as very masculine'. Many women who responded wanted more aesthetically pleasing glasses. Additionally, *The Gender Pint Gap* found that 20% of women didn't

Amy Rankine, beer academic researcher, leader of forages, fermentation classes,
wild food courses, walks and workshops, and Women in Beer member.

drink beer because they were concerned about calories or weight gain.
Respondents said that beer was very gaseous and made them feel bloated.
A further 17% didn't drink beer because they were concerned with 'being
judged by others', which is an unreasonable concern given what we have
just seen. This was reflected in another report by Dea Latis in 2019, *The Beer
Agender*, in which women who drank beer were viewed in a negative light.
As Smith says:

> It [beer] wasn't seen as ladylike. It wasn't seen as a drink for women.
> A really interesting one for me was how females viewed other females
> who drank beer and they put them in a lower socio-economic group, a
> lower class of group. Words that came out were they are dowdy, they
> don't look after themselves. And I just thought, this is women judging
> women, so imagine what men think like about women drinking beer.

So, we have this combination of classism and internalised misogyny
permeating the idea that beer is not for women. This idea that beer is
strongly associated with masculinity, and is seen as being unladylike or
unfeminine, permeated the interviews, with many telling me that they
had personal experience of these attitudes. Emma Inch of *Fermentation Beer
and Brewing Radio* said, 'I remember when I was about 18 or whatever and
the assumptions all the time when you drank beer. Even landlords were

reluctant to sell pints of beer to women, they only wanted to sell halves. And so that has changed.' Natalya Watson, author, Beer Sommelier, and Cicerone, told me that when she was getting into beer she was also told that drinking beer wasn't ladylike, 'and I can imagine I'm not the only person to have been told that'. She certainly was not.

Women Who Write About Beer

'I went to my first Great British Beer Festival in 2005, and I just fell in love with cask ale at that point,' Ruvani de Silva tells me about her motivation to start beer writing. It was this love of cask that motivated her to get more involved, volunteering for CAMRA, seeking out this kind of beer everywhere and 'getting a bit nerdy about it'. Then she found herself visiting the United States for work, where she could find all sorts of craft beers to sample: 'I'd just scoop them all up, and you could buy them as singles, which was very exciting.' When back home in the UK, she would seek out these American craft beers, and soon found herself becoming a huge fan of more local brews when they began to be made. 'I was all over it very early on,' she told me. She even joined a group, Boozers Without Borders, which helped raise money for refugees by running craft beer tasting events and tours in London. All the while, she was still volunteering for CAMRA, 'I was just very into the scene. Loved it.'

And then she made the move to Texas. At first, because she didn't have a work permit, she wasn't able to look for a job, so she started her blog, *craftbeeramethyst.com*, in which she wrote about her experiences with local breweries and beer events. Later, after finally receiving her work permit, she didn't want to go back to her old career in PR. But her previous career had given her expertise in the art of pitching, and so she started pitching beer stories, sending out articles to publications, before finally getting a few bites. From there, her love for beer just grew and grew, launching de Silva into a very successful career trajectory as a food and drinks writer with a particular soft spot for beer.

De Silva posts about a range of topics on her personal blog, and for other publications such as *PorchDrinking.com* and the *Houston Chronicle*. She is an expert at recommending the most interesting venues to her local readers in Texas, including an April 2023 article for *Good Beer Hunting* about the Whip In, an Austin institution purchased by an Indian immigrant family in 1986 who, as de Silva elucidated, 'transformed it into a unique combination of craft beer mecca, Tex-Mex-Indian fusion restaurant, South Asian supermarket, and live music venue'. These are the sorts of human interest stories that de Silva explores with readers, drawing them into the local beer scene.

De Silva also tackles some of the broader issues in the brewing industry. Her articles on topics relating to diversity and inclusion have peppered this book, and she tells me that these are two of the main themes in her writing. She didn't set out to write specifically about diversity and inclusion but found herself frequently talking about them. 'But obviously as a woman of colour, a queer woman of colour [...] you go places and you can tell if a place isn't inclusive.' During the course of her writing career she has found herself thinking more and more about the places in which she was

Ruvani de Silva, freelance beer writer and educator, and founder of the South Asian Beer Club.

drinking beer, or even the beer and breweries themselves. As she says, 'what are these places really like?' She began to identify gaps or issues in the beer industry at large, and told me that there wasn't anyone talking about these issues in Texas, especially about the role of other South Asians in the beer scene.

Her research and writing also led to her launching the South Asian Beer Club. It began with a project looking to find other South Asian women who drink beer, and quickly evolved into a dedicated beer group supporting South Asian people in the beer industry around the world; a place for them to compare notes, support each other, and maybe even work together. In fact, in April 2023 they announced a collaboration brew with the formerly named Chicago Brewseum, now called the Beer Culture Center. The beer, called Subcontinental Jackfruit Lager, brought together four different South-Asian owned breweries in the United States: Roughhouse Brewing, Misfit Outpost, Windmills USA, and Azadi Brewing.

De Silva is one of many talented women who write about beer; women like Jessica Boak (or Slack) of *Boak and Bailey*, and many others too numerous to name in this book. In some ways these writers hark back to the women who wrote guidebooks on how to homebrew in the early modern period, or even those aletasters of medieval England, Scotland and Wales who evaluated the local brews.

It is these women who write about beer and educate others about it who are part of the push for a more inclusive and diverse industry. Authors like Melissa Cole, whom de Silva credits as one of her biggest influences, are now household names for many of us. And while there are, today, plenty of women in the beer writing world, women have been writing about beer for centuries, as we saw in chapter four. More recently, in the 20th century, women entered the beer writing world through publications like CAMRA's *Good Beer Guide*, when Andrea Gillies was appointed editor in 1988. In the *Guide*, authors like Katherine Adams, Virginia Matthews and Roz Morris wrote about public houses in the UK with wit and flare. Gillies edited the *Guide* again the following year, then Jeff Evans took over the role. The current editor, Emma Haines, took over the reins from Roger Protz in 2019.

Speaking of CAMRA, Laura Hadland quite literally wrote the book on it, including an entire chapter on the women of the organisation. Fittingly named *50 Years of CAMRA*, her biography of the organisation had her travelling all over the country to conduct oral history interviews for the book. Hadland told me the story of Laura Craft, the 30,000th CAMRA member, who had gone to a festival with her boyfriend and joined the organisation on a whim. Craft is still a member and married to that very boyfriend.

Coming from a background in history and museum work, it's the human stories like this that really appeal to Hadland, focusing her on the people in the industry. As she said, 'I get really drawn into stuff and fall down rabbit holes all the time [...] I was gone for days just digging, digging, digging for more.' Hadland certainly succeeded in relaying these human stories to readers in her book on CAMRA's 50-year history. It won the prestigious 'Best Beer Book in the World, 2022' by Gourmand International Awards.

Hadland has written extensively for CAMRA, contributing to the *Good Beer Guide* amongst other projects, and is currently working on a history of CAMRA's Great British Beer Festival. She also does freelance work for an array of publications including *Glug Magazine* and *The Telegraph*. Hadland writes on topics such as beer education, helping people navigate the many styles and flavours, 'because, I think, beer is quite confusing. And you can't know everything'. Importantly, returning to those women of CAMRA who Hadland included in her work, she credits them with paving the way, 'I think I'm probably hanging on the tailcoats of the women who've gone before. There are women writers who have laid a path for me and others like me to follow. They have made my experience easier.'

Laura Hadland, freelance food and drinks writer, author of *50 Years of CAMRA*, and Creative Director of Thirst Media.

Another woman who has worked with CAMRA is Emma Inch. She married her love of beer with her work and created the first beer radio show on FM in the UK on Radio Reverb. And it has carried on from there. As a podcaster on *Fermentation Beer and Brewing Radio*, Inch weaves together stories of local breweries for her niche podcast audience. In fact, having a smaller, more dedicated group of listeners was something that really appealed to her. As she noted, 'you are right in people's heads'. But it isn't just about storytelling; educating audiences about beer is also a key part of podcasts, both on and off the air. Importantly, Inch also works with people, training and mentoring to help them with their own beer writing or podcasting.

Emma Inch, an award-winning freelance beer writer, former chair of the British Guild of Beer Writers, and podcaster at *Fermentation Beer and Brewing Radio*.

On *A Woman's Brew*, Joanne Love and Tori Powell often focus episodes on education, teaching their listeners about beer styles or brewing techniques. Importantly, they also conduct interviews, sharing experiences of how brewers got started in the industry and how they make it work. Elsewhere, Love runs her online beer education programme, *Love Beer Learning*, where she teaches interested attendees all about the brew. Like women's beer groups, women's beer communicators focus on the importance of education to their audiences. Through new media like podcasts or online courses, beer education reminds us of those women writing books for

Joanne Love and Tori Powell of *A Woman's Brew*, a craft beer podcast.
Love also runs *LoveBeerLearning*, a beer education platform.

housewives or servants in the 1600s and 1700s, adding to the legacy of centuries of women's brewing knowledge.

Love is in good company. Aside from her hugely important consultancy work, Jane Peyton is a drinks writer and podcaster, having written *The Philosophy of Beer* and *Beer o'Clock*. Peyton also famously founded the School of Booze in 2008 with the intent to run corporate beer tastings. Having spent years teaching people about alcoholic drinks, she has developed an online learning platform designed for people in the hospitality industry to educate them on beer, cider, and wine.

Like Peyton and Love, Natalya Watson has also launched her own online school of learning, Virtual Beer School, catering to the general population who simply want to expand their knowledge base. Watson is the author of *Beer: Taste the Evolution in 50 Styles*. The book was a deep dive into the history of modern beer styles and how to drink them, 'A taster's guide through the history of beer,' she told me. Her book was published on 19 March 2020, just before the UK went into lockdown, meaning that she wasn't able to do any kind of a launch. But what she did do was a virtual book club. She would take a chapter a week and take participants through the various bits of the book that didn't survive the final edit, as well as other research that she had

Jane Peyton, founder of the School of Booze, writer of many books including *Philosophy of Beer* and *Drink: A Tippler's Miscellany*, beer educator and podcaster.

since carried out. At the end of this, people wanted to continue; they wanted to keep up the social connections that had been built during lockdown.

Watson decided to build something else. She crowdsourced topics such as Japanese or French beer styles, or how to become a Beer Sommelier. By the end, people told her they would pay her. And so Virtual Beer School was born. We can almost imagine Watson's school being the natural successor to Eliza Smith's 1727 *The Complete Housewife*. Indeed, if Smith had been able to teach a class about what she had told readers in her book, it would likely mirror Watson's, or Love's, or Peyton's.

Another thing that Love, Peyton and Watson, as well as many other women I interviewed have in common is certification. Watson is a Beer Sommelier and Advanced Cicerone, while Love is a Certified Cicerone. We learned earlier about those women who brew and the courses available to them to further their knowledge of the process, like those attended by Apiwe Nxusani-Mawela or Nidhi Sharma. Jane Peyton has multiple accreditations, including Beer and Cider Sommelier. She was able to use this as a way to increase her credibility as a beer expert, including hosting the Guinness

Natalya Watson, beer educator and author of *Beer: Taste the Evolution in 50 Styles*, founder of Virtual Beer School and *Beer with Nat* podcast, Beer Sommelier and Advanced Cicerone.

World record-breaking largest beer tasting tutorial in the world, which had 1,236 attendees. And though she hasn't experienced sexism inside the industry, she told me, outside of it is a different ball game:

> Within the general population yes, I have encountered sexism from men making silly comments, or making an assumption I know nothing about beer. Quite often they try to enlighten me about beer despite them not being in the beer industry or having any accredited knowledge, and knowing that I am an experienced beer educator and communicator. If I am hosting an event I deal with it by inviting them to come and take over from me and do the presentation. That always shuts them up.

*   *   *

On the surface, this chapter perhaps appears to be the most disparate, weaving together mismatched pieces of an increasingly complicated puzzle. However, the stories of women who malted, harvested hops, and women who drank the final product are not so very unrelated, as we have seen. After all, beer could not exist without hops and malt, and if no one drank it then hop pickers and maltsters would have all been out of a job. But it's also because, as the other chapters have shown us, women have always been central to these roles, and have more in common than we may initially assume. From buying and selling malt in the 16th century to enjoying a few pints with their local women's beer group in the 21st, there is very little that women have not influenced in some way in the history of this ubiquitous brew.

There is no point in the history of British beer that women were not part of the story. They were poor widows with disabilities who brewed as a way to sustain themselves when other jobs were beyond their capabilities. They were Jewish women who brewed to maintain their families. They were desi pub owners who created important cultural homes. They were housewives from different backgrounds who brewed to make extra income for their families. They were lesbian women who owned spaces where people brewed and served ale. They were servants, of a range of ethnicities, races, and religions, who assisted their employers with the brewing tasks. They were wealthy heiresses who ran massive brewing enterprises. They were Traveller and Romani women who picked hops alongside their families. They were canning line operatives who were critical parts of their respective unions. They were all kinds of women who stepped up to take over men's jobs at the outbreak of the First World War. And today they *are* finance officers, bottle shop owners, IT support staff, social media marketers, bartenders, beer judges, activists, chefs, writers, drinkers, maltsters, and, of course, brewers. This is as true now as it was in the medieval period. The history of beer in Britain is the history of women, full stop.

RECIPES

'It is granted on all hands,
that, according to the common saying,
good eating deserves good drinking'

ELIZA SMITH, *The Complete Housewife:
Or, Accomplished Gentlewoman's Companion*, 1727

Apple Fritters

In true modern blogger fashion, I am going to start my recipe selection with an essay nattering on incessantly about all the minutiae I can think of before finally giving you the actual ingredients and how to make it. Do I sound bitter? Maybe a little. But in all seriousness, I'm giving you a brief history of these recipes so you have some idea of the context.

Virtually every collection of historical recipes contains at least one for ale-battered apple fritters. From the medieval period, a recipe from *The Forme of Cury*, dating to 1390, is called 'Frytour of Pasternakes of Apples', and I would be lying if I said I wasn't drawn to this one initially because of the ingredients 'pasternakes' and 'skyrwater'. Come for the carrots, stay for the parsnips, which are the translations of these words, respectively. I made this, with a few modifications for the apples especially, for my blog a few years ago and it was very good. Recipes for these apple fritters also appear in those books written by and for housewives. Hannah Woolley's 1670 *The Cook's Guide* contains two recipes for apple fritters, both involving a posset of cream and ale (see below). Janet Maule's recipe book also includes some apple fritters involving ale and sherry. Eliza Smith's 1766 *The Complete Housewife* included one that was particularly easy to follow.

I've created my favourite version below, which is a mix of *The Forme of Cury*, Smith, Maule's and Woolley's, plus some toppings of my own design. A word of warning, however: I am not a chef or professional cook; this is

merely my home-cook approximation, so I can't guarantee results. However, it's fun to try these at home. See it as a way to connect with those women of the past whom you've just read about. That said, you will need to be mindful of food safety practices.

A few points of interest before proceeding. I recommend using a malt-forward beer for this recipe, and the others. Something like an English mild or any wheat beer. Malty lagers also work really well. As for the apples themselves, I like using honey crisp or gala. Granny Smiths are nice as well. But use your personal favourite, and bear in mind that the dish will be sweetened with toppings.

So without further ado, here is my attempt at apple fritters.

Ingredients

8 egg yolks and 4 egg whites
Approx 1l of cream
Pint of ale
240g flour
4 apples
Nutmeg, cinnamon, ginger, salt to taste
Neutral oil of your choice for frying
Toppings (various)

Method

1. Clean, core and peel the apples. Slice horizontally about ¼-in thick.
2. Add the cream and beer to a pan. Heat it until just below boiling.
3. Beat your eggs together, add slowly to the cream and beer, making sure that it doesn't start turning into scrambled eggs.
4. Add spices to the mixture.
5. Remove from heat.
6. In a bowl, add the flour. Slowly add to this your egg/cream/ beer mixture. Combine until the batter is fairly thick.
7. In another pan heat up the neutral oil of your choice.
8. Dip apples in the batter.
9. Fry the apples in the oil for approximately 3–5 minutes depending on size of your slices and how tender you want them to be.
10. Remove from heat. Serve with toppings of your choice.
    I liked mine with some drizzled honey and a bit of cinnamon.
    Would also be lovely with ice cream or custard.

Cock Ale

This is one of those drinks with a strange name and a bizarre mishmash of ingredients. To address the elephant in the room, early modern people were well aware of the somewhat scandalous nature of the name of the ale. The 1811 *Dictionary of Buckish Slang, University Wit, And Pickpocket Eloquence* defined it as a 'provocative drink', though perhaps it was more provocative in terms of the ingredients, which involved boiling a rooster in ale, hence the name. To this is added raisins, dates, mace, nutmeg, and some higher proof alcohol, all of which seems to make sense. But boiling a chicken in it? Perhaps it's a throwback to Elynour Rummyng and her hen's droppings ale, but less likely to kill you from salmonella. Alas, this is also without the added benefit of making you look two or three years younger.

This drink seemed like a unique concoction, so naturally I had to make it, thinking it was not going to be particularly pleasant. More fool me. It is delicious. To be fair, though, it has been made for centuries, well into the modern era, so I should have been clued in that there must have been something to it. Unlike the myriad of foods that shouldn't, but in fact do, taste just like chicken, this one decidedly does not. Instead, the chicken adds a richness to the drink, the fat rendering into the ale and making it creamier and fuller bodied. The spices and beer itself cover up any kind of poultry flavour in my experience, making this a lovely drink to reheat and enjoy on a cold day.

The recipe below is a combination of one from the 16th-century *The Closet of the Eminently Learned Sir Kenelme Digbie Kt. Opened*, Eliza Smith's 1766 *The Complete Housewife*, and Hannah Woolley's 1670 *The Accomplish'd lady's delight*. All three recipes are remarkably similar with only the spices changing to some degree. As with all these recipes, I recommend using a malt-forward ale, and I would also suggest getting your chicken pre-murdered.

Ingredients

2 raw chicken thighs
2 pints of ale
Small handful of raisins (40g)
Small handful of dates (40g)
Mixed spice or pumpkin spice mix to taste
2 shots of cream sherry

Method

1. Thoroughly sanitise (not just wash) several bottles for the finished cock ale before refrigeration. You can find the chemicals for this at your local homebrew shop.
2. Boil the chicken thighs in the ale until fully cooked. Separate (incidentally these make a delicious dinner base). Leave to cool.
3. Mix the raisins, dates and spices together with a mortar and pestle or food processor.
4. Add this mixture to two shots of cream sherry.
5. Add this to the chicken and ale mixture.
6. Decant into the sanitised bottles and leave in your fridge for several days to properly combine. Then enjoy!

Beer tray from The Netherlands.

Posset

Like the other recipes here, posset appears in nearly all of the recipe books that we have explored thus far, with each book having its own signature version. At its core, a posset is cream and egg yolks mixed and heated to form a type of custard, to which spices such as cinnamon and nutmeg are added, as well as ale. It is thick and heavy and generally served in a glass. Possets used to be a very popular dessert, in part because they tasted nice, but also because they were used as a kind of comforting medication for those who were ill. They even had their own glassware. Posset itself dates back at least to the medieval period, and, like the others we have investigated, features prominently in all those books for and by housewives. Merryell Williams' *Book of Recipes* had two recipes for posset, one with and one without milk. Mrs Johnson's recipes for the Fletcher of Saltoun family from the 18th century contained one for 'Ane Eating Posset'. Eliza Smith had two recipes, one for an oatmeal sack posset, and one for a posset with ale. And Edward Allde's 1588 *The good hous-wiues treasurie Beeing a verye necessarie booke instructing to the dressing of meates. Hereunto is also annexed sundrie holsome medicines for diuers diseases* also contained one.

Early 18th-century posset pot with cover, Staffordshire, England.

I've made my own version using a combination of these recipes. As with the other recipes, I have made this before on my blog. After some experimenting, I've decided on the following recipe for you. I opted to make one with milk, but there are some you can make without. As mentioned before, this one contains eggs that may be undercooked, so make and eat this at your own risk. Always use safe food practices, nd if you are not certain or haven't cooked this before, use pasteurised eggs (available in supermarkets).

Ingredients

1 pint of ale
8 eggs – yolks and whites
1 pint cream
1 pint milk
50g of grated bread (just let some dry out a bit and grate it into your mix, or add unseasoned breadcrumbs)
120g sugar
Cinnamon and nutmeg to taste
2 shots of sherry or brandy

Method

1. Add milk and cream together on the stove. Heat until boiling.
2. Add spices, grated bread, and sugar.
3. Mix well until sugar is dissolved. Make sure milk does not curdle.
4. Beat your eggs together in a separate heatproof bowl.
5. Add ale, sherry/brandy to egg mixture.
6. Pour the boiling milk mixture into the ale, sherry/brandy mix. Mix back and forth between the two to make it nice and frothy.
7. Drink.

Bibliography

Introduction

BENNETT, Judith. 'Remembering Elizabeth Etchingham and Agnes Oxenbridge.' In Noreen Giffney, Michelle M. Sauer, and Diane Watt (eds.) *The Lesbian Premodern*, pp. 131–143. Palgrave Macmillan, 2011.

BLAIR, Thomas L. *Black Britannia: From Slavery to Freedom in the 18th Century*, The Black London eMonograph Series, 2013.

COLUMBIA LAW SCHOOL. 'Kimberlé Crenshaw on Intersectionality, More than Two Decades Later.' Columbia Law School Website. 7 June 2017. https://www.law.columbia.edu/news/archive/kimberle-crenshaw-intersectionality-more-two-decades-later

GATTUSO, Reina. 'The Return of Japan's Female Sake Brewers.' Atlas Obscura, 13 July 2020. https://www.atlasobscura.com/articles/women-sake-brewers-in-japan.

GERZINA, Gretchen Holbrook. *Black London: Life before Emancipation*, Rutgers University Press, 1995.

HAYASHIDA, Frances. 'Chicha Histories: Pre-Hispanic Brewing in the Andes and the Use of Ethnographic and Historical Analogues'. In Justin Jennings and Brenda J. Bowser (ed.) *Drink, Power, and Society in the Andes*, pp. 233–256. University Press of Florida, 2009.

KAUFMANN, Miranda. *Black Tudors: The Untold Story*. Simon and Schuster, 2017.

KELLOGG, Susan. *Weaving the Past: A History of Latin America's Indigenous Women from the Prehispanic Period to the Present*, Oxford University Press, 2005.

LAYCOCK, Stuart. *All the Countries We've Ever Invaded: And the Few We Never Got Round To*. History Press, 2013.

MARCHÉ, Montaz. 'Uncovering Black Women in Eighteenth- and Nineteenth-Century Britain.' History, 28 October 2019. https://www.ucl.ac.uk/history/news/2019/oct/uncovering-black-women-eighteenth-and-nineteenth-century-britain

NUBIA, Onyeka. *Blackamoores: Africans in Tudor England, Their Presence, Status and Origins*, 2013.

NUBIA, Onyeka. 'Blacks Britannia: Diversity in Medieval and Early Modern England.' Medievalists.net. 10 November 2021: https://www.medievalists.net/2022/08/blacks-britannica-diversity-in-medieval-and-early-modern-england

OLUSOGA, David. *Black and British: A Forgotten History*. Pan Macmillan, 2016.

OTELE, Olivette. *African Europeans: An Untold Story*. Basic Books, 2020.

SCATTERGOOD, John (ed. and introduction). 'The *Tunning of Elinor Rumming*', in John Scattergood (ed.) *The Complete English Poems of John Skelton*. Harmondsworth, 1983.

SHACKELL, James. '"After Every Challenge, I Get Stronger." Meet the Middle East's First Female Brewer.' Intrepid Travel Blog (blog), 12 December 2022. https://www.intrepidtravel.com/adventures/meet-the-middle-easts-first-female-brewer

SKELTON, John. 'The Tunning of Elynour Rummyng', in Marie Loughlin, Sandra Bell, and Patricia Brace (ed.) *The Broadview Anthology of Sixteenth-Century Poetry and Prose*, pp. 1–8. Broadview Press, Petersborough, Ontario, 2011.

The Ancient Laws and Customs of The Burghs of Scotland Vol. I A.D. 1124–1424. John Greig & Son, 1868.

CHAPTER ONE
Of Pints and Plagues

'Are People Really Moving out of Cities? – Moving Outside London | Leaders,' *Leaders.co.uk*
1 April 2021: https://www.leaders.co.uk/advice/are-people-really-moving-out-cities-20210401

BARROW, J. S., J. D. Herson, A. H. Lawes, P. J. Riden and M. V. J. Seaborne. 'Economic infrastructure and institutions: Craft guilds', in A. T. Thacker and C. P. Lewis (eds.). *A History of the County of Chester: Volume 5 Part 2, the City of Chester: Culture, Buildings, Institutions*, pp. 114–124 Victoria County History, 2005. On *British History Online*: http://www.british-history.ac.uk/vch/ches/vol5/pt2/pp114–124

BAKER, Stephanie Marie. *Brewing and Baking in Scotland, 1406–1513*, University of Stirling, MPhil, April 2022.

BALL, Mia. *The Worshipful Company of Brewers: a Short History.* Hutchinson Benham Ltd., 1977.

BEDINGTON, Ed. 'Three Quarters of Pubs facing extinction,' *MorningAdvertiser.co.uk*, August 23rd, 2022. https://www.morningadvertiser.co.uk/Article/2022/08/23/Three-quarters-of-pubs-likely-to-close-in-energy-crisis

BENNETT, Judith. *Ale, Beer and Brewsters in England: Women's work in a changing world 1300–1600.* Oxford University Press, 1996.

Britannia Ryans Removals. 'Are Brits Selling Up and Leaving Major UK Cities Post Lockdown?' *Britannia Movers International*, 12 January 2023. https://www.britannia-movers.co.uk/coronavirus-news/are-brits-selling-up-and-leaving-major-uk-cities-post-lockdown

BROWN, James. 'How the Bubonic Plague Changed Drinking Habits.' *The Conversation*, n.d. https://theconversation.com/how-the-bubonic-plague-changed-drinking-habits-160840

BURTON, Kristen. *The Citie Calls for Beere: The Introduction of Hops and the Foundation of Industrial Brewing in London 1200–1700.* Unpublished MA Thesis, Oklahoma State University, 2010.

CHANCE, Eleanor, Christina Colvin, Janet Cooper, C J Day, T G Hassall, Mary Jessup and Nesta Selwyn. 'Craft Guilds', in A History of the County of Oxford: Volume 4, the City of Oxford, ed. Alan Crossley and C R Elrington (London, 1979), pp. 312–327. On *British History Online* http://www.british-history.ac.uk/vch/oxon/vol4/pp312–327

CLARKE, Daniel, Vaughan Ellis, Holly Patrick-Thomson, and David Weir. *Researching Craft Beer: Understanding Production, Community and Culture in an Evolving Sector.* Emerald Group Publishing, 2021.

Close the Gap and Engender. 'Joint Briefing on the Impact of Covid-19 on Young Women's Employment, Financial Security, and Mental Health.' November, 2021. https://www.engender.org.uk/content/publications/Close-the-Gap-and-Engender-Joint-briefing-on-the-impact-of-Covid-19-on-young-women.pdf

Contributors to Wikimedia projects. 'Select Historical Documents of the Middle Ages/Book I/The Statute of Laborers.' *Wikisource, the Free Online Library.* 15 August 2016. https://en.wikisource.org/wiki/Select_Historical_Documents_of_the_Middle_Ages/Book_I/The_Statute_of_Laborers

COWAN, Mairi. *Death, Life and Religious Change in Scottish Towns c. 1350–1560.* Manchester University Press, 2013.

DAVIES, Rob. 'Pub Closures Rise Sharply amid Warning over Planned Business Rate Change.' *The Guardian*, 18 September 2023. https://www.theguardian.com/business/2023/sep/18/pub-closures-rise-sharply-amid-warning-over-planned-business-rate-change

DE PAZ NIEVES, Carmen, Isis Gaddis, Miriam Muller. 'Gender and COVID-19: What have we learnt, one year later'. In *Policy Research Working Paper* 9709, June 2021. https://openknowledge.worldbank.org/server/api/core/bitstreams/c84090d9-5647-5a38-8217-8fb921c7198a/content

DONNACHIE, Ian. *History of the Brewing Industry in Scotland*. John Donald Publishers Ltd., 1979.

FRENCH, Katherine L. *The Good Woman of the Parish: Gender and Religion After the Black Death*, University of Pennsylvania Press, 2008.

GLEISS, Barbara. *Women in Public Houses: A Historic Analysis of The Social and Economic Role of Women Patronising English Public Houses, 1880s–1970s*. Unpub. PhD Thesis, University Wien, 2009.

HANAWALT, Barbara. *'Of Good and Ill Repute': Gender and Social Control in Medieval England*. Oxford University Press, 1998.

'Has the Pandemic Ended the Allure of Big Cities?', *Frontier Economics*, n.d. https://www.frontier-economics.com/uk/en/news-and-articles/articles/article-i8141-has-the-pandemic-ended-the-allure-of-big-cities

HUTTON, Georgina. 'Hospitality Industry and Covid-19.' Research Briefing to House of Commons, May 11th, 2022. https://researchbriefings.files.parliament.uk/documents/CBP-9111/CBP-9111.pdf

JONES, Daisy. 'How Alcohol Lost Its Cool', *vice.com*, 1 September 2022. https://www.vice.com/en/article/xgyg5q/drinking-isnt-cool-anymore

'Katherine Petirson [18462]' 8 August 1483 Tax Assessment E 179/180/111 in The National Archives. In *England's Immigrants 1330–1550: Resident Aliens in the Late Middle Ages*. University of York, The National Archives, Humanities Research Institute, University of Sheffield, Funded Arts & Humanities Research Council. February 2012-February 2015. https://www.englandsimmigrants.com/document/649

'Katherine Servaunt [32531],' Tax Assessment 16 x 25 June 1483, The National Archives E 179/242/25. In *England's Immigrants 1330 – 1550: Resident Aliens in the Late Middle Ages*. University of York, The National Archives, Humanities Research Institute, University of Sheffield, Funded Arts & Humanities Research Council. February 2012-February 2015. https://www.englandsimmigrants.com/person/32531

KELLY, Luke. 'Direct and indirect impacts of the Covid-19 pandemic on women and girls,' K4D Helpdesk Report, 13 August 2021. https://opendocs.ids.ac.uk/opendocs/bitstream/handle/20.500.12413/16995/1038_covid_impact_on_women_girls.pdf

LANGLAND, William, and George Economou (trans.). *William Langland's "Piers Plowman": The C Version*. University of Pennsylvania Press, 1996.

LONDON CITY HALL. 'Half of Londoners Wanting to Move Home Want out of London,' n.d. https://www.london.gov.uk/press-releases/assembly/escaping-the-city-post-covid

MAITLAND, F.W., ed. *Select Pleas of the Crown: Volume 1 – A.D. 1200–1225*. Bernard Quaritch, 1888.

MARKHAM, Gervase. *The English Housewife*. McGill-Queen's Press, 1994.

METCALFE, Caroline. 'William Porlond clerk to the Craft and Fraternity of the Brewers of London', in *Transactions of the London and Middlesex Archaeological Society*, 64 (2013), pp. 267–284.

New Food. 'How Has COVID-19 Impacted the UK Brewing and Distilling Industries?' *New Food Magazine*, May 20, 2020. https://www.newfoodmagazine.com/article/110366/how-has-covid-19-impacted-the-uk-brewing-and-distilling-industries

'Ordinance of Labourers 1349.' *Britannia: Sources of British History*: https://web.archive.org/web/20140701104840/http://britannia.com/history/docs/laborer1.html

PATTINSON, Ron, 'Hop Additions – is this the end,' *Shut Up About Barclay Perkins*. Tuesday, 9 November 2010. https://barclayperkins.blogspot.com/2010/11/hop-additions-is-this-end_09.html

PATTINSON, Ron, 'Scottish Ale,' *Shut Up About Barclay Perkins*, Friday, 19 October 2007. https://barclayperkins.blogspot.com/2007/10/scottish-ale.html

RIGHTS OF WOMEN, 'Rights of Women Survey Reveals Online Sexual Harassment Has Increased, as Women Continue to Suffer Sexual Harassment Whilst Working through the Covid-19 Pandemic.' 2021. https://opendocs.ids.ac.uk/opendocs/bitstream/handle/20.500.12413/16995/1038_covid_impact_on_women_girls.pdf

ROULET, Thomas J. and Joel Bothellod. 'Viewing Covid Turmoil through a Black Death Lens.' In *Academy of Managament Insights.* https://journals.aom.org/

ROWLANDS, Samuel. *A Terrible Battell Betweene the Two Consumers of the Whole World: Time and Death*, 1606.

RUDDICK, Graham. 'Cities are regaining their allure after Covid, and we should be glad that they are,' *TheTimes.co.uk*, 14 February 2022. https://www.thetimes.co.uk/article/cities-are-regaining-their-allure-after-covid-and-we-should-be-glad-that-they-are

RYLANDS, W. H. (ed.), *The Ars Moriendi, Editio Princeps, circa 1450, a Reproduction of the Copy in the British Museum.* 1881.

'Salisbury: Merchant and craft guilds to 1612,' in Elizabeth Crittall (ed.) *A History of the County of Wiltshire: Volume 6*, pp. 132–136. London, 1962. On *British History Online* http://www.british-history.ac.uk/vch/wilts/vol6/pp. 132–136

SAUER, Michelle M. *Gender in Medieval Culture.* Bloomsbury, 2015.

SENN, Mark A. 'English Life and Law in the Time of the Black Death,' in *Real Property, Probate, and Trust Journal*, Vol. 38, No. 3, pp.507–588 (Fall, 2003).

SIBA – the Voice of British Brewing. 'COVID-19 Brewing Industry Survey Results + Infographic – SIBA – The Voice Of British Brewing,' 23 April 2020. https://www.siba.co.uk/coronavirus-covid-19-latest-advice-guidance-for-brewers/covid-19-brewing-industry-survey-results-infographic

SIBA, The Society of Independent Brewers, *The SIBA Craft Beer Report 2022*, 2022.

SIDDERS, Jack. 'Londoners Leaving the City in Droves as Covid Trend Persists.' Bloomberg.Com, 31 July 2022. https://www.bloomberg.com/news/articles/2022-07-31/londoners-leaving-the-city-in-droves-as-covid-trend-persists

SMITH, Christian, 'Number of pubs in England and Wales falls to lowest on record,' *thedrinksbusiness.com*, 4 July 2022. https://www.thedrinksbusiness.com/2022/07/number-of-pubs-in-england-and-wales-falls-to-lowest-on-record

THATCHER, Nikkie, '"Business Closures time-bomb next year" warning issued,' *MorningAdvertiser.co.uk*, 27 October 2021. https://www.morningadvertiser.co.uk/Article/2021/10/27/How-many-breweries-closed-in-2020

The Ancient Laws and Customs of The Burghs of Scotland Vol. 1 A.D. 1124–1424. John Greig & Son, 1858.

TOBYN, Graeme. 'How England first managed a national infection crisis: Implementation of the Plague Orders of 1578 compared with COVID-19 Lockdown March to May 2020' in *Social Sciences and Humanities Open 3 No. 1* (12 January 2021).

TUSSER, T. *Five Hundred Points of Good Husbandry…: Together with a Book of Huswifery.* English Dialect Society, 1878.

UNGER, Richard W. *Beer in the Middle Ages and the Renaissance.* University of Pennsylvania Press, 2013.

VAN DEKKEN, Marjolein, *Brewing, Distilling and Serving Working Women in Dutch Drink Industry, 1500–1800.* PhD., University of Utrecht, 2009.

VAN DEKKEN, Marjolein. *Brewing, Roasting and Serving: Production and Sale of Drink by Women in the Northern Netherlands, circa 1500–1800.* Amsterdam University Press, 2010.

VAUGHAN, Theresa. 'The Alewife: Changing Images and Bad Brews' in *AVISTA Forum Journal* Vol. 21 No. 1/2 (2012), pp. 34–41.

WADE, Lizzie. 'The Black Death May Have Transformed Medieval Societies in Sub-Saharan Africa', *Science.org*, 6 March 2019. https://www.science.org/content/article/black-death-may-have-transformed-medieval-societies-sub-saharan-africa

YOUNGS, Deborah. 'The Townswomen of Wales: Singlewomen, Work and Service, *c.*1300–*c.*1550' in Helen Fulton (ed.) *Urban Culture in Medieval Wales* ebook. University of Wales Press, 2012.

CHAPTER TWO

Rules, Regulations, and How to Blithely Ignore Them

'Anne Core Petition/Appeal 1667 (Michaelmas),' Petition/Appeal in Lancaster Records Office QSP 311/2. In *Intoxicants & Early Modernity England, 1580–1740 database*. University of Sheffield Department of History, The Victorian and Albert Museum, and Digital Humanities Institute|Sheffield. Funded ESRC and AHRC. V. 1.0: https://www.dhi.ac.uk/intoxicants/record.jsp?&source=petition&petition_ID=6

BENNETT, Judith. *Ale, Beer and Brewsters in England: Women's work in a changing world 1300–1600*, Oxford University Press, 1996.

BAILON, William Paley (ed.), *Court Rolls of the Manor of Wakefield Vol. I 1274–1297*, The Yorkshire Archaeological Society, Record Series vol. 29, 1901.

'Cicely Collier Petition/Testimonial 1655 Midsummer' Petition/Testimonial in Lancaster Records Office QSP 116/19. In *Intoxicants & Early Modernity England, 1580–1740 database*. University of Sheffield Department of History, The Victorian and Albert Museum, and Digital Humanities Institute, Sheffield. Funded ESRC and AHRC. V. 1.0: https://www.dhi.ac.uk/intoxicants/record.jsp?&source=petition&petition_ID=57

Corporation, City of London, and John Carpenter (ed.). *Liber Albus: The White Book of the City of London*, Richard Griffin and Company, 1861.

'Dorothy Hall Petition/Testimonial 1667 (Easter)' Petition/Testimonial in Lancaster Records Office QSP 304/5. In *Intoxicants & Early Modernity England, 1580–1740 database*. University of Sheffield Department of History, The Victorian and Albert Museum, and Digital Humanities Institute, Sheffield. Funded ESRC and AHRC. V. 1.0: https://www.dhi.ac.uk/intoxicants/record.jsp?&source=petition&petition_ID=79

EBELING, Jennie R., and Michael M. Homan, 'Baking and Brewing Beer in the Israelite Household: A Study of Women's Cooking Technology,' in B.A. Nakhai (ed.), *The World of Women in the Ancient and Classical Near East*. Cambridge Scholars Press, 2008.

EWAN, Elizabeth. '"For Whatever Ales Ye": Women as Consumers and Producers in Later Medieval Scottish Towns,' in Elizabeth Ewan and Maureen M. Meikle (eds.), *Women in Scotland: c.1100–c.1750*. Tuckwell Press, 1999.

Extracts from the Council of register of the Burgh of Aberdeen: 1398–1570. The Spalding Club, 1844.

FRANCK, Richard. *Northern Memoirs, Calculated for the Meridian of Scotland: Wherein Most Or All of the Cities, Citadels, Seaports, Castles, Forts, Fortresses, Rivers and Rivulets Are Compendiously Described: Together with Choice Collections of Various Discoveries, Remarkable Observations, Theological Notions … : To Which Is Added the Contemplative & Practical Angler …* Printed for author, sold by Henry Mortlock, 1694.

FRANKOT, Edda, Anna Havinga, Claire Hawes, William Hepburn, Wim Peters, Jackson Armstrong, Phil Astley, Andrew Mackillop, Andrew Simpson, Adam Wyner, (eds.), *Aberdeen Registers Online: 1398–1511* (Aberdeen: University of Aberdeen, 2019), https://www.abdn.ac.uk/aro (12 October 2022).

GUNN, Steven (2017). *Sixteenth-century English accident inquests*. [Data Collection]. Colchester, Essex: UK Data Archive. 10.5255/UKDA-SN-852155. https://reshare.ukdataservice.ac.uk/852155

HANNA, Ralph. 'Brewing Trouble: On Literature and History- and alewives,' in Barbara Hanawalt and David Wallace (eds.) *Bodies and Disciplines: Intersections of Literature and History in the 15th Century*, pp. 1–18. University of Minnesota Press, 1996.

HILL, Rosalind. 'The Theory and Practice of Excommunication in Medieval England,' *History* 42, no. 144 (February 1, 1957), pp. 1–11.

Historical Manuscripts Commission, 'The corporation of Lincoln: Registers, vol. V (1599–1638)', in *The Manuscripts of Lincoln, Bury St. Edmunds Etc. Fourteenth Report, Appendix; Part VIII*, pp. 75–102. Her Majesty's Stationary Office, 1895. On *British History Online*. http://www.british-history.ac.uk/hist-mss-comm/vol37/pt8/pp. 75–102.

HUNT, Pauline, 'Fiona has a head for ale,' in *Cambridge Daily News*, September 5th, 1974. https://www.britishnewspaperarchive.co.uk/viewer/bl/0003740/19740905/004/0004

'Jane Smith Petition/Appeal 1646,' Petition/Appeal, Lancaster Records Office QSB 1/277/55. In *Intoxicants & Early Modernity England, 1580-1740 database*. University of Sheffield Department of History, The Victorian and Albert Museum, and Digital Humanities Institute|Sheffield. Funded ESRC and AHRC. V. 1.0: https://www.dhi.ac.uk/intoxicants/record.jsp?&source=petition&petition_ID=25

'John Harrison and Joshua Taylor Complaint Against Katherine Blomiley of Chorlton 1656,' Petition/Complaint in Lancaster Records Office QSP 132/9. In *Intoxicants & Early Modernity England, 1580-1740 database*. University of Sheffield Department of History, The Victorian and Albert Museum, and Digital Humanities Institute|Sheffield. Funded ESRC and AHRC. V. 1.0: https://www.dhi.ac.uk/intoxicants/record.jsp?&source=petition&petition_ID=60

JOHNSON, Lizabeth. 'Sex and the Single Welshwoman: Prostitution and Concubinage in Late Medieval Wales,' in *The Welsh History Review/Clychgrawn Hanes Cymru* Vol. 27 No. 2. (December 2014), pp. 253–281.

LINDSAY, David. *Ane Satyre Of The Thrie Estaitis*. Canongate Books, 2012

MATTHEWS, John Hobson (ed.), 'Glamorgan Calendar Rolls and Gaol Files: 1542-94', in *Cardiff Records: Volume 2*. Cardiff Records Committee, 1900.

MAYHEW, Nicholas. 'The Status of Women and brewing of ale in medieval Aberdeen' *Review of Scottish Culture* 10, 1996–7, pp. 16–21.

PRESTWICH, Michael. *York Civic Ordinances, 1301*. Borthwick Publications, 1976.

PUGH, Ralph Bernard. *A History of the Country of Cambridge and the Isle of Ely: Index to Volumes I-IV*. University of Oxford Press, 1960.

RIGG, J. M. (ed). 'Select Pleas, Starrs, and Other Records from the Rolls of the Exchequer of the Jews, A. D. 1220-1284.' *Harvard Law Review* 15, no. 8 (1 April 1902): 681.

ROTH, Pinchas, 'Medieval English Rabbis: Image and Self-Image,' in Early Middle English, Vol. 1, No. 1, (2019) pp. 17–33.

ROTH, Pinchas, and Ethan Zadoff. 'The Talmudic Community of Thirteenth-Century England' in Sarah Rees Jones and Sethina Watson (eds) *Christians and Jews in Angevin England: The York Massacre of 1190, Narratives and Contexts*. Boydell & Brewer, 2013.

SMITH, Llinos Beverley. 'Towards a history of women in late medieval Wales,' in M. Roberts and S. Clarke (eds), *Women and Gender in Early Modern Wales*, pp. 14–49. University of Wales Press, 2000.

SMITH, Llinos Beverley. 'In Search of an Urban Identity: Aspects of Urban Society in Late Medieval Wales,' in Helen Fulton (ed) *Urban Culture in Medieval Wales* ebook. University of Wales Press, 2012.

STEVENS, Matthew Frank. 'Women Brewers in Fourteenth Century Ruthin.' In *Denbighshire Historical Society Transactions 55*, pp. 15–31 (2006).

'Susan Lunt Appeal 1628 (Midsummer),' Petition/Appeal, Lancaster Records Office QSB 1/43/53, In *Intoxicants & Early Modernity England, 1580-1740 database*. University of Sheffield Department of History, The Victorian and Albert Museum, and Digital Humanities Institute, Sheffield. Funded ESRC and AHRC. V. 1.0: https://www.dhi.ac.uk/intoxicants/record.jsp?&source=petition&petition_ID=123

The Ancient Laws and Customs of The Burghs of Scotland Vol. I A.D. 1124-1424. John Greig & Son, 1868.

The Ancient Laws and Customs of The Burghs of Scotland Vol. II A.D. 1424-1707. John Greig & Son, 1910.

THOMAS, Wilma R. *Women in the rural society of south-west Wales, c.1780-1870.* PhD Thesis, Swansea University, 2003.

THOMPSON, A. Hamilton (ed.) *Visitations of Religious Houses in the Diocese of Lincoln Vol. II: Records of Visitations held by William Alnwick Bishop of Lincoln* A.D. 1436 to A.D. 1449. Lincoln Record Society, 1918.

'Widow Rosbotham Petition 1650', Petition/Application, Lancaster Records Office QSP 27/26. In *Intoxicants & Early Modernity England, 1580-1740 database.* University of Sheffield Department of History, The Victorian and Albert Museum, and Digital Humanities Institute, Sheffield. Funded ESRC and AHRC. V. 1.0: https://www.dhi.ac.uk/intoxicants/record.jsp?&source=petition&petition_ID=3

YOUNGS, Deborah. 'The Townswomen of Wales: Singlewomen, Work and Service, c.1300–c.1550' in Helen Fulton (ed) *Urban Culture in Medieval Wales* ebook. University of Wales Press, 2012.

CHAPTER THREE

This Beer Can Kill You

'A Surgeon's Advice to Mothers: The Milk', in Isabella Beeton and Samuel Beeton, (eds). *The Englishwoman's Domestic Magazine Vol. 7*, pp. 149–152. S.O. Beeton, 1858.

ALEXANDRE, Anais. *Potions, Elixirs & Brews: A Modern Witches' Grimoire of Drinkable Spells.* Watkins Media Limited, 2020.

'Agnes Finnie' in Julian Goodare, Lauren Martin, Joyce Miller and Louise Yeoman. *The Survey of Scottish Witchcraft.* (2003). http://www.shca.ed.ac.uk/witches

ANON. *A Closet for Ladies and Gentlewomen, Or, the Art of Preseruing, Conseruing and Candying. With the Manner Howe to Make Diuers Kinds of Syrups: And All Kind of Banqueting Stuffes. Also Diuers Soueraigne Medecines and Salves,* Etc. Printed by F. Kingston for Arthur Johnson, 1608.

ANON. *A true relation of the araignment of eighteene vvitches. that were tried, convicted, and condemned, at a sessions holden at St. Edmunds-bury in Suffolke, and there by the iudge and iustices of the said sessions condemned to die, and so were executed the 27. day of August 1645. As also a list of the names of those that were executed, and their severall confessions before their executions. VVith a true relation of the manner how they find them out. The names of those that were executed. Mr. Lowes parson of Branson. Thomas Evered a cooper with Mary his wife. Mary Bacon. Anne Alderman. Rebecca Morris. Mary Fuller. Mary Clowes. Margery Sparham Katherine Tooley. Sarah Spinlow. Iane Limstead. Anne Wright. Mary Smith. Iane Rivert. Susan Manners. Mary Skipper. Anne Leech.* Printed in London by I.H. 1645.

ANON. *The apprehension and confession of three notorious witches. Arreigned and by iustice condemned and executed at Chelmes-forde, in the Countye of Essex, the 5. day of Iulye, last past. 1589. With the manner of their diuelish practices and keeping of thier spirits, whose fourmes are heerein truelye proportioned.* Printed by E. Allde, 1589.

APPLEBY, John, Will Stahl-Timmins 'Consumption, flux, and dropsy: counting deaths in 17th century London,' *BMJ: British Medical Journal (Online)* Vol 363 (Dec. 12th, 2018).

BENNETT, Judith. *Ale, Beer and Brewsters in England: Women's work in a changing world 1300-1600.* Oxford University Press, 1996.

'Bessie Wright' in Julian Goodare, Lauren Martin, Joyce Miller and Louise Yeoman. *The Survey of Scottish Witchcraft.* 2003. http://www.shca.ed.ac.uk/witches

BROWN, James. 'Trouble Brewing: Ale, Beer, and Witchcraft.' *Intoxicating Spaces,* 18 March 2021. https://www.intoxicatingspaces.org/2021/03/18/trouble-brewing-ale-beer-and-witchcraft

BICKERDYKE, John. *The Curiosities of Ale & Beer: An Entertaining History: Illustrated with over Fifty Quaint Cuts.* Swan Sonnenschein & Co., 1886.

BURKE, Peter, *Eyewitnessing: The Use of Images as Historical Evidence*. Cornell, 2000.

Calendar of Essex Assize File, Assizes held at Chelmsford, July 4th, 1560: 'Indictment of John Samond. 4 July 1560', Essex Records Office. ASS 35/2/5/8.

'Catherine MacTargett' in Julian Goodare,, Lauren Martin, Joyce Miller and Louise Yeoman. *The Survey of Scottish Witchcraft*. 2003. http://www.shca.ed.ac.uk/witches

CLARK, Andrew (ed.). *Full Text of 'The Life and Times of Anthony Wood, Antiquary, of Oxford 1623–1695*. Clarendon Press, 1891.

COLLINS, J. W. (ed). *Mother Red Cap*. J. W. Collins, 1843.

CUNNINGHAM, Scott. *Cunningham's Encyclopedia of Magical Herbs*. Llewellyn Worldwide, 2012.

DAVIS, James. *Medieval Market Morality: Life, Law and Ethics in the English Marketplace 1200–1500*. Cambridge University Press, 2012.

Dea Latis. *The Beer Agender: A further study into female attitude and behaviours towards beer 2019*. 2019: https://dealatisuk.files.wordpress.com/2019/09/68c83-0e690-the-beer-agender-digital.pdf

Dea Latis. *The Gender Pint Gap: A study into GB female attitudes and behaviours towards beer*. 2018: https://dealatisuk.files.wordpress.com/2019/09/4dec5-86c7b-gender-pint-gap-report_dea-latis_may-2018.pdf

DI SIMPLICIO, Oscar, 'On the Neuropsychological Origins of Witchcraft Cognition: The Geographic and Economic Variable,' Ch. 28 in Brian P. Levack (ed). *The Oxford Handbook of Witchcraft in Early Modern Europe and Colonial America* ebook. Oxford University Press, 2013.

DUNBAR, William. 'Poems Comic, Satiric and Parodic', in John Conlee (ed), *William Dunbar: The Complete Works*. Medieval Institute Publications, 2004. https://d.lib.rochester.edu/teams/text/conlee-dunbar-complete-works-poems-comic-satiric-and-parodic

DYER, Peter. 'The 1900 Arsenic Poisoning Epidemic.' In *Brewery History Number 130*, pp. 65–85.

GASKILL, Malcolm. *Witchcraft: A Very Short Introduction*. Oxford University Press, 2010

GASKILL, Malcolm, 'Witchcraft Trials in England,' in Ch. 16. Brian P. Levack (ed). *The Oxford Handbook of Witchcraft in Early Modern Europe and Colonial America* ebook. Oxford University Press, 2013.

GASKILL, Malcolm, 'Witchcraft and Evidence in Early Modern England,' in *Past and Present*, No. 198, February 2008, pp. 33–70.

GILL, Miriam. 'Female Piety and Impiety: Selected Images of Women and Their Reception in Wall Paintings in England After 1300' in Samantha J. E. Riches and Sarah Salih (eds.) *Gender and Holiness: Men, Women, and Saints in Late Medieval Europe*, pp. 101–120. Routledge, 2002.

GILL, Miriam. *Late Medieval Wall Painting in England: Content and Context (c.1300–1530)*. PhD Thesis, Courtauld Institute of Art, University of London, 2002.

GLASS, David Victor. 'John Graunt and His Natural and Political Observations', *Notes and Records of the Royal Society of London*, Vol. 19, No 1 (June 1964), pp. 63–100.

GOODARE, Julian. 'The Framework for Scottish Witch-Hunting in the 1590s,' *The Scottish Historical Review 81*, no. 2 (January 1, 2002), pp. 240–50.

GOODARE, Julian. 'Witchcraft in Scotland,' Ch. 17 in Brian P. Levack (ed.). *The Oxford Handbook of Witchcraft in Early Modern Europe and Colonial America* ebook. Oxford University Press, 2013.

GRAUNT, John. *Natural and political observations mentioned in a following index, and made upon the bills of mortality by John Graunt ... ; with reference to the government, religion, trade, growth, ayre, diseases, and the several changes of the said city*. Thomas Roycroft for John Martin, James Allestry, and Thomas Dicas, 1662.

GUILEY, Rosemary, *The Encyclopedia of Witches, Witchcraft and Wicca*. Facts on File, 2008.

HANAWALT, Barbara. *Of Good and Ill Repute': Gender and Social Control in Medieval England*. Oxford University Press, 1998.

HARRISON, William. *A Description of Elizabethan England: Written for Holinshed's Chronicles.* P. F. Collier and Son Company, 1909.

'Helen Clark' in Julian Goodare, Lauren Martin, Joyce Miller and Louise Yeoman. *The Survey of Scottish Witchcraft.* 2003. http://www.shca.ed.ac.uk/witches

HOGGARD, Brian. 'The Archaeology of Counter-Witchcraft and Popular Magic' in Owen Davies and Willem de Blecourt eds. *Beyond the Witch Trials: Witchcraft and Magic in Enlightenment Europe.* Manchester University Press, 2004.

'How Beer Can Benefit Your Health', *NBCNew.com,* 2 June 2018. https://www.nbcnews.com

HUGHES, David. *"A Bottle of Guinness Please": The Colourful History of Guinness.* Phimboy, 2006.

'Issobel Griersoune' in Julian Goodare, Lauren Martin, Joyce Miller and Louise Yeoman. *The Survey of Scottish Witchcraft.* 2003 http://www.shca.ed.ac.uk/witches/.

'Isobell Young' in Julian Goodare, Lauren Martin, Joyce Miller and Louise Yeoman. *The Survey of Scottish Witchcraft.* 2003 http://www.shca.ed.ac.uk/witches/.

'Jean Woodrow' in Julian Goodare, Lauren Martin, Joyce Miller and Louise Yeoman. *The Survey of Scottish Witchcraft.* 2003 http://www.shca.ed.ac.uk/witches/.

'Johnnet Wischert' in Julian Goodare, Lauren Martin, Joyce Miller and Louise Yeoman. *The Survey of Scottish Witchcraft.* 2003 http://www.shca.ed.ac.uk/witches

KELYNACK, Dr., and William Kirby. *Arsenical Poisoning in Beer Drinkers 1901.* Bailliere, Tindall & Cox, 1901.

LANGLAND, William, and George Economou. *William Langland's "Piers Plowman": The C Version.* University of Pennsylvania Press, 1996.

LEVACK, Brian. *The Witch-hunt in Early Modern Europe.* Harlow, 2006.

LYDGATE, John. 'Ballad on an Ale Seller,' *Sheffield Hallam University Website*: https://teaching.shu.ac.uk/ds/sle/altered/selections/early/lydgate.htm

LYDGATE, John. 'Put Thieving Millers and Bakers in the Pillory', p.56. in Frederick J. Furniville (ed.) *Political, Religious, and Love Poems.* Kegan Paul, Trench, Trubner for the Early English Text Society, 1866.

MACK, Laura, Zach Williams. "The Best Post-Workout Beers to Celebrate Your Gains." *Thrillist,* 10 March 2020. https://www.thrillist.com/health/nation/beer-after-workout-exercise

McFARLANE, Alan, *Witchcraft in Tudor and Stuart England: A Regional and Comparative Study 2nd edition with introduction by James Sharpe* Routledge, London, 1999.

'Marable Coupe,' in Julian Goodare, Lauren Martin, Joyce Miller and Louise Yeoman. *The Survey of Scottish Witchcraft.* 2003 http://www.shca.ed.ac.uk/witches/.

'Margaret Abernethy,' in Julian Goodare, Lauren Martin, Joyce Miller and Louise Yeoman. *The Survey of Scottish Witchcraft.* 2003 http://www.shca.ed.ac.uk/witches/.

'Margaret Finlasoun,' in Julian Goodare, Lauren Martin, Joyce Miller and Louise Yeoman. *The Survey of Scottish Witchcraft.* 2003 http://www.shca.ed.ac.uk/witches/.

MARTIN, Lynn A. *Alcohol, Sex and Gender in Late Medieval and Early Modern Europe.* Springer, 2001.

Mercury News and Bay Area News Group. 'Medicinal Beer? New Study Shows Maybe the Ancient Nubians Were onto Something.' *The Mercury News,* February 26, 2011. https://www.mercurynews.com/2011/02/26/medicinal-beer-new-study-shows-maybe-the-ancient-nubians-were-onto-something

MICKEY, Thomas J., *Deconstructing Public Relations: Public Relations Criticism.* Lawrence Erlbaum Associates, 2003.

PELLING, Margaret, Frances White, 'CHAIRE, Catherine', in *Physicians and Irregular Medical Practitioners in London 1550–1640 Database.* 2004. on *British History Online* http://www.british-history.ac.uk/no-series/london-physicians/1550-1640/chaire-catherine

POOLE, Robert. *The Lancashire Witches: Histories and Stories.* Manchester University Press, 2013.

'Rosin,' *Dictionary of Traded Goods and Commodities 1550–1820*. University of Wolverhampton, 2007. On *British History Online*. https://www.british-history.ac.uk/no-series/traded-goods-dictionary/1550-1820/rosin-royal-plums

Royal Commission on Arsenic Poisoning Arising from the Consumption of Beer and Other Articles of Food Or Drink: Minutes of Evidence and Appendices : Evidence Received in 1901, Together with Appendices 1 to 15, and Index, 1903.

SAUER, Michelle M. *Gender in Medieval Culture*. Bloomsbury, 2015.

SHARPE, James, 'Introduction' in Alan McFarlane (author), *Witchcraft in Tudor and Stuart England: A Regional and Comparative Study*. Routledge, 1999.

SHARPE, James. 'Introduction,' in Robert Poole (author) *The Lancashire Witches: Histories and Stories*. Manchester University Press, 2013.

SHAW, Lucy. 'UK's First "Medicinal" Mushroom Beer Launches,' *The Drinks Business*, September 17, 2020. https://www.thedrinksbusiness.com/2020/09/uks-first-medicinal-mushroom-beer-launches

SKELTON, John 'The Tunning of Elynour Rummyng', in Marie Loughlin, Sandra Bell, and Patricia Brace (ed.) *The Broadview Anthology of Sixteenth-Century Poetry and Prose*, pp. 1–8. Broadview Press, 2011.

SPENCE, Elizabeth Isabella. *Summer Excursions through parts of Oxfordshire, Gloucestershire, Warwickshire, Staffordshire, Herefordshire, Derbyshire and South Wales vol 1*. Longman, Hurst, Rees and Ormer, 1809.

SMITH, Eliza. *The Compleat Housewife: Or, Accomplish'd Gentlewoman's Companion*. Andrews Mcmeel+ORM, 2012.

SUGGETT, Richard. *Welsh Witches: Narratives of Witchcraft and Magic in 16th and 17th Century Wales*. University of Pennsylvania Press, 2018.

SUGGETT, Richard, *A History of Magic and Witchcraft in Wales*. History Press Limited, 2008. Suhr, Carla. 'Publishing for the Masses: Early Modern English Witchcraft Pamphlets' in *Neuphilologische Mitteilungen*, Vol. 113, No. 1 (2012), pp. 118–121.

SWAIN, John. *Witchcraft, Economy and Society in the Forest of Pendle*. Winchester University Press, 2013.

'The Cookes Plaie' in Maurice Hussey (ed). *The Chester Mystery Plays*. Heinemann Educational Books, 1964.

UNKNOWN, *Receipt Book*, 1660s–1680s. LUNA Folger Digital Image Collection. V. A. 697, File Name 166210. https://luna.folger.edu/luna/servlet/detail

WADE, Christina. 'Nope, Medieval Alewives Aren't The Archetype For The Modern Pop Culture Witch.' *Braciatrix*, 27 October 2017. https://braciatrix.com/2017/10/27/nope-medieval-alewives-arent-the-archetype-for-the-modern-pop-culture-witch

WASHINGTON-HARMON, Taylyn. 'Beer May Be a Better Post-Workout Drink Than We Previously Thought,' *Men's Health*, 19 August 2021. https://www.menshealth.com/health

WILLIAMS, Laura, Zack Mack, 'The Best Post-Workout Beers to Celebrate Your Gains.' *Thrillist*, March 10, 2020. https://www.thrillist.com/health/nation/beer-after-workout-exercise

WILLIAMS, Merryell, *Book of Recipes*, Late 17th/early 18th century. Llyfrgell Genedlaethol Cymru – The National Library of Wales, Peniarth MS 513D. https://www.library.wales/discover-learn/digital-exhibitions/manuscripts/early-modern-period/merryell-williamss-book-of-recipes

WOOD, Anthony A. *The Life and Times of Anthony Wood: Antiquary, of Oxford, 1632–1695, Described by Himself*. Clarendon Press, 1891.

W. W. *A true and iust recorde, of the information, examination and confession of all the witches, taken at S. Ofes in the countie of Essex whereof some were executed, and other some entreated according to the determination of lawe. Wherein all men may see what a pestilent people witches are, and how vnworthy to lyue in a Christian Commonwealth. Written orderly, as the cases were tryed by euidence, by W. W.* Printed Thomas Dawson, 1582.

CHAPTER FOUR
Homebrewing Housewives

'Ann Tartary' Baptismal Record, Saint Helen Bishopsgate, 26 November 1746.London Metropolitan Arches Data Collections, Z/PROJECT/BAL/C/P69/HEL/A/002/MS06831/003/9. In Switching the Lens – Rediscovering Londoners of African, Caribbean, Asian and Indigenous Heritage, 1561 to 1840. London Metropolitan Archives, Funded in part by British Library as Black and Asian Londoner Project. 2000- (ongoing). https://search.lma.gov.uk

AUSTEN, Jane. 'Letter to Cassandra Austen October 7th, 1808', p. 13. in Edward Hugessen Brabourne, *Letters of Jane Austen: Edited with an Introduction and Critical Remarks by Edward, Lord Brabourne Vol. II.* Richard Bentley & Son, 1884.

AUSTEN, Jane. 'Letter to Cassandra Austen, December 9th, 1808,' p.39 in Edward Hugessen Brabourne, *Letters of Jane Austen: Edited with an Introduction and Critical Remarks by Edward, Lord Brabourne Vol. II,* Richard Bentley & Son, 1884.

AUSTEN, Jane. 'Letter March 9th, 1814,' p. 233 in Edward Hugessen Brabourne, *Letters of Jane Austen: Edited with an Introduction and Critical Remarks by Edward, Lord Brabourne Vol. II,* Richard Bentley & Son, 1884.

BLAIR, Thomas L. *Black Britannia: From Slavery to Freedom in the 18th Century.* The Black London eMonograph Series, Editions Blair, 2013.

'Charlotte Harris,' in P. Thompson and T. Lummis (2009). *Family Life and Work Experience Before 1918,* 1870–1973. [data collection]. 7th Edition. UK Data Service. SN: 2000, DOI: http://doi.org

COLE, Melissa. *The Beer Kitchen: The Art and Science of Cooking and Pairing with Beer.* Hardie Grant Publishing, 2018.

DAWSON, Thomas. *The Good Housewife's Jewel.* Southover Historic Cookery & H, 1996.

DAWSON, Thomas(?). *A Good Huswifes Handmaide for the Kitchin Containing Manie Principall Pointes of Cookerie, As well How to Dresse Meates, After Sundrie the Best Fashions Vsed in England and Other Countries.* Richard Jones, 1594.

DEAN, Darron, Andrew Hann, Mark Overton, and Jane Whittle. *Production and Consumption in English Households 1600-1750.* Routledge, 2012.

DIGBY, Kenelm. *The Closet of Sir Kenelm Digby, Knight, Opened.* Philip Lee Warner, 1910.

'Elizabeth' Burial Record, 2 August 1665, Saint Andrew, Holborn, London Metropolitan Archives Data Collections Z/PROJECT/BAL/C/P82/AND/A/010/MS06673/004/2. In Switching the Lens – Rediscovering Londoners of African, Caribbean, Asian and Indigenous Heritage, 1561 to 1840. London Metropolitan Archives, Funded in part by British Library as Black and Asian Londoner Project. 2000- (ongoing). https://search.lma.gov.uk

'Elizabeth Eade,' in P. Thompson and T. Lummis (2009). *Family Life and Work Experience Before 1918,* 1870–1973. [data collection]. 7th Edition. UK Data Service. SN: 2000, DOI: http://doi.org

FLETCHER OF SALTOUN FAMILY. *Anonymous Recipe Book of the Fletcher of Saltoun Family.* Complied by Mrs. Johnston, 1700–1799, National Library of Scotland MS. 17857. https://digital.nls.uk/recipes/browse/archive

'Florence Kate Johnson,' in P. Thompson and T. Lummis (2009). *Family Life and Work Experience Before 1918,* 1870–1973. [data collection]. 7th Edition. UK Data Service. SN: 2000, DOI: http://doi.org

'Frauncis' Burial Record, 3 March 1597, Saint Botolph Aldgate. London Metropolitan Archives Data Collections, Z/PROJECT/BAL/C/P69/BOT2/A/003/MS9223/4. In Switching the Lens – Rediscovering Londoners of African, Caribbean, Asian and Indigenous Heritage, 1561 to 1840. London Metropolitan Archives, Funded in part by British Library as Black and Asian Londoner Project. 2000- (ongoing). https://search.lma.gov.uk/scripts/mwimain.dll

GLASSE, Hannah. *The Art of Cookery made Plain and Easy.* Cottom and Stewart, 1805.

HACKETT, Rosalind I. J. *Art and Religion in Africa*. Cassell, 1999.

HARRISON, William. *A Description of Elizabethan England: Written for Holinshed's Chronicles*. P. F. Collier and Son Company, 1909

'Jane Poole Plaintiff/ Sarah Heyman Witness Deposition 1685,' Depositions and Examinations Chester Quarter Sessions 1685 in Chester Records Office, ZQSF 83/50. In *Intoxicants & Early Modernity England, 1580-1740 database*. University of Sheffield Department of History, The Victorian and Albert Museum, and Digital Humanities Institute|Sheffield. Funded ESRC and AHRC. V. 1.0: https://www.dhi.ac.uk/intoxicants/record.jsp?&source=courtpaper&courtpaper_ID=1142

KENDALL, 'The Role of Izangoma in Bringing the Zulu Goddess Back to Her People' *The Drama Review*, Volume 43, Issue 2 (162), (Summer 1999) pp. 94–117.

'Maria Morton' Baptismal Record, May 13th, 1830, Saint John at Hackney, London Metropolitan Archives Data Collections Z/PROJECT/BAL/M/P79/JN1/033/1061. In Switching the Lens – Rediscovering Londoners of African, Caribbean, Asian and Indigenous Heritage, 1561 to 1840. London Metropolitan Archives, Funded in part by British Library as Black and Asian Londoner Project. 2000- (ongoing). https://search.lma.gov.uk

MARCHÉ, Montaz. 'A focus on black women in eighteenth-century Britain,' *History Matters Journal* 1, no. 1 (2020): 42–51.

MARCHÉ, Montaz. 'Uncovering Black Women in Eighteenth- and Nineteenth-Century Britain.' *History*, October 28, 2019. https://www.ucl.ac.uk/history/news/2019/oct/uncovering-black-women-eighteenth-and-nineteenth-century-britain

MAULE, Janet, *Janet Maule's Recipe Book*, c.1701, National Library of Scotland, Acc. 12242. https://digital.nls.uk/recipes/browse/archive

McCULLA, Theresa. 'Patsy Young – American Brewer, Fugitive From Slavery – Good Beer Hunting,' *Good Beer Hunting*, March 10, 2022. https://www.goodbeerhunting.com/blog/2021/9/14/patsy-young-american-brewer-fugitive-from-slavery

'Miss Slamon,' in P. Thompson and T. Lummis (2009). *Family Life and Work Experience Before 1918, 1870–1973*. [data collection]. 7th Edition. UK Data Service. SN: 2000, DOI: http://doi.org

'Mr. Griffiths,' in P. Thompson and T. Lummis (2009). *Family Life and Work Experience Before 1918, 1870–1973*. [data collection]. 7th Edition. UK Data Service. SN: 2000, DOI: http://doi.org

'Mrs. Harris,' in P. Thompson and T. Lummis (2009). *Family Life and Work Experience Before 1918, 1870–1973*. [data collection]. 7th Edition. UK Data Service. SN: 2000, DOI: http://doi.org

'Mrs. Mainwarning,' in P. Thompson and T. Lummis (2009). *Family Life and Work Experience Before 1918, 1870–1973*. [data collection]. 7th Edition. UK Data Service. SN: 2000, DOI: http://doi.org

MOYLE, John. *Chirurgus Marinus: Or, the Sea-Chirurgion. Being Instructions to Junior Chirurgic Practitioners, Who Design to Serve at Sea in This Imploy. in Two General Parts... . the Fourth Edition, Newly Corrected and Inlarged*. Gale Ecco, Print Editions, 2018.

Old Bailey Proceedings, London Lives, 1690–1800, t18171203-165 (www.londonlives.org, version 1.1, 17 June 2012) 3 December 1817, George Fawcett.

OLUSOGA, David. *Black and British: A Forgotten History*. Pan Macmillan, 2016.

ORLIN, Lena Corwin, 'Anne by Indirection', Shakespeare Quarterly 65, no. 4 (Winter 2014), pp. 421–454.

'Paul's Impromptu' in Isabella Beeton and Samuel Beeton (eds.) *The Englishwoman's Domestic Magazine* v. 1. 1852–1856, p. 236.

PLAT, Hugh. *Delights for ladies to adorn their persons, tables, closets, and distillatories, with beauties, banquets, perfumes, and waters*. Printed by Peter Short, 1602.

PENNEY, Norman. *The Household Account Book of Sarah Fell of Swarthmoor Hall*. Cambridge University Press, 2014.

'Robert Bracken,' in P. Thompson and T. Lummis. (2009). *Family Life and Work Experience Before 1918, 1870–1973.* [data collection]. 7th Edition. UK Data Service. SN: 2000, DOI: http://doi.org/ 10.5255/UKDA-SN-2000-1

SAMBROOK, Pamela. *Country House Brewing in England, 1500-1900.* Bloomsbury Academic, 2003.

'Sarah-Tachcanah,' Baptismal Record, Saint James Clerkenwell, 24 December 1715. London Metropolitan Archives Data Collections Z/PROJECT/BAL/M/P76/JS1/008/0371. In Switching the Lens – Rediscovering Londoners of African, Caribbean, Asian and Indigenous Heritage, 1561 to 1840. London Metropolitan Archives, Funded in part by British Library as Black and Asian Londoner Project. 2000– (ongoing). https://search.lma.gov.uk

SMITH, Eliza. *The Compleat Housewife: Or, Accomplish'd Gentlewoman's Companion.* Andrews McMeel Publishing, 2012.

'Sophia Young', 4 June 1819, Baptismal Record, Saint Luke, Chelsea, London Metropolitan Archives Data Collections Z/PROJECT/BAL/M/P74/LUK/190/0212. In Switching the Lens – Rediscovering Londoners of African, Caribbean, Asian and Indigenous Heritage, 1561 to 1840. London Metropolitan Archives, Funded in part by British Library as Black and Asian Londoner Project. 2000– (ongoing). https://search.lma.gov.uk/

'Susannah York' Baptismal Record, Saint James the Great, Friern Barnet, 8 August 1792. London Metropolitan Archives Data Collections Z/PROJECT/BAL/M/DRO/012/I/A/01/002/1101. In Switching the Lens – Rediscovering Londoners of African, Caribbean, Asian and Indigenous Heritage, 1561 to 1840. London Metropolitan Archives, Funded in part by British Library as Black and Asian Londoner Project. 2000– (ongoing). https://search.lma.gov.uk/scripts

'The Englishwoman's Conversazione,' in Isabella Beeton and Samuel Beeton, (eds.). *The Englishwoman's Domestic Magazine* Series 2, Vol. 4, (November 1861), p. 48.

'Things Worth Knowing: A Pleasant Drink for Warm Weather' in in Isabella Beeton and Samuel Beeton, (eds). *The Englishwoman's Domestic Magazine.* No. 4, Vol. 7 (August, 1858), p. 127.

'Things Worth Knowing: To Cure Sweet Hams,' in Isabella Beeton and Samuel Beeton, (eds.). *The Englishwoman's Domestic Magazine.* No. 3 Vol. 8 (July 1858), p. 92.

'Things Worth Knowing: To Make Ginger Beer' Isabella Beeton and Samuel Beeton, (eds.). *The Englishwoman's Domestic Magazine* No. 2 Vol. 6 (1857). p. 94.

'Things Worth Knowing: To make Malt Wine,' in Isabella Beeton and Samuel Beeton, (eds.). *The Englishwoman's Domestic Magazine.* No. 5, Vol. 8 (September 1859), p. 155.

THOMAS, Wilma R. *Women in the rural society of south-west Wales, c.1780–1870.* PhD Thesis Swansea University: https://cronfa.swan.ac.uk/Record/cronfa42585

VAN BEEK, Walter. 'The Gender of Beer: Beer Symbolism among the Kapsiki/Hig and the Dogon' in Wulf Schiefenhövel, Helen Macbeth (eds.), *Liquid Bread: beer and Brewing in Cross-Cultural Perspective,* ebook. Berghahn Books, 2011.

'WANTED, – A MAID SERVANT, of a middle age.' Advertisement. *Oxford Journal,* May 4th, 1776. https://www.britishnewspaperarchive.co.uk/viewer/BL/0000073/17760504/010/0002

'William Lily to Elias Ashmole, 1662,' p. 842 in *Elias Ashmole: His Autobiographical and Historical Notes, his Correspondence, and Other Contemporary Sources Relating to his Life and Work,* ed. C. H. Josten, 5 vols (Oxford: OUP, 1967), vol. 3.

'William Lily to Elias Ashmole, April 19th, 1675,' pp. 1424–5 in *Elias Ashmole: His Autobiographical and Historical Notes, his Correspondence, and Other Contemporary Sources Relating to his Life and Work,* ed. C. H. Josten, 5 vols (Oxford: OUP, 1967), vol. 4.

WILLIAMS, Merryell, *Book of Recipes,* Late 17th/early 18th century. Llyfrgell Genedlaethol Cymru – The National Library of Wales, Peniarth MS 513D. https://www.library.wales/discover-learn/ digital-exhibitions/manuscripts/early-modern-period/merryell-williamss-book-of-recipes

WOOLLEY, Hannah. *The Accomplish'd Lady's Delight in Preserving, Physick, Beautifying, Cookery, and Gardening: Containing, I. The Art of Preserving and Candying Fruits and Flowers... II. The Physical Cabinet: Or, Excellent Receipts in Physick and Chyrurgery... III. The Compleat Cook's Guide... IV. The Lady's Diversion in Her Garden...* Printed B. Harris, 1675.

WOOLLEY, Hannah, *The Compleat Servant-Maid; or, The young maidens tutor Directing them how they may fit, and qualifie themselves for any of these employments. Viz. Waiting woman, house-keeper, chamber-maid, cook-maid, under cook-maid, nursery-maid, dairy-maid, laundry-maid, house-maid, scullery-maid. Composed for the great benefit and advantage of all young maidens.* (T. Passinger, at the Three Bibles on London Bridge, 1677. https://quod.lib.umich.edu

WOOLLEY, Hannah. *The Cook's Guide: Or, Rare Receipts for Cookery: Published and Set Forth Particularly for Ladies and Gentlwomen; Being Very Beneficial for All Those That Desire the True Way of Dressing of All Sorts of Flesh, Fowles, and Fish; the Best Directions for All Manner of Kickshaws, and the Most Ho-Good Sawces: Whereby Noble Persons and Others in Their Hospitalities May Be Gratified in Their Gusto's. Never Before Printed. By Hannah Wolley,* Printed for Peter Dring at the Sun in the Poultry, next door to the Rose-Tavern, 1664.

WOOLLEY, Hannah. *The Queen-like Closet or Rich Cabinet stored with all manner of rare receipts for preserving, candying & cookery. Very pleasant and beneficial to all ingenious persons of the female sex. By Hannah Wolley.* Printed for R. Lowndes at the White Lion in Duck-Lane, near West-Smithfield, 1670.

WHITTLE, Jane, 'Housewives and Servants in Rural England, 1440–1650: Evidence of Women's Work from Probate Documents,' in *Transactions of the Royal Historical Society*, Vol. 15 (2005). pp. 51–74.

CHAPTER FIVE

Workin' 9 to Last Orders

'A Raid on Some Shebeens in Glasgow' 20 February 1871, in Thomas Lampray, The Brewers Guardian: A First Class Paper, Devoted to the Protection of Brewers' Interests in Licensing, Legal, and Parliamentary Matters, REVIEW OF THE MALT, HOP AND SUGAR TRADES, & WINE AND SPIRIT TRADES' RECORD, Vol 1. The Offices, London, 1871.

'ADULTERATION AND DILUTION OF BEER AND SPIRITS BY PUBLICANS' January 31st, 1893, *The Brewers Guardian: A First Class Paper, Devoted to the Protection of Brewers' Interests in Licensing, Legal, and Parliamentary Matters, REVIEW OF THE MALT, HOP AND SUGAR TRADES, & WINE AND SPIRIT TRADES' RECORD*, Vol 23 (January to December 1893). The Offices, London, 1893.

'Ann Lloyd Testimony in Defamation Case, St. John The Baptist, Chester, 1713,' Depositions & Examinations Church Court Deposition St. John The Baptist, Chester, Chester Records Office EDC 5/1713/5 (unfold.) Brandrett c. Moulson. In *Intoxicants & Early Modernity England, 1580–1740 database.* University of Sheffield Department of History, The Victorian and Albert Museum, and Digital Humanities Institute|Sheffield. Funded ESRC and AHRC. V. 1.0: https://www.dhi.ac.uk/intoxicants/record.jsp?&source=courtpaper&courtpaper_ID=505

'Anne Woosencroft Defendant, Manchester, 1623,' Depositions & Examinations, Manchester Quarter Session 1623, GMCRO GB127.MS fol. 110v. In *Intoxicants & Early Modernity England, 1580–1740 database.* University of Sheffield Department of History, The Victorian and Albert Museum, and Digital Humanities Institute|Sheffield. Funded ESRC and AHRC. V. 1.0: https://www.dhi.ac.uk/intoxicants/record.jsp?&source=courtpaper&courtpaper_ID=1220

'Barmaid Attacked: Desperate Affray In An Inn.' *Portsmouth Evening News*, 4 October 1905. https://www.britishnewspaperarchive.co.uk/viewer/bl/0000290/19051004/200/0008

BENNETT, Judith. *Ale, Beer and Brewsters in England: Women's work in a changing world 1300–1600.* Oxford University Press, 1996.

199

BENNETT, Robert J, Harry Smith, Piero Montebruno and Carry van Lieshout 'Changes in Victorian entrepreneurship in England and Wales 1851–1911: Methodology and business population estimates' in *Business History* Vol 64, No. 7, (2022), pp. 1211–1243

'BIRMINGHAM: Interesting to Publicans' October 1st, 1877, *The Country Brewers' Gazette: The Official Organ of the Country Brewers' Society* Vol 1. No. 3 (London, 1877).

BRESSEY, Caroline. 'Geographies of Belonging: white women and black history.' in *Women's History Review Vol 22 No. 4 (2013)* pp. 541–558.

'Bristol's First Coloured Barmaid.' *Bristol Evening Post*, August 12th, 1967. https://www. britishnewspaperarchive.co.uk/viewer/bl/0004769/19670812/010/0010

BROWN, Frank. 'WANTED, Coloured Lady for Barmaid.' Advertisement, *The Stage*, February 15th, 1889. https://www.britishnewspaperarchive.co.uk/viewer/bl/0001179/18890215/041/0015

BROWNHILL, Mr. 'Wanted, Coloured Lady as Barmaid.' Advertisement, *The Stage*, April 6th, 1899. https://www.britishnewspaperarchive.co.uk/viewer/bl/0001179/18990406/060/0021

BROWN, James R. *The landscape of drink: inns, taverns and alehouses in early modern Southampton.* PhD thesis, University of Warwick, 2007.

BROWN, Rebecca. 'I've Never Known Sexual Harassment Like When I Was A Barmaid.' *Lappthebrand*, 21 April 2021. https://www.lappthebrand.com/blogs/perspectives/i-ve-never-known-sexual-harassment-like-when-i-was-a-barmaid

BURTON, Kristen. *The Citie Calls for Beere: The Introduction of Hops and the Foundation of Industrial Brewing in London 1200–1700.* Unpublished MA Thesis, Oklahoma State University, 2010.

Castle Music Hall, Nuneatou. 'WANTED, a coloured young lady as BARMAID.' Advertisement, *Liverpool Mercury*, 23 March 1875. https://www.britishnewspaperarchive.co.uk/viewer/ bl/0000081/18750323/081/0005

'Catherine Holland Testimony in Immorality Case Against Joseph Tovey, 1649–1667,' Depositions & Examinations Church Court Deposition Chester Records Office EDC 5/1667/24 (unfold.) Office c. Tovey. In *Intoxicants & Early Modernity England, 1580–1740 database.* University of Sheffield Department of History, The Victorian and Albert Museum, and Digital Humanities Institute|Sheffield. Funded ESRC and AHRC. V. 1.0: https://www.dhi.ac.uk/intoxicants/record. jsp?&source=courtpaper&courtpaper_ID=466&keyword=public%20house

'CHARGE OF ADULTERATING ALE AT SHIFNAL' April 3rd, 1871, Thomas Lampray, *The Brewers Guardian: A First Class Paper, Devoted to the Protection of Brewers' Interests in Licensing, Legal, and Parliamentary Matters, REVIEW OF THE MALT, HOP AND SUGAR TRADES, & WINE AND SPIRIT TRADES' RECORD*, Vol 1. The Offices, London, 1871.

CHESHIRE, Edward, 'The Results of the Census of Great Britain in 1851, with a Description of the Machinery and Processes Employed to Obtain the Returns; also an Appendix of Tables of Reference' in *Journal of the Statistical Society of London*, Vol 17, No. 1 (March 1854) pp. 45–72.

CLARK, Alice M. *The Working Life of Women in the Seventeenth Century.* Routledge EBooks. Informa, 2013.

CLARK, Peter, "The Alehouse and Social Integration in English Towns, 1500–1700.' In Maurice Garden, Yves Lequin (eds.) *Habiter La Ville: xve-xxe siècles.* Online versions. Presses universitaires de Lyon, 1984.

'COUNTY OF LONDON SESSIONS', June 20th, 1893, in *The Brewers Guardian: A First Class Paper, Devoted to the Protection of Brewers' Interests in Licensing, Legal, and Parliamentary Matters, REVIEW OF THE MALT, HOP AND SUGAR TRADES, & WINE AND SPIRIT TRADES' RECORD*, Vol 23 (January to December 1893). The Offices, London, 1893.

DE SILVA, Ruvani. 'Electric Sparks – How the Brown Gradient Beer Wenches Are Transforming Utah's Beer Scene – Good Beer Hunting,' *Good Beer Hunting*, 15 May 2022. https://www. goodbeerhunting.com/blog/2022/4/12/electric-sparks-how-the-brown-gradient-beer-wenches-are-transforming-utahs-beer-scene

DE SILVA, Ruvani. 'The Sound of Silence: Burnout and Allyship in Beer DEI,' *craftbeeramethyst*, 12 April 2023. https://craftbeeramethyst.com/the-sound-of-silence-burnout-and-allyship-in-beer-dei

'Effect of the Forbes Mackenzie Act', 20 March 1871, in Thomas Lampray, *The Brewers Guardian: A First Class Paper, Devoted to the Protection of Brewers' Interests in Licensing, Legal, and Parliamentary Matters, REVIEW OF THE MALT, HOP AND SUGAR TRADES, & WINE AND SPIRIT TRADES' RECORD*, Vol 1. The Offices, London, 1871.

'England and Wales Census, 1851'. Database with images. *FamilySearch*. http://FamilySearch.org: 18 July 2022. From '1851 England, Scotland and Wales census'. Database and images. *findmypast*. http://www.findmypast.com : n.d. Citing PRO HO 107. The National Archives of the UK, Kew, Surrey.

'Felonious Assault on a Married Woman.' *West Kent Guardian*, October 16th, 1852. https://www.britishnewspaperarchive.co.uk/viewer/bl/0000307/18521016/015/0003

GLEISS, Barbara, *Women in Public Houses: A Historic Analysis of The Social and Economic Role of Women Patronising English Public Houses, 1880s–1970s*. PhD Thesis, University Wien, 2009.

GREEN, Isaac. 'Wanted, a good ATTRACTION, for a Bar.' Advertisement, *The Era*, 20 June 1880. https://www.britishnewspaperarchive.co.uk/viewer/bl/0000053/18800620/048/0019

GREGORY, Ruby. 'Barmaid Who Was Sexually Assaulted Told She Can "Expect to Get Touched"', *WalesOnline*, October 12, 2022. https://www.walesonline.co.uk/news/uk-news/barmaid-who-sexually-assaulted-told-25241315

HANAWALT, Barbara. '*Of Good and Ill Repute': Gender and Social Control in Medieval England*. Oxford University Press, 1998.

'HEAVY PENALTIES FOR SELLING WITHOUT A LICENSE,' February 20th, 1871', in Thomas Lampray, *The Brewers Guardian: A First Class Paper, Devoted to the Protection of Brewers' Interests in Licensing, Legal, and Parliamentary Matters, REVIEW OF THE MALT, HOP AND SUGAR TRADES, & WINE AND SPIRIT TRADES' RECORD*, Vol 1. The Offices, London, 1871. *Coplestone*

HODGKINSON, J. H. 'WANTED, Coloured Lady as Barmaid.' Advertisement, *Liverpool Daily Post*, June 12th, 1893. https://www.britishnewspaperarchive.co.uk/viewer/bl/0000647/18930612/002/0002

HOWSAM, Leslie. 'Legal Paperwork and Public Policy: Eliza Orme's Professional Expertise in Late-Victorian Britain.' in Heidi Egginton and Zoë Thomas, eds. *Precarious Professionals: Gender, Identities and Social Change in Modern Britain*. University of London Press, 2021.

INCH, Emma. 'Passion, Pride and Protest. Pt.1 – CAMRA – Campaign for Real Ale,' 8 February 2022. https://camra.org.uk/learn-discover/discover/passion-pride-and-protest-pt-1

'Jane Ashton Plaintiff Church Court Deposition Bowdon, Altrincham, Bucklow, Cheshire, 1718,' Church Court Depositions & Examinations Boiwdon, Altrincham, Bucklow, Cheshire 1718 in Chester Records Office EDC 5/1718/10; 1719/8 (unfold.) Ashton v. Clayton. In *Intoxicants & Early Modernity England, 1580–1740 database*. University of Sheffield Department of History, The Victorian and Albert Museum, and Digital Humanities Institute|Sheffield. Funded ESRC and AHRC. V. 1.0: https://www.dhi.ac.uk/intoxicants/record.jsp?&source=courtpaper&courtpaper_ID=507

JESUDASON, David. *Desi Pubs: A guide to British-Indian Pubs, Food & Culture*. Camra Books, 2023.

JESUDASON, David. 'Desi Style — The History and Significance of England's Anglo-Asian Pubs,' *Pellicle*, 2 June 2021. https://www.pelliclemag.com/home/2021/5/31/desi-style-the-history-and-significance-of-englands-anglo-asian-pubs

'Joan Walley Plaintiff Church Court Deposition Tarporley, Cheshire February 18th, 1576', Church Court Depositions & Examinations, February 18th, 1576 Tarporley, Cheshire, in Chester Records Office EDC 5/1575/22 Walley c Dawson. In *Intoxicants & Early Modernity England, 1580–1740 database*. University of Sheffield Department of History, The Victorian and Albert Museum, and Digital Humanities Institute|Sheffield. Funded ESRC and AHRC. V. 1.0: https://www.dhi.ac.uk/intoxicants/record.jsp?&source=courtpaper&courtpaper_ID–5

'John Withers Plaintiff Church Court Deposition Tarporley, Cheshire, 1665', in Church Court
Depositions & Examinations Tarporley, Cheshire 1665, in Chester Records Office, EDC
5/1665/32 (unfold.) Wither c. Radley. In *Intoxicants & Early Modernity England, 1580–1740*
database. University of Sheffield Department of History, The Victorian and Albert Museum,
and Digital Humanities Institute|Sheffield. Funded ESRC and AHRC. V. 1.0: https://www.
dhi.ac.uk/intoxicants/record.jsp?&source=courtpaper&courtpaper_ID=152

LEACH, Arthur Francis. *Beverley Town Documents*, Selden Society, Vol. XIV. Bernard Quaritch, 1900.

LUCKETT, Mr. 'WANTED, Coloured Lady, as Barmaid.' Advertisement, *The Era*, 8 June 1895.
https://www.britishnewspaperarchive.co.uk/viewer/bl/0000053/18950608/112/0024

MARTIN, Lynn A. *Alcohol, Sex and Gender in Late Medieval and Early Modern Europe*. Springer, 2001.

'Margaret Burscough Testimony, Thurstaston, Cheshire 1680,' Church Court Depositions &
Examination in Chester Records Office EDC 5/1680/4 Office c. Groome. In *Intoxicants & Early*
Modernity England, 1580–1740 database. University of Sheffield Department of History, The
Victorian and Albert Museum, and Digital Humanities Institute, Sheffield. Funded ESRC
and AHRC. V. 1.0: https://www.dhi.ac.uk/intoxicants/record.jsp?&source=courtpaper&courtpaper_
ID=297

'Margaret Maddock Plaintiff Theft Case, Manchester 1620', Depositions & Examinations
Manchester Quarter Sessions, GMCRO GB 127.MS, fol. 83v. In *Intoxicants & Early Modernity*
England, 1580–1740 database. University of Sheffield Department of History, The Victorian
and Albert Museum, and Digital Humanities Institute, Sheffield. Funded ESRC and AHRC.
V. 1.0: https://www.dhi.ac.uk/intoxicants/record.jsp?&source=courtpaper&courtpaper_
ID=1213&keyword=public%20house

Mass-Observation, *The Pub and The People: A Worktown Study*. London Victor Gollancz Ltd, 1942.

M. G. 'AS BARMAID, a respectable young Person of colour.' Advertisement, *Morning Advertiser*,
February 12th, 1850. https://www.britishnewspaperarchive.co.uk/viewer/bl/0001427/18500212/
053/0001

Middlesex Sessions: Sessions Papers – Justices Working Documents, 1st October, 1697.
on London Lives, 1690–1800, (www.londonlives.org, version 1.1, 17 June 2012).
London Metropolitan Archives, LMSMPS500520054

Middlesex Sessions: Sessions Papers – Justices Working Documents, June 26th, 1708.
on London Lives, 1690–1800, (www.londonlives.org, version 1.1, 17 June 2012).
London Metropolitan Archives, LMSMPS500990071.

Middlesex Sessions: Sessions Papers – Justices Working Documents, December 1716.
on London Lives, 1690–1800, (www.londonlives.org, version 1.1, 17 June 2012).
London Metropolitan Archives, LMSMPS501580055.

Middlesex Sessions: Sessions Papers – Justices Working Documents, 13th September, 1717.
on London Lives, 1690–1800, (www.londonlives.org, version 1.1, 17 June 2012).
London Metropolitan Archives, LMSMPS501640049

Middlesex Sessions: Sessions Papers – Justices Working Documents, 20th January, 1718.
on London Lives, 1690–1800, (www.londonlives.org, version 1.1, 17 June 2012).
London Metropolitan Archives, LMSMPS501680058

MILES, Henry Downes. esq (compiler), *The London and Suburban Licensed Victuallers' Hotel, & Tavern*
Keepers' Directory together with a List of the Brewers, Maltsters, Hop Factors, Distillers & Rectifiers of
the United Kingdom. Henry Downes Miles, 1874. https://play.google.com/books/reader

'Miscellanous Items' 24 1871, Thomas Lampray, *The Brewers Guardian: A First Class Paper, Devoted to*
the Protection of Brewers' Interests in Licensing, Legal, and Parliamentary Matters, REVIEW OF THE
MALT, HOP AND SUGAR TRADES, & WINE AND SPIRIT TRADES' RECORD, Vol 1. The
Offices, London, 1871.

ROBERT, Edwin, Courtney Brinkworth, Jeremey Sumner, Wycherley Gibson, 'William Dreede of Banbury Innholder, buried, 12th April, 1639', in *The Banbury Wills and Inventories: 1591-1620*, Banbury Historical Society Part 1 of the Banbury Wills and Inventories. Banbury Historical Society, 1976.

ROBINSON, Jane. *Mary Seacole: The Charismatic Black Nurse Who Became a Heroine of the Crimea.* Hachette UK, 2019.

Royal Commission on Labour. *The Employment of Women. Reports by Miss Eliza Orme, Miss Clara E. Collet, Miss May E. Abraham, and Miss Margaret H. Irwin (Lady Assistant Commissioners), on the Conditions of Work in Various Industries in England, Wales, Scotland, and Ireland*, 1893.

'Provincial Intelligence' 15 May 1871, Thomas Lampray, *The Brewers Guardian: A First Class Paper, Devoted to the Protection of Brewers' Interests in Licensing, Legal, and Parliamentary Matters, REVIEW OF THE MALT, HOP AND SUGAR TRADES, & WINE AND SPIRIT TRADES' RECORD*, Vol 1. The Offices, London, 1871. *AGNES HILL*

SEACOLE, Mary. *Wonderful Adventures of Mrs. Seacole in Many Lands.* DigiCat, 2022.

SHEPARD, Alexandra. 'Crediting Women in the Early Modern English Economy,' *History Workshop Journal* 79, no. 1 (April 1, 2015), pp. 1–24.

SMITH, Harry, Piero Montebruno and Carry van Lieshout 'Changes in Victorian entrepreneurship in England and Wales 1851–1911: Methodology and business population estimates' in *Business History* Vol 64, No. 7, (2022), pp. 1211–1243.

'SOUTHWARK. Conviction of a Chandler's shopkeepers for selling Beer without a License', 18 December 1871. Thomas Lampray, *The Brewers Guardian: A First Class Paper, Devoted to the Protection of Brewers' Interests in Licensing, Legal, and Parliamentary Matters, REVIEW OF THE MALT, HOP AND SUGAR TRADES, & WINE AND SPIRIT TRADES' RECORD*, Vol 1. The Offices, London, 1871.

'SUNDAY TRADING PROSECUTION AT BEVERLY' 3 April 1871, in Thomas Lampray, *The Brewers Guardian: A First Class Paper, Devoted to the Protection of Brewers' Interests in Licensing, Legal, and Parliamentary Matters, REVIEW OF THE MALT, HOP AND SUGAR TRADES, & WINE AND SPIRIT TRADES' RECORD*, Vol 1. The Offices, London, 1871.

Taylor, Matthew. 'Nurse Is Greatest Black Briton.' *The Guardian*, February 10, 2004. https://www.theguardian.com/uk/2004/feb/10/britishidentity.artsandhumanities

'The Case of Criminal Assault At Thornthwaite.' *Westmoreland Gazette*, December 27th, 1862. https://www.britishnewspaperarchive.co.uk/viewer/bl/0000399/18621227/014/0005

'The Future of the Licensing Question,' 18 September 1871, Thomas Lampray, *The Brewers Guardian: A First Class Paper, Devoted to the Protection of Brewers' Interests in Licensing, Legal, and Parliamentary Matters, REVIEW OF THE MALT, HOP AND SUGAR TRADES, & WINE AND SPIRIT TRADES' RECORD*, Vol 1. The Offices, London, 1871. p. 276

'The Letting of Public Houses,' 13 February 1871, in Thomas Lampray, *The Brewers Guardian: A First Class Paper, Devoted to the Protection of Brewers' Interests in Licensing, Legal, and Parliamentary Matters, REVIEW OF THE MALT, HOP AND SUGAR TRADES, & WINE AND SPIRIT TRADES' RECORD*, Vol 1. The Offices, London, 1871.

'The RAID AGAINST Widows or PUBLICANS AT MARLBOROUGH', 2 October 1871, in Thomas Lampray, *The Brewers Guardian: A First Class Paper, Devoted to the Protection of Brewers' Interests in Licensing, Legal, and Parliamentary Matters, REVIEW OF THE MALT, HOP AND SUGAR TRADES, & WINE AND SPIRIT TRADES' RECORD*, Vol 1. The Offices, London, 1871.

TOWERS, Engine Inn, Pelton, S. O. 'Coloured BARMAID wanted.' *Yorkshire Post and Leeds Intelligencer*, 23 September 1910, https://www.britishnewspaperarchive.co.uk/viewer/bl/0000687/19100923/091/0002

'Ursula Malpas Plaintiff Church Court Deposition Weaverham, Cheshire 1670,' Church Court
    Depositions & Examinations, 1670 in Chester Records Office EDC 5/1670/66 (unfol.) Malpas
    c. Litler. In *Intoxicants & Early Modernity England, 1580–1740 database*. University of Sheffield
    Department of History, The Victorian and Albert Museum, and Digital Humanities
    Institute, Sheffield. Funded ESRC and AHRC. V. 1.0: https://www.dhi.ac.uk/intoxicants/
    record.jsp?&source=courtpaper&courtpaper_ID=290
'Wanted, A Young Coloured Woman As Barmaid for a Vault.' Advertisement, *Liverpool Daily Post*,
    11 May 1864. https://www.britishnewspaperarchive.co.uk/viewer/bl/0000197/18640511/
    054/0003
Whitehall Evening Post. 'Thursday's Post.' *Derby Mercury*, 11 May 1732. https://www.
    britishnewspaperarchive.co.uk/viewer/bl/0000189/17320511/017/0004
Wikipedia contributors. "Mary Phillips (Suffragette)." Wikipedia, 5 August 2022. https://en.
    wikipedia.org/wiki/Mary_Phillips_(suffragette).
'Women's Rights' January, 30th, 1871, in Thomas Lampray, *The Brewers Guardian: A First Class Paper,*
    Devoted to the Protection of Brewers' Interests in Licensing, Legal, and Parliamentary Matters,
    REVIEW OF THE MALT, HOP AND SUGAR TRADES, & WINE AND SPIRIT TRADES' RECORD,
    Vol 1. The Offices, London, 1871.

CHAPTER SIX
'Til Death Do Us Part

'A dreadful accident is reported from Landore, in South Wales', 11 June 1887 in *Staffordshire Chronicle*,
    https://www.britishnewspaperarchive.co.uk/viewer/bl/0001944/18870611/084/0007
'At last a chance of peace at brewery.' *Newcastle Journal*, 26 January 1966. https://www.
    britishnewspaperarchive.co.uk/viewer/bl/0002240/19660126/033/0003
'A Tory Candidate and Female Brewery Workers.' *Edinburgh Evening News*, 28 November 1899.
    https://www.britishnewspaperarchive.co.uk/viewer/bl/0000452/18991128/039/0003
AURORA, 'Ladies Column.' *Hendon & Finchley Times*, 7 April 1916. https://www.
    britishnewspaperarchive.co.uk/viewer/bl/0001599/19160407/015/0002
BALL, Mia. *The Worshipful Company of Brewers: a Short History*. Hutchinson Benham Ltd, 1977.
'Bankrups this week.' *Ipswitch Journal*, 19 February 1726. https://www.britishnewspaperarchive.
    co.uk/viewer/bl/0000191/17260219/009/0004
'Bankrupts.' *Newcastle Courant*, 20 August 1763. https://www.britishnewspaperarchive.co.uk/
    viewer/bl/0000085/17630820/001/0002
BARLOW, Ellen. 'How Beer and Brewing Kept the Country House Running at Temple Newsam,'
    Museum Crush, March 1st, 2018. https://museumcrush.org/how-beer-and-brewing-kept-the-
    country-house-running-at-temple-newsam
BENNISON, Brian Robert, *The Brewing Trade in North East England, 1869–1939*, PhD thesis,
    University of Newcastle Upon Tyne, July 1992.
'Bigger Pay Packets.' *Liverpool Echo*, 13 December 1962. https://www.britishnewspaperarchive.co.uk/
    viewer/bl/0000271/19621213/094/0007
'Bolney and Twineham Conservative and Unionist Association: Speeches by Mr. H. S. Cautley
    and Lieut.-Colonel Rawson.' *Mid Sussex Times*, 3 March 1908. https://www.
    britishnewspaperarchive.co.uk/viewer/bl/0001598/19080303/212/0008
'Brewery Women Sacked.' *Coventry Evening Telegraph*, 9 February 1967. https://www.
    britishnewspaperarchive.co.uk/viewer/bl/0000769/19670209/594/0042
'Brewery Workers' New Agreement.' *Burton Observer and Chronicle*, 24 January 1946.
    https://www.britishnewspaperarchive.co.uk/viewer/bl/0003310/19460124/006/0001

Calendar of Wills Proved and Enrolled in the Court of Husting, London: Part 2, 1358–1688, ed. R. R. Sharpe. Her Majesty's Stationery Office, 1890. On *British History Online* http://www.british-history.ac.uk/court-husting-wills/vol2

Census of Production (1907) Preliminary Tables: Summarising the Results of the Returns Received under the Census of Production Act, 1906. Darling & Son, 1909. https://escoe-website.s3.amazonaws.com/wp-content/uploads/2018/10/19190412/1907-Census-of-Production-Preliminary-Tables-Part-1.pdf

'Control Board Again on the Warpath; Women as Brewery Workers.' *Burton Observer and Chronicle*, 8 June 1916. https://www.britishnewspaperarchive.co.uk/viewer/bl/0003309/19160608/058/0003

CORNELL, Martyn, 'Benskins of Watford – Brewery History Society Wiki', *Brewery History Society Journal*, No. 51, (November, 1987). http://breweryhistory.com

CORNWALLIS, Caroline Frances, 'Letter of Caroline Francis Cornwallis to Miss Frere, June 23rd, 1830,' p. 126 in *Selections from the Letters of Caroline Frances Cornwallis*. Trübner and Co, 1864,

DEARING, John (ed) Penelope Starr and Philip Vaughn (assistant eds), *The History of Reading Society: The Reading Book of Days*, The History Press, Stroud, 2013.

Devanha Brewery Ltd., 'Wanted women for bottle-washing.' *Aberdeen Evening Express*, 22 April 1914. https://www.britishnewspaperarchive.co.uk/viewer/bl/0000445/19140422/094/0001

'Draymen Bid to Start Lorry Strike', *Newcastle Journal*, 17 January 1966. https://www.britishnewspaperarchive.co.uk/viewer/bl/0002240/19660117/083/0007

'Edward William, Brewer, Will 1666' 1666, Llandof, Glamorgan, in Llyfrgell Genedlaethol Cymru – The National Library of Wales. https://viewer.library.wales

'Falkirk.' *Dundee Advertiser*, 9 March 1865. https://www.britishnewspaperarchive.co.uk/viewer/bl/0000295/18650309/047/0004

FITCH, Robert. 'Norwich Brewers' Marks and Trade Regulations' pp. 313–330 in *Norfolk Archaeology or Miscellaneous Tracts Relating to THE ANTIQUITIES OF THE COUNTY OF NORFOLK* Vol V. Norwich. Norfolk and Norwich Archaeological Society, 1859.

'Glamorgan Calendar Rolls and Gaol Files: 1783–99' pp. 232–250 in John Hobson Matthews, *Cardiff Records: Volume 2*, Cardiff Records Committee, 1900. On *British History Online* http://www.british-history.ac.uk/cardiff-records/vol2/pp232–250

GLUCKSMANN, Miriam, 'In a Class of Their Own? Women Workers in New Industries in Inter-War Britain', in *Feminist Review No. 24* (Autumn 1986), pp. 7–37.

'Interview with Charlotte Donohoe,' *Brewing Stories: An Oral History of 3 London Breweries*, digital:works with support from Fuller's Brewery, Chiswick Archives, Richmond Local Studies Centre, and Wandsworth Heritage Service: https://www.brewingstories.org.uk/

'Interview with Christine Hooper,' *Brewing Stories: An Oral History of 3 London Breweries*, digital:works with support from Fuller's Brewery, Chiswick Archives, Richmond Local Studies Centre, and Wandsworth Heritage Service: https://www.brewingstories.org.uk/

'Interview with Denise Annon', *Brewing Stories: An Oral History of 3 London Breweries*, digital:works with support from Fuller's Brewery, Chiswick Archives, Richmond Local Studies Centre, and Wandsworth Heritage Service: https://www.brewingstories.org.uk

'Interview with Maureen Barney,' *Brewing Stories: An Oral History of 3 London Breweries*, digital:works with support from Fuller's Brewery, Chiswick Archives, Richmond Local Studies Centre, and Wandsworth Heritage Service: https://www.brewingstories.org.uk

'Interview with Sila Singh' *Brewing Stories: An Oral History of 3 London Breweries*, digital:works with support from Fuller's Brewery, Chiswick Archives, Richmond Local Studies Centre, and Wandsworth Heritage Service: https://www.brewingstories.org.uk

'Interview with Val Hobson,' *Brewing Stories: An Oral History of 3 London Breweries*, digital:works with support from Fuller's Brewery, Chiswick Archives, Richmond Local Studies Centre, and Wandsworth Heritage Service: https://www.brewingstories.org.uk

'Lack of Support end Vaux Strike.' *Newcastle Journal*, 27 January 1966. https://www.britishnewspaperarchive.co.uk/viewer/bl/0002240/19660127/005/0001

LEWIS, George P. 'A Female worker roll vats of beer into a storage house at a Staffordshire brewery in September 1918,' September 1918, *The Employment of Women in Britain 1914–1918*, part of the Imperial War Museum Photograph Archive Collection Q28339 https://commons.wikimedia.org/wiki/File:The_Employment_of_Women_in_Britain,_1914-1918_Q28339.jpg

LEWIS, George P. 'A group of female works in the grounds of a Staffordshire brewery in September 1918,' September 1918, *The Employment of Women in Britain 1914–1918*, part of the Imperial War Museum Photograph Archive Collection Q28341 https://commons.wikimedia.org/wiki/File:The_Employment_of_Women_in_Britain,_1914-1918_Q28341.jpg

LEWIS, George P. 'Female vat house workers clean pager store casks at a brewery, probably in Cheshire, September 1918,' September 1918, *The Employment of Women in Britain 1914–1918*, part of the Imperial War Museum Photograph Archive Collection Q28332 https://commons.wikimedia.org/wiki/File:The_Employment_of_Women_in_Britain,_1914-1918_Q28332.jpg

LEWIS, George P. 'Female workers filling barrels with beer at a Stafford brewery in September 1918,' September 1918, *The Employment of Women in Britain 1914–1918*, part of the Imperial War Museum Photograph Archive Collection Q28338 https://commons.wikimedia.org/wiki/File:The_Employment_of_Women_in_Britain,_1914-1918_Q28338.jpg

LEWIS, George P. 'Female workers label bottles of lager using machinery at a Cheshire brewery, September 1918,' September 1918, *The Employment of Women in Britain 1914–1918*, part of the Imperial War Museum Photograph Archive Collection Q28330 https://commons.wikimedia.org/wiki/File:The_Employment_of_Women_in_Britain,_1914-1918_Q28330.jpg

LEWIS, George P. 'Female worker packing bottles of lager beer in a pasteurizer in a Cheshire brewery, September 1918,' September 1918, *The Employment of Women in Britain 1914–1918*, part of the Imperial War Museum Photograph Archive Collection Q28328 https://commons.wikimedia.org/wiki/File:The_Employment_of_Women_in_Britain,_1914-1918_Q28328.jpg

LEWIS, George P. 'Female workers roll casks of beer across the floor at a brewery in Cheshire, September 1918,' September 1918, *The Employment of Women in Britain 1914–1918*, part of the Imperial War Museum Photograph Archive Collection Q28336 https://commons.wikimedia.org/wiki/File:The_Employment_of_Women_in_Britain,_1914-1918_Q28336.jpg

LEWIS, George P. 'Two female war workers use large wooden funnels to place dry hops into casks at a brewery in Cheshire, September 1918,' September 1918, *The Employment of Women in Britain 1914–1918*, part of the Imperial War Museum Photograph Archive Collection Q28334 https://commons.wikimedia.org/wiki/File:The_Employment_of_Women_in_Britain,_1914-1918_Q28334.jpg

LISTER, Anne. *The Secret Diaries Of Miss Anne Lister: Vol. 1: I Know My Own Heart.* Hachette UK, 2010.

MILES, Henry Downes. esq (compiler), The London and Suburban Licensed Victuallers' Hotel, & Tavern Keepers' Directory together with a List of the Brewers, Maltsters, Hop Factors, Distillers & Rectifiers of the United Kingdom, London, Henry Downes Miles, 1874. https://play.google.com/books/reader

Mitchells & Butlers Ltd. Cape Hill Brewery Birmingham, 'Vacancies for Women on Part-time Brewery Work,' Advertisement, *Evening Dispatch*, 20 December 1941. https://www.britishnewspaperarchive.co.uk/viewer/bl/0000671/19411220/139/0004

'Mother Tells Vaux Chairman: I Will Drive Beer Truck.' *Newcastle Journal*, 25 January 1966. https://www.britishnewspaperarchive.co.uk/viewer/bl/0002240/19660125/078/0007

'Mr. Malcolm Mitchell, Hon. Sec. Men's League.' *Vote*, 15 October 1910. https://www. britishnewspaperarchive.co.uk/viewer/bl/0002186/19101015/036/0012

Mrs. Burgham, 'Redbrook Brewery', advertisement, *Monmouthshire Beacon*, 27 November 1869. https://www.britishnewspaperarchive.co.uk/viewer/bl/0001272/18691127/014/0001

'National Union of General Workers: Branch Formed for Berwick.' *Berwick Advertiser*, 2 April 1920. https://www.britishnewspaperarchive.co.uk/viewer/bl/0000717/19200402/040/0003

NICHOLLS, Horace. 'A Female worker at work in the cellar of a London brewery,' First World War, *The Employment of Women in Britain 1914-1918*, part of the Imperial War Museum Photograph Archive Collection Q31065 https://commons.wikimedia.org/wiki/File:The_ Employment_of_Women_in_Britain,_1914-1918_Q31065.jpg

NICHOLLS, Horace. 'A Female worker cleaning casks at a London brewery,' First World War, *The Employment of Women in Britain 1914-1918*, part of the Imperial War Museum Photograph Archive Collection Q31064 https://commons.wikimedia.org/wiki/File:The_Employment_of_ Women_in_Britain,_1914-1918_Q31064.jpg

NICHOLLS, Horace. 'A Female worker correcting the main in the refrigerating room of a London brewery,' First World War, *The Employment of Women in Britain 1914-1918*, part of the Imperial War Museum Photograph Archive Collection Q31067 https://commons.wikimedia.org/wiki/ File:The_Employment_of_Women_in_Britain,_1914-1918_Q31067.jpg

NICHOLLS, Horace. 'A Female worker cutting out casks in the cooperage of a London brewery,' First World War, *The Employment of Women in Britain 1914-1918*, part of the Imperial War Museum Photograph Archive Collection. Q31071 https://commons.wikimedia.org/wiki/ File:The_Employment_of_Women_in_Britain,_1914-1918_Q31071.jpg

NICHOLLS, Horace. 'A Female worker cutting out casks in the cooperage of a London brewery,' First World War, *The Employment of Women in Britain 1914-1918*, part of the Imperial War Museum Photograph Archive Collection Q31074 https://commons.wikimedia.org/wiki/ File:The_Employment_of_Women_in_Britain,_1914-1918_Q31074.jpg

NICHOLLS, Horace. 'A Female worker feeding wet hops to the driers in a London brewery,' First World War, *The Employment of Women in Britain 1914-1918*, part of the Imperial War Museum Photograph Archive Collection Q31072 https://commons.wikimedia.org/wiki/File:The_ Employment_of_Women_in_Britain,_1914-1918_Q31072.jpg

NICHOLLS, Horace. 'A Female worker hopping casks at a London Brewery,' First World War, *The Employment of Women in Britain 1914-1918*, part of the Imperial War Museum Photograph Archive Collection. Q31063. https://commons.wikimedia.org/wiki/File:The_Employment_ of_Women_in_Britain,_1914-1918_Q31063.jpg

NICHOLLS, Horace. 'A Female worker in the cooperage of a London brewery,' First World War, *The Employment of Women in Britain 1914-1918*, part of the Imperial War Museum Photograph Archive Collection Q31077 https://commons.wikimedia.org/wiki/File:The_Employment_of_ Women_in_Britain,_1914-1918_Q31077.jpg

NICHOLLS, Horace. 'A group of female employees at a London brewery,' First World War, *The Employment of Women in Britain 1914-1918*, part of the Imperial War Museum Photograph Archive Collection Q31061 https://commons.wikimedia.org/wiki/File:The_Employment_of_ Women_in_Britain,_1914-1918_Q31061.jpg

PROTZ, Roger. *The Family Brewers of Britain: A Celebration of British Brewing Heritage*, Camra Books, 2020.

REDMOND, Nicholas, 'Amey's Brewery Ltd - Brewery History Society Wiki,' n.d., http:// breweryhistory.com/wiki/index

'Sepia Postcard showing group of catering staff outside bass brewery. 7 men standing behind 3 seated women'. In National Brewery Collection. 1890. Ref: BAH/BAS/BASSTAFF/86.0137.00: https://www.nbcarchives.co.uk/collections/getrecord/GB2779_BAH_BAS_BASSTAFF_86_0137_00#

The Brewery, 'One or Two Respectable Women Wanted,' Advertisement, *Falkirk Herald*, 14 April 1894. https://www.britishnewspaperarchive.co.uk/viewer/bl/0000467/18940414/040/0001

'The Directory of Wholesale Brewers in the United Kingdom', pp. 351–371 in *Brewers' Almanack and Wine & Spirit Trade Annual 1915*. The Review Press Limited, 1915. https://www.google.ie/books/edition/Brewers_Almanack_and_Wine_Spirit_Trade

The John Gray Centre, 'Brewing in Dunbar,' *johngraycentre.org*, n.d. https://www.johngraycentre.org/places/1-places/towns-villages/dunbar-2/brewing-in-dunbar

'Trade Unions and Non-Federated Employers.' The *Oxford Chronicle and Reading Gazette*, 19 March 1920. https://www.britishnewspaperarchive.co.uk/viewer/bl/0000989/19200319/181/0016

Tyne Brewery, 'Scottish and Newcastle Breweries Males and Females Required for Tyne Bottling Factory,' Advertisement, *Newcastle Evening Chronicle*, 20 May 1966. https://www.britishnewspaperarchive.co.uk/viewer/bl/0000726/19660520/502/0016

UNKNOWN 'A Bottling Machine Watched Over by a Single Woman Worker' In National Brewery Collection. unspecified. Ref. BAH/JOU/JOUPROC/86.2349.02. https://www.nbcarchives.co.uk/collections/getrecord/GB2779

UNKNOWN. 'PHOTOGRAPH SHOWING BASS BRY TAILORING AND CLOGGING DEPT MEMBERS. 2 WOMEN & 7 MEN, 1 MAN IN SUIT. BUILDING NOW HOUSES BASS MUSEUM LIBRARY AND EDUCATION DEPT'. In National Brewery Collection. Unspecified, 1960. Ref. BAHBAS/BASSTAFF/86.0765.00 https://www.nbcarchives.co.uk/collections/getrecord/GB2779

'Untitled.' *Staffordshire Chronicle*, 11 June 1887. https://www.britishnewspaperarchive.co.uk/viewer/bl/0001944/18870611/084/0007

W. A. Falconar & Co. Limited, in 14 March 1893, *The Brewers Guardian: A First Class Paper, Devoted to the Protection of Brewers' Interests in Licensing, Legal, and Parliamentary Matters, REVIEW OF THE MALT, HOP AND SUGAR TRADES, & WINE AND SPIRIT TRADES' RECORD*, Vol 23 (January to December 1893). The Offices, 1893.

'Wife Sold for £12.' *Manchester Evening News*, 20 March 1907. https://www.britishnewspaperarchive.co.uk/viewer/bl/0000272/19070320/163/0006

'Wills: 1618–1700', pp. 119–138 in John Hobson Matthews (ed.). *Cardiff Records: Volume 3*, (Cardiff Records Office, 1901. On *British History Online* http://www.british-history.ac.uk/cardiff-records/vol3/pp119–138.

'Women as Brewery Clerks.' *Manchester Evening News*, 20 March 1907. https://www.britishnewspaperarchive.co.uk/viewer/bl/0000272/19070320/163/0006

'Women Brewery Workers' Strike.' *Coventry Evening Telegraph*, 2 June 1960. https://www.britishnewspaperarchive.co.uk/viewer/bl/0000769/19600602/204/0018

Women in Industry: Report of the War Cabinet Committee on Women in Industry and Appendices: Summaries of Evidence &c. Vol 2. H. M. Stationary Office, London, 1919.

'Women May Join Brewery Strike.' *Sunday Sun*, 23 January 1966. https://www.britishnewspaperarchive.co.uk/viewer/bl/0001723/19660123/133/0011

'World War I: 1914–1918, Striking Women', n.d. https://www.striking-women.org/module/women-and-work/world-war-i-1914-1918

YULE, G. Udny, 'Statistics of Production and the Census of Production Act (1906)' in *Journal of Royal Statistical Society* Vol. 70, No. 1 (March 1907), pp. 52–99.

CHAPTER SEVEN
Beyond Breweries

ADAMS, Tim, 'Hopsters meet hipsters as East End families relive the exodus to Kent' in *The Observer: Agriculture*, September 13th, 2014. https://www.theguardian.com/science/2014/sep/13/hopsters-hipsters-london-kent-hop-picking-beer

'A New Demand for the Munitions, Ale: Women as Maltsters.' *Yorkshire Evening Post*, 19 May 1917. https://www.britishnewspaperarchive.co.uk/viewer/bl/0000273/19170519/105/0005

'Annual Hop Invasion Starts.' *Tonbridge Free Press*, 27 August 1943. https://www.britishnewspaperarchive.co.uk/viewer/bl/0004173/19430827/044/0004

BENNETT, Judith. *Ale, Beer and Brewsters in England: Women's work in a changing world 1300–1600*. Oxford University Press, 1996.

BERKELEY, George, Monck and Eliza Berkeley (ed), *Poems: by the late George-Monck Berkeley, Esq. ... With a preface by the editor, consisting of some anecdotes of Mr. Monck Berkeley and several of his friends.* J. Nichols, 1797.

BICKERDYKE, John. *The Curiosities of Ale & Beer: An Entertaining History: Illustrated with over Fifty Quaint Cuts.* Swan Sonnenschein & Co., 1886.

BOOTH, Charles. *Life and Labour of the People in London.* Macmillian, 1903.

Bourne Farm, Sandhurst. 'Men and Women wanted for Hop-picking by machine.' Advertisement, *Sevenoaks Chronicle and Kentish Advertiser*, 27 July 1962. https://www.britishnewspaperarchive.co.uk/viewer/bl/0001068/19620727/202/0012

'Brewery Women Under Notice.' *Sheffield Independent*, 5 March 1917. https://www.britishnewspaperarchive.co.uk/viewer/bl/0001464/19170305/068/0003

'Burton Brewery Workers' Wages.' *Burton Observer and Chronicle*, 18 December 1941. https://www.britishnewspaperarchive.co.uk/viewer/bl/0003310/19411218/149/0007

'Burton Women Maltster's Severe Injuries.' *Burton Observer and Chronicle*, 11 January 1919. https://www.britishnewspaperarchive.co.uk/viewer/bl/0003310/19190111/040/0003

'Burton Workers Union.' *Burton Daily Mail*, 25 October 1915. https://www.britishnewspaperarchive.co.uk/viewer/bl/0001119/19151025/078/0004

COLE, Melissa, 'The Everyone Welcome Initiative: What's This All About,' *everyonewelcomeinitiative.com*, 28 June 2018. https://everyonewelcomeinitiative.com/author/melissacolebeer

'Cranbrook.' *West Kent Guardian*, 16 October 1852. https://www.britishnewspaperarchive.co.uk/viewer/bl/0000307/18521016/015/0003

Dea Latis. *The Beer Agender: A further study into female attitude and behaviours towards beer 2019*. 2019: https://dealatisuk.files.wordpress.com/2019/09/68c83-0e690-the-beer-agender-digital.pdf

Dea Latis. *The Gender Pint Gap: A study into GB female attitudes and behaviours towards beer.* 2018: https://dealatisuk.files.wordpress.com/2019/09/4dec5-86c7b-gender-pint-gap-report_dea-latis_may-2018.pdf

Derek Evans Studio, photographer, from *Herefordshire Life through a Lens*. https://herefordshirehistory.org.uk/archive/herefordshire-life-through-a-lens/: 'Baby Sitting in a Hop Crib in Marden with Women Pick Hops', 20 September 1967; 'Children, Hop Pickers and a Tractor in a Herefordshire Hop Yard, 1966.' 24 September 1966; 'Families of Butler Brothers Sitting Around a Campfire after Hop Picking', 1950s/1960s; 'Hop Picking mother (Pearly Butler) and child (Rosie) from the Roma community at Claston Farm, Dormington.' Claston Farm, Dormington, 1957; 'Mother by Hop Crib and Baby in Hop Crib, Withington, Herefordshire 1968'; 'Napping Boy in a Hop Yard at Hoddels Farm, Herefordshire, 1960'; 'Roma Child Rosie Butler with Mud Pies in a Herefordshire Hop Yard', Claston Farm, Dormington, 1950s/1960s; 'Women and Children Hop Picking at Hoddels Farm, Herefordshire, 1960'.

DUCKWORTH, George H., *Notebook: Police District 11 [Poplar and Limehouse], District 12 [Bow and Bromley] and District 13 [South Hackney and Hackney]* BOOTH/B/346. 1897.

DUCKWORTH, George H. *Notebook: Police District 32 [Trinity Newington and St Mary Bermondsey], District 33 [St James Bermondsey and Rotherhithe], District 34 [Lambeth and Kennington], District 35 [Kennington (2nd) and Brixton], District 41 [St Peter Walworth and St Mary Newington], District 42 [St George Camberwell], District 45 [Deptford],* BOOTH/B/365, 1899.

'Edinburgh Women Visit A Brewery.' *Edinburgh Evening News*, 24 May 1927. https://www.britishnewspaperarchive.co.uk/viewer/bl/0000452/19270524/170/0006

'Elizabeth Helin/Deposition & Examination Case of Theft 1601', in *Quarter Sessions, Chester 1601* held at Chester Records Office/Chester Archives and Local Studies, ZQSE 6/11 In *Intoxicants & Early Modernity England, 1580–1740 database.* University of Sheffield Department of History, The Victorian and Albert Museum, and Digital Humanities Institute|Sheffield. Funded ESRC and AHRC. V. 1.0: https://www.dhi.ac.uk/intoxicants/record.jsp?&source=courtpaper&courtpaper_ID=787

FACER, Ruth. *Mary Bacon's World: A Farmer's Wife in Eighteenth-Century Hampshire.* Threshold Press Limited, 2010.

FORD MANOR FARM, Hoath. 'Wanted: Women for Training Hops.' *Herne Bay Press,* 6 May 1966. https://www.britishnewspaperarchive.co.uk/viewer/bl/0003424/19660506/303/0008

'Foreman Maltster' Advertisement, *The Scotsman,* 23 November 1917. https://www.britishnewspaperarchive.co.uk/viewer/bl/0000540/19171123/006/0001

GALLOWAY, Jim. 'The malt trade in later medieval England' Conference paper delivered at Leeds IMC, Univ. of Leeds, UK, July 2016. https://www.academia.edu/34719195/The_malt_trade_in_later_medieval_England

GLEISS, Barbara, *Women in Public Houses. A Historic Analysis of The Social and Economic Role of Women Patronising English Public Houses, 1880s – 1970s.* Pub. PhD Thesis, Universitat Wien, 2009.

GUTZKE, David. *Women Drinking out in Britain since the Early Twentieth Century.* Manchester University Press, 2016.

HADLOW PLACE FARM, Golden Green, Tonbridge. 'Women Wanted for Hop-Picking Machine.' Advertisement. *Sevenoaks Chronicle and Kentish Advertiser,* 26 August 1955. https://www.britishnewspaperarchive.co.uk/viewer/bl/0001068/19550826/257/0016

'Hartlake Memorial: Hop-picking,' *BBC,* n.d. https://www.bbc.co.uk/kent/voices/hartlake/hop_picking.shtml

'Hops Crop Up to Standard.' *Kington Times,* 8 September 1951. https://www.britishnewspaperarchive.co.uk/viewer/bl/0002545/19510908/004/0001

'Hygienic Hop Picking.' *Belfast Telegraph,* 25 August 1937. https://www.britishnewspaperarchive.co.uk/viewer/bl/0002318/19370825/136/0006

J. K. 'War Time in the Hopyards: Busy, But Peaceful, Scenes.' *Evesham Standard & West Midland Observer,* 16 September 1939. https://www.britishnewspaperarchive.co.uk/viewer/bl/0002560/19390916/031/0002

Kentish Express, 'Ashford.' *Canterbury Journal, Kentish Times and Farmers' Gazette,* 21 September 1872. https://www.britishnewspaperarchive.co.uk/viewer/bl/0001404/18720921/030/0003

LANGHAMER, Claire '"A Public House Is for All Classes, Men and Women Alike": Women, Leisure and Drink in Second World War England', *Women's History Review,* 12 (2003).

Letter from Lettice Kynnersley, Badger, to Walter Bagot, Blithfield, 1608? September 14: autograph manuscript signed, Papers of the Bagot family of Blithfield, Staffordshire. Transcription by Early Modern Manuscripts Online (EMMO). MS L.a.598, Folger Shakespeare Library, Washington, DC. https://emmo.folger.edu/view/La598/regularized

'Letter from Mrs. Donnellan to Mrs. Elizabeth Montagu, December 28th, 1747,' in Matthew Montagu (ed) *The Letters of Mrs. Elizabeth Montagu, with some of the letters of her correspondence*' Vol. 2. T. Cadell and W. Davies, 1809.

LONDON, Jack, and Alexander Masters (ed). *The People of the Abyss* (Hesperus Press, 2013).

L. U. HUBBLE and Son, China Farm, Harbledown, Canterbury. '2 to 3 Women required for Hop-picking Machine Work in September.' Advertisement. *Herne Bay Press*, 18 August 1972. https://www.britishnewspaperarchive.co.uk/viewer/bl/0003424/19720818/164/0013

'Magistrates' Clerk's Office.' *South Eastern Gazette*, 18 October 1853. https://www. britishnewspaperarchive.co.uk/viewer/bl/0001098/18531018/092/0005

'Mary Bacon/Baachelor of Yarmouth' in *Port Book Great Yarmouth, Norfolk, England. November 11th, 1678*. Held at the National Archives, E 190/496/22. In *Intoxicants & Early Modernity England, 1580–1740 database*. University of Sheffield Department of History, The Victorian and Albert Museum, and Digital Humanities Institute, Sheffield. Funded ESRC and AHRC. V. 1.0: https://www.dhi.ac.uk/intoxicants/record.jsp?&source=consignment&consignment_ID=13134

MARKHAM, Gervase. *The English Housewife*. McGill-Queen's Press, 1994.

Mass-Observation, *The Pub and The People: A Worktown Study*. London Victor Gollancz Ltd, 1942.

'Mechanical Hop-picking,' *Leeds Mercury*, 18 September 1922. https://www. britishnewspaperarchive.co.uk/viewer/bl/0000748/19220918/101/0006

'Mechanical Hop Picking.' *The Sphere*, 28 September 1957. https://www.britishnewspaperarchive. co.uk/viewer/bl/0001861/19570928/041/0038

MILNE, Alison. 'The Birth of Crafty Maltsters'. *Crafty Maltsters*, 10 May 2019. https://www. craftymaltsters.co.uk

Mr. H. C. Seppings Wright (artist). 'With The Distressed Hop-pickers in Kent.' *Illustrated London News*, 11 September 1897. https://www.britishnewspaperarchive.co.uk/viewer/BL/0001578/18970911/050/0019

PATTINSON, Ron, 'Cowsheds,' *Shut Up About Barclay Perkins*, 29 June 2007. https://barclayperkins. blogspot.com

PENNEY, Norman. *The Household Account Book of Sarah Fell of Swarthmoor Hall*. Cambridge University Press, 2014.

REG SPELLER/Fox Photos/Getty Images, 'A Franciscan friar and nun walk with hop pickers' children at Paddock Wood, Kent,' Getty Images, 1934. From Uren, Amanda. 'c.1900–1949 Hop pickers: Families Migrate to Harvest the Bitter Bud.' *Mashable*, 12 June 2017. https:// mashable.com/feature/hop-pickers

REG SPELLER/Fox Photos/Getty Images, 'Hop pickers' children watch as a Franciscan friar puts up a notice of a church service.' Kent, Getty Images, 1933. From Uren, Amanda. 'c.1900–1949 Hop pickers: Families Migrate to Harvest the Bitter Bud.' *Mashable*, 12 June 2017. https:// mashable.com/feature/hop-pickers

'Rural Hop Pickers'. *Pall Mall Gazette*, 8 October 1874. https://www.britishnewspaperarchive.co.uk/ viewer/BL/0000098/18741008/018/0010

SAUER, Michelle M. *Gender in Medieval Culture*, Bloomsbury, 2015.

SHARPE, Pamela, "The Female Labour Market in English Agriculture during the Industrial Revolution: expansion or contraction?' in *The Agricultural History Review* Vol. 47, No. 2, (1999), pp. 161–181.

SKELTON, John. 'The Tunning of Elynour Rummyng,' pp. 1–8 in Marie Loughlin, Sandra Bell, and Patricia Brace (eds.) *The Broadview Anthology of Sixteenth-Century Poetry and Prose*, Broadview Press, 2011.

SIMNETT, J. S (?). 'Women Maltsters, Bass'. Photograph. Bass Holdings Ltd. Collection. In National Brewery Collection. 6 March 1917. Ref: BAH/BAS/BASSTAFF/86.0141.02. https://www.nbcarchives.co.uk/collections/getrecord/GB2779

'Smell of Barley Recalled.' *Newark Advertiser*, 17 February 1968. https://www.britishnewspaperarchive.co.uk/viewer/bl/0003436/19680217/151/0009

SMITH, George, 'Hop-picking', Oil on Canvas, 1714–1776. Midstone Museum and Bentlif Art Gallery. https://artuk.org/discover/artworks/hop-picking-76789

STOPES, H. *Malt and Malting: An Historical, Scientific, and Practical Treatise, Showing, as Clearly as Existing Knowledge Permits, What Malt Is, and How to Make It. With Full Descriptions of All Buildings and Appliances, Together with Detailed Definitions of Every Matter Connected Therewith, Illustrated by 150 Woodcuts*, Lyon, 1885.

The Ancient Laws and Customs of The Burghs of Scotland Vol. I A.D. 1124–1424. John Greig & Son, 1868.

'THE HOP-PICKING SEASON', 1 October 1877, *The Country Brewers' Gazette: The Official Organ of the Country Brewers' Society* Vol 1. No. 3 (London, 1877).

'The Hopping Season: Cheery Crowds on Special Trains, East Enders' Holiday Outing.' *Halifax Evening Courier*, 24 August 1932. https://www.britishnewspaperarchive.co.uk/viewer/bl/0003295/19320824/052/0002

The Universal British Directory 1793–1798, Michael Winton, 1993.

Unknown. 'Bass Women Maltsters'. Photograph. Bass Holdings Ltd. Collection. In National Brewery Collection. unspecified. Ref: BAH/BAS/BASSTAFF/86.0141.02. https://www.nbcarchives.co.uk/collections/getrecord

UREN, Amanda. "*c.* 1900–1949 Hop pickers: Families Migrate to Harvest the Bitter Bud." *Mashable*, June 12, 2017. https://mashable.com/feature/hop-pickers

WHARTON, Betty *The Smiths of Ryburgh*. Crisp Malting Ltd, 1990.

WHITTLE, Jane, 'Housewives and Servants in Rural England, 1440–1650: Evidence of Women's Work from Probate Documents,' in *Transactions of the Royal Historical Society*, Vol. 15 (2005). pp. 51–74.

'WOMEN AND ALCOHOL', 20 February 1871, Thomas Lampray, *The Brewers Guardian: A First Class Paper, Devoted to the Protection of Brewers' Interests in Licensing, Legal, and Parliamentary Matters, REVIEW OF THE MALT, HOP AND SUGAR TRADES, & WINE AND SPIRIT TRADES' RECORD*, Vol 1. The Offices, London, 1871.

'Women & The War.' *Westminster Gazette*, 11 July 1916. https://www.britishnewspaperarchive.co.uk/viewer/bl/0002947/19160711/028/0004

'Women Hop Pickers.' *Vote*, 9 September 1921. https://www.britishnewspaperarchive.co.uk/viewer/bl/0002186/19210909/010/0003

Women Maltsters.' *Birmingham Daily Gazette*, 14 October 1916. https://www.britishnewspaperarchive.co.uk/viewer/bl/0000669/19161014/131/0005

'Women Maltsters.' *Burton Observer and Chronicle* 8 June 1916. https://www.britishnewspaperarchive.co.uk/viewer/bl/0003309/19160608/059/0003

'Women Visit A Brewery: And Receive a Sample!' *West Middlesex Gazette*, 15 August 1936. https://www.britishnewspaperarchive.co.uk/viewer/bl/0002564/19360815/090/0007

Index

1522 Alehouse Licensing Act, 53, 77
1828 Alehouses Act, 113
1830 Beerhouse Act, 113
1851 General Census of Great Britain, 116
1881 Census of England, Wales, and Scotland, 150
1917 Report of the War Cabinet Committee of Women in Industry, 134
1908 Census of Production in the United Kingdom, 131
50 Years of CAMRA, 172–3

A

A closet for ladies and gentlewomen, 80
A Terrible Battell Betweene Two Consumers of the Whole World: Time and Death (*see also* Samuel Rowland), 14–15
A Woman's Brew podcast (*see also* Powell, Tori and Love, Joanne), 10, 38, 88, 144, 174–5
Aberdeen Council Registers, 48–50
    women brewing in, 48–50
    laws, 49–50
    breaking assize in, 49–50
    singlewomen, 49–50
Adedipe, Helena, 10, 28–9, 30, 37, 99, 100, 124, 144
administration, women in, 38, 126, 136
adulterators of ale
    brewers, 65
    early modern, 65
    19th century publicans, 115
adverts
    for female brewing servants, 98
    for barmaids of colour, 119–120
    for breweries, 128, 131, 133–5
    for hop pickers, 158–160
    beer advertising and sexism, 167–9

Aitken and Co. 134–5
alcohol-free beer (*see* Drop Bear Beer Company)
ale-sellers
    women tavern owners, 5, 15, 54, 58–60, 68–9, 111–16
    family publicans, 109–10, 112–13
    hucksters and regrators, 110
    in literature, 5, 15, 63–9
    licensing, 58–60, 105–7, 113–15
ale brewers vs beer brewers
    immigrants, 18–19
    introduction of hops, 18–21, 23–4
    laws, 21
    guilds, 21–4
alehouses
    in literature, 5, 15, 63–9
    women working in, 17, 106–10, 116–22
    women owners, 5, 15, 54, 58–60, 68–9
    women attending, 122, 161–70
alestake
    use of, 46
    witches and, 67
aletasters
    assize and, 51, 53, 172
    breaking laws, 45, 51
Ane Satyre of the Thrie Estaits, 47
Ankerwyke Priory, 46
Annon, Denise, 136
anti-semitism
    and witch depictions, 67–8
    medieval laws, 44
appeasement with ale
    witches in England, 69
    witches in Scotland, 77–8
Ars Moriendi, 14
arsenic (*see* poison)

Arsenical Poisoning in Beer Drinkers, 75
art
    depictions of female brewers in, 63–5
    doom paintings, 64
Ashmole, Elias, (*see* Lily, William)
Ashton, Jane, 105–6
assize of ale, 22
    women brewers breaking in; England, 45–6;
        Scotland, 48–50; Wales, 51
    aletasters, 45, 51, 53, 172
    ordinances, 45–6, 48–50

B
Bacon, Mary, (farmer), 154–5
Bacon, Mary, (who imported hops), 155
bans
    women banned selling ale, 23, 107, 110–11
    women banned brewing, 25, 48–9, 107, 130–1
barmaids, 17, 107–9, 120–2
    attacks on, 107–9, 117–19
    racism in adverts, 119–120
    low pay and poor conditions, 116–120
    Eliza Orme, 116–18
Barney, Maureen, 136
beer advertising
    medical claims, 81–2
    sexism in, 168
beer brewing
    introduction of hops, 18–21, 23–4
    conflict with ale brewers, 18–21, 23–4
    impact on women brewers, 18–24
Beer Culture Center, 4, 172
beer education, 162–163, 173–177
beer houses (*see also* alehouses), 165
Beer Sommelier, 52, 170, 176, 177
beer writing, 170–3
Beer: Taste the Evolution in 50 Styles, 175, 177
Beeton, Samuel and Isabella (*see*
    Englishwoman's Domestic Magazine)
Belle, Dido Elizabeth, 86
Bennett, Judith, 16–18, 20, 22, 27, 45, 50, 51, 60,
    107, 148
Benskin's Brewery, 129
Berkeley, Eliza, 153–4
Bickerdyke, John, 78, 149
Bill to Restrict Barmaids, 118

Black Death
    arrival of, 11, 13–14
    impact, 13–18
    quarantine, 14
    alehouses, 13–14, 17
    pigeons and medical cures, 14
blogging (*see* beer writing)
Booth, Charles (see *The Life and Labour of
    the People of London*)
Borough Brewery, 129
bottle shop, 32–4, 121–2, 178
bottling lines, 27, 131–7
braggot, 87–8
Brave Noise (*see also* Eliot, Ash), 10, 145–6
Brew4Change Africa, 145
Brewer's Guardian, 113–5
brewer's marks 126–7
Brewery History, the Journal for the Brewery
    History Society, 128–9
brewery tours
    modern women's beer groups, 161–2
    early 20th century, 161–2
brewing
    dangers of, 54–55, 97
    at home, 16–18, 43–4, 45–57, 83–98
    industrial, 123–44
    small scale commercial, 16–18, 45–62, 123–5
Brewing Stories: An Oral History of 3 London Breweries,
    135–6
Bressey, Caroline, 119
brooms
    and witches, 66–7
Brown, James, 15, 69, 108
Burton, Kristen, 17, 20–1, 104

C
*Calendar of Wills Proved and Enrolled in the
    Court of Husting, London*, 125
CAMRA, 4, 130, 170, 172–5
Campbell, Lynsey, 10, 31, 57
capotian hat, 68
care work, 37–8, 144
Carlsberg and Tuborg, 135
cask ale, 52, 92, 96, 133–4, 170
catering department, 131, 134
Cathars, 66

Catholics, 110–11, 158

cats, 66, 73

cauldrons, 60, 67, 90

Chain, Talia 10, 41–3, 84, 160

Chaucer, 66

cheating alewives
in literature, 5, 15, 63–9
in England, 45–6
in Scotland, 48–50
in Wales, 50

Chester Mystery Plays, 64

Chicago Brewseum (*see* Beer Culture Center)

childcare (*see* care work)

chores
brewing as part of, 84–5, 89–98

christening, 116

Cicerone, 170, 176, 177

Closet Brewing, 10, 28, 40, 74, 84, 137–8, 141, 163

cock ale, 81, 91, 182–3

Cole, Melissa, 89, 172

concubinage, (*see* also sex work), 51

cooking
with ale or beer, 85–90, 94–5, 98–9
books on 44, 85–90

cooper, 74, 133, 151, 161

Cornell, Martyn, 19, 128, 129

Cornwallis, Caroline Frances, 127

coronavirus
and Black Death parallels 24–40
economic impact; on pubs, 32–6; on
breweries, 24–32; on drinking, 24–5, 30–2;
bar workers, 37
historically marginalised groups, 26–7,
36–40

Corporation of Lincoln Registers, 54

cost of living crisis, 38–9

Country Brewer's Gazette, 114–15

cows, 60–2, 94
Puggy the cow, 60–2

cowsheds, 165–6

craft beer
women in breweries, 31–2, 139, 141
women and, 34, 40, 56, 121–2, 139
changes needed, 36, 139–146

Crafty Maltsters, 153

cuckstool, 48

Curiosities of Ale and Beer (*see* Bickerdyke, John)

cursed beer and ale, 73–7

cwrw bach, 60

D

Dea Latis, 10, 52, 103, 168–9

defamation (*see* slander)

*Delights for ladies to adorn their persons, tables,
closets, and distillatories, with beauties,
banquets, perfumes, and waters*, 89

demons and alewives, 5, 63–5, 66–70

Description of Elizabethan England, 64–5, 93

Desi Pubs (*see* David Jesudason)

de Silva, Ruvani, 10, 84, 91, 122, 144, 170–2

destruction of ale/beer by witches, 73–7

diod faen, 84, 100

disability
historical women brewing with, 55–7, 58
modern breweries and, 57–8

Dogon, 86

doughnuts, 87

Doom Painting (*see* art)

Drop Bear Beer Company, 10, 30, 37, 40, 74, 84, 139–141

drinking
women and beer, 161–170
women drinking in public 122, 163–171

Drummond, Joelle, 10, 30, 40, 74, 139–141,

drunkenness, 58, 105, 108

ducking stool (*see* cuckstool)

Duckworth, George, 165

Dunbar, William, (see *The Devil's Inquest*)

Dyffryn Clwyd, 50

E

Edinburgh, 24, 28, 35, 48, 114, 117, 137, 141

Edinburgh Women's Citizen's, Association, 161

Eko Brewery, 10, 28–30, 37, 40, 84, 99–101, 124, 144

Eliot, Ash, (*see* also Brave Noise), 10, 145–6

energy crisis (*see* cost of living crisis)

England's Immigrants Database, 19–20

Englishwoman's Domestic Magazine, 82, 94–5, 96

Ewan, Elizabeth, 16, 24, 48

F

false measures, 15, 48–9, 59, 64, 107

familiars (witches), 66

Family Life and Work Experience Before 1918, 83–4
fermentation, 89, 92, 95, 169
Fermentation Beer and Brewing Radio (*see* Inch, Emma)
fish, 91, 99, 149
Five Hundred Points of Good Husbandry … together with a Book of Huswifery, 20
Five Points Brewing Company 37–9, 55–6, 121
Flemish Ale, 19–20
Fletcher of Saltoun Family (*see* Mrs Johnston)
folk magick, 69
Fuller's Brewery, 135–6

G
gaol (*see* jail)
Gaskill, Malcolm, 72–3
Gentleman Jack, (*see* Lister, Anne)
Gilreath, Elicia, 4, 39–40
ginger beer, 83, 84, 95
Girton Brewery, 129
Glamorgan Calendar Rolls and Gaol Files: 1542, 94, 53
Glasladies Beer Society, 10, 142, 162
Glasse, Hannah, 96
Gleiss, Barbara, 16, 18, 107, 118, 167
goddess, 67, 86, 123
Good Beer Guide, 172–3
Graunt, John (*see* *Natural and Political Observations mentioned in a flowing index and made upon the Bills of Mortality*)
Gray, Jules, 10, 32–6, 120
Grevell, Margaret, 73
guilds
  in England, 21–3
  London, 21–2
  Edinburgh, 24
  Oxford, 22
  Wales, 24
Guinness, 82, 166
Gundry, Ann, 128–9
Gutzke, David, 164–6

H
Hadland, Laura, 10, 104, 172–3
Hanawalt, Barbara, 109
Hartley House, 118

Harrison, William, 65
Hell, 46
  alewives in, 63–5
herbs
  in medicinal beers, 14, 80–1
  in beer recipes, 23
Hobson, Val, 136
homebrewing, 24, 41
  and early modern period, 51, 85–7, 91–5
  19th and 20th centuries, 83–5, 91–5
  female servants and, 86–7, 93–4, 96–98
  women's books on, 87–92, 94–5
  modern women brewing, 41, 51, 74, 84, 90, 99, 139
hoop, on the, 125
Hop Hideout (*see* Gray, Jules)
Hop Picker's Specials (*see* hop picking)
hop-picking, 154–161
  conditions, 156–8
  hoppers hospitals, 157
  families, 158
  trains, 156
  diseases, 157
  in art, 155, 156, 157
  women and, 154–161
  Catholic families, 158
  Traveller and Romani families, 158–9
Hopkins, Matthew, Witch Finder General, 72
hops (*see also* beer)
  picking, 154–161
  introduction, 18–21, 23–4
  in beer, 18–24
  and women, 18–24
  Scotland, 23–4
  Wales, 24
Household Account Book of Sarah Fell of Swarthmoor Hall, 93, 149–150
housewife
  and brewing (*see* homebrewing), 51, 85–7, 91–5
  books for, 87–92, 94–5
hucksters, 110
Hull Brewers' Guild, 22
husbandman, 85, 110
husbands
  owning public houses with wives, 109–10
  brewing with wives, 18, 20, 22–3, 28, 41, 48–9, 85, 99

I

illegal drinking establishments (*see* shebeens)

immigrants
in medieval, 18–20
in early modern, 85–6, 98, 100
modern period, 26, 100

Inch, Emma, 10, 37, 74, 84, 91, 104, 144, 169, 174

Industrial revolution
impact on brewing, 11, 128
women owning industrial breweries, 128–131
women working in industrial breweries, 131–2

inheritance
women owning breweries through, 125, 128–131

International Women's Collaboration Brew Day, 91

Intoxicants and Early Modernity: England, 1580-1740 database, 53–5, 58–9, 97, 105–6, 110, 149

Israelite brewing, 44

IT workers, 136

J

jail, 53, 59, 115

Jesudason, David, 104

Jewish brewing traditions
ancient, 44
medieval, 43–4
modern, 41–3

Johanna St. John, 80–1

John Gray Centre, 4, 127, 134

John Joule and Sons Ltd., 135

Joy Barber, Doreen, 10, 37–9, 55, 56, 121

Juliana of Ravenesfeud, 45

K

Kempe, Margery, 47

King James I, 72

Kings Arms Public House, 165

Knights Templar, 66

kosher brewing (*see* Jewish brewing)

L

lab technicians, 134

Lady Holmbey's Scotch Ale, 90

laws, 16–17
against women brewing, 23, 25, 48–9, 107, 110–11, 130–1
against Jewish people brewing, 43–4
against Catholics having alehouses, 110–11
assize of ale, 15–16, 45–51
malting, 148

laws of the gilde of Scotland, 148

Leges Quatour Burgiorum, 48

letters
from women, 94–5, 96, 98, 127, 147
about malting, 147–8, 151
about brewing, 93, 96, 98, 127

LGBTQ+ pubs, 104

Liber Albus, 48

licensing, 44, 53–60
of alehouses 105–6, 113–14

Licoricia of Winchester (*see* Jewish brewing traditions)

Lily, William, 93

Lister, Anne, 124–5, 138

living wage, 58, 140

lockdown (*see* coronavirus)

London, 13, 19, 20, 35, 41, 58, 71–2, 83, 86, 107, 109, 112, 116–18, 156–7, 160–1, 165–6, 167, 170
brewing guilds in, 21–2, 148
women brewers in, 20, 28–30, 58, 76, 86, 98, 125, 133, 135–6

London Lives 1690-1800: Crime Poverty and Social Policy in the Metropolis project, 98

Love Beer Learning, 174

Love, Joanne (*see also A Woman's Brew*), 10, 38, 144, 161, 174–5

Lydgate, John, 64–5

Lyndesay, Sir David, (*see Ane Satyre of the Thrie Estaits*)

M

machine picking hops (*see* hops)

maleficium (*see* witchcraft)

malt, 12, 20, 49, 55, 56, 64, 65, 73, 78, 80–2, 87, 90–1, 93, 95
women making in medieval, 147–9
women making early modern, 92, 110, 149–150
women making modern era, 129, 133, 150–3
current women in malt, 153

malt tonic, 81–2

Malt and Malting, an Historical, Scientific, and Practical Treatsie, 150

Marker, Mary, 126

marketing, women in, 10, 25, 38–9, 56, 120, 121, 132, 138, 140, 146, 153, 166

Markham, Gervase, 14, 148, 162

Marlborough, 113–114

   raids on widows, 114

marriage, 64, 117, 137, 138, 155, 173

   impact on women who brewed, 16–18, 22–3, 41, 49–50

masculinisation of beer drinking in public, 163–8

masculinsation of beer, 164, 168–9

masculinsation of brewing, 16–24, 27

mash in, 73, 90–1, 123

Mass-Observation, 116, 166–7, 223

maternity policy, 144

Mayhew, Nicholas, 16, 48

Mbaba Mwana Waresa, 86

McCulla, Theresa, 86–7

McNena, Sarah, 74, 139–141

mead, 90, 96

Meantime Brewing Company, 10, 57, 124-4, 142–3

Medicinal beer, 80–2

memento mori, 14–15

Mendoza, Monica, 10, 162

Merryell Williams *Book of Recipes*, 80–1, 87–8, 99, 184

Messrs Allsopp Brewery, 132

methiglin (*see* mead)

Middlesex Sessions, 106, 110

military (*see also* World War I and World War II), 21, 133–5

Misericord (*see* art)

Moonwake Brewing Company, 38, 120

Mother Bunch, 90

Mother Louse, 62, 68

Mother Red Cap, 69

Mrs Johnston, 90

murder 72, 81, 73–4

N

National Brewery, 129

National Brewery Centre Archives, 134

Natural and Political Observations mentioned in a flowing index and made upon the Bills of Mortality, 71–2

nettles, brewing with, 42, 83–4, 100

Neville, Sydney, 166

nightclubs, 58, 120

Northern Memoirs, 60–2

Norwich Cathedral (*see* art)

nuns, 46–7, 158

Nxusani-Mawela, Apiwe, (*see also* Tolokazi Beer Company), 10, 25–6, 100, 145, 176

O

Ordinance of Labourers 1349, 17

Orme, Eliza, (*see also* barmaids), 116–18

Oxford Brewer's Guild, 22–3

P

Parnall, Hester, (*see* St Austell brewery), 130

Pattinson, Ron, 24, 128, 165–6

Pease, Elizabeth, 127

Peckover, Judeth, 126

petitions for alehouses, 53, 55–9, 105–6,111

   women with disabilities, 55–57

   women in poverty, 54–55

Peyton, Jane, 10, 91, 168–9, 175, 176–7

Physicians and Irregular Medical Practitioners in London 1550-1640 database, 76

Piers Plowman, 17

Plague Orders 1578, 15, 32

Plat, Sir Hugh, 89–90

podcasts, 4, 8, 10, 38, 65, 84, 174–5, 176

Poems (*see* Berkeley, Eliza)

poison

   arsenic, 75

   witchcraft, beer and, 73–5

   strychnine, 81

police, 165

posset, 80, 87, 93, 180, 184–5

poverty

   brewing and, 54–8

Powell, Tori, 10, 88, 144, 174–5

Prabhu, Nix, (*see also* GlasLadies Beer Society), 10, 142, 162–3

Prentice, Joan, 71

Protz, Roger, 130, 172
public houses, 11, 17, 24, 32–8, 51–2, 55, 103–5,
111–22, 116, 128–9, 162–8, 170
pumpkin beer, 87–8
punishment of alewives (*see* also cuckstool)
England, 45–8
Scotland, 48–50
Wales, 51
purging ale, 81, 93
Put Thieving Millers and Bakers in the Pillory
(*see* Lydgate, John)

Q
quarantine, 15, 25, 26, 27, 32
Queer Brewing Project, 137

R
Rankine, Amy, 10, 168–9
Reading Book of Days, 128–9
Recipe Book of Janet Maule, 90, 180
recipes
for beer or ale 18, 41, 74, 79, 89–5
for foods with ale or beer, 87–9, 179–185
for medicines, 79–82
Redbrook Brewery, 128
regrators (*see* hucksters)
regulations (*see* laws)
religious brewing
nuns and, 46–7
Jewish brewing traditions, 41–4
reputation, 70
importance of, 53–4, 77, 105–6
lawsuits to defend, 58, 105
and alehouses, 58–9, 77, 105–6
Romani community
and hop picking, 158–9, 178
Romyng, Alianora, 6–7, 8
Rowland, Samuel, 14–15
Rummyng, Elynour, 5, 8, 69, 81, 182
Running Horse, 6–7
rural brewing, 60, 87, 124–5
versus urban brewing 21–3
in the early modern period, 87–98, 147–150
Ruthin, 50–1

S
Sabbath, 67, 105
Sadeh Farm and Lone Goat Brewing Company
(*see also* Chain, Talia), 10, 41–3, 47, 60, 160
Saint Brigid, 63
sales, women in, 136, 140, 146
salt (*see* adulteration)
Sambrook, Pamela, 94
Sauer, Michelle, 16, 18, 21, 27, 164
School of Booze, 168, 175–6
Seacole, Mary, 111–12
secretaries in breweries, 134
Select pleas, stars, and other records from the rolls of
the Exchequer of the Jews, A.D. 1220–1284, 44
servants
female servants and brewing, 11, 47, 85–7, 91,
93, 96–8, 100, 174, 178
and alehouses, 107–9
and malting, 147–9
adverts for, 98
hop picking, 154
sex work 51, 106–9
sexual abuse, 107–9
sexual harassment, 107–9, 118–9
Sharma, Nidhi, (*see also* Meantime Brewery Co),
10, 57, 123–4, 142–4, 176
shareholders
women in breweries, 130–1, 135
chairwomen (*see* Parnall, Hester)
Sharpe, James, 17
Sharpe, Pamela, 154
shebeens, 114–15
Sheffield 15, 32–6, 53, 119, 120, 135, 152
Shepard, Alexandra, 109–10
Sinclair, Sarah, 10, 38, 120–1
Singh, Sila, 136
single women, 21, 49–50, 108, 126–7
Skelton, John (*see also* Rummyng, Elynour), 5, 8,
69, 81, 182
Slander, 105–6, 164
Smith, Annabel, 10, 52, 103, 168–9
Smith, Eliza, 81, 91–3
Smith, George, 155
snobbery, 17, 165
Society for Independent Brewers, 26, 31–2, 34,
36, 38

South Africa, 25–6, 100–1, 145

South Asian Beer Club, 122, 171–2

Spence, Elizabeth Isabella (see *Summer Excursions through parts of Oxfordshire, Gloucestershire, Warwickshire, Staffordshire, Herefordshire, Derbyshire and South Wales*)

St Austell Brewery, 130

St Laurence's Church in Ludlow (see art)

Staffordshire, 70, 134–5, 184

Statutes of Labourers 1351, 17

Stevens, Lizzie, 10, 28, 137–8, 141

Stevens, Lucy, 10, 28, 137–8, 141

Stevens, Matthew Frank, 16, 50–1

stout, 82, 84, 92, 99, 101, 129, 163, 166

strychnine, (see poison)

suffragettes, 116–18, 130

Summer Excursions through parts of Oxfordshire, Gloucestershire, Warwickshire, Staffordshire, Herefordshire, Derbyshire and South Wales, 70–1

Survey of Scottish Witches database, 77–79

Swansea (see Drop Bear Beer Company)

Switching the Lens – Rediscovering Londoners of African, Caribbean, Asian and Indigenous Heritage 1561 to 1840 database, 86

T

Tassin, Amélie, (see also Women in Beer), 10, 38–9, 121–2, 132, 144, 162–3

Temple Newsam (see Pease, Elizabeth)

The Accomplish'd lady's delight in preserving, physick, beautifying, and cookery (see Woolley, Hannah)

The Art of Cookery made plain and easy (see Glasse, Hannah)

The Beer Agender, 168–9

The Book of Margery Kempe, 47

The Closet of Sir Kenelm Digby Knight Opened, 90, 182

The Compleat servant-maid (see Woolley, Hannah)

The Complete Housewife (see Smith, Eliza)

The Cook's guide (see Woolley, Hannah)

The Devil's Inquest, 65

The Directory of Wholesale Brewers in the United Kingdom, 129

The Employment of Women in Britain 1914-1918, 133–4

The English Huswife, 14, 148–9

The Family Brewers of Britain: A Celebration of British Brewing Heritage (see Protz, Roger)

The Gender Pint Gap, 168–9

The Life and Labour of the People of London, 165–6

The Pub and The People, 4, 116, 166–7

The queen-like closet (see Woolley, Hannah)

The Smiths of Ryburgh, 153

Thomas, Wilma, 60, 97

tippling house (see alehouse)

Tolokazi Beer Company, 10, 25–6, 40, 100–1, 145

Tosafists (see Jewish brewing traditions)

Traveller community and hop picking, 158–9, 178

Tusser, Thomas, (see *five hundred points of good husbandry*)

U

Unger, Richard, 19, 22

unions
strikes, 135
women in, brewery unions, 132, 135, 136

Universal British Directory 1793-1798, 150

urban brewing, 17, 18–21, 23, 27, 50, 97–8, 128–137
versus rural brewing, 21–3

V

vats, 5, 123

Vaughan, Theresa, 16

Vaux Brewery, 135

vinegar, 95, 154

Virtual Beer School, 175–7

W

W. A. Falconer and Co, Ltd, 129–130

Walker, Ann, 125, 138

Walley, Joan, 105

Warn & Sons, 128

Watney, Combe, Reid and Co Ltd, 133–4, 161

Watson, Natalya, 10, 170, 175–7

Wharton, Betty, (see The Smiths of Ryburgh)

Whittle, Jane, 94, 97, 149

widows, 16–18, 20–3, 48–50, 54–5, 57, 59, 110–11, 113–14, 127, 128, 161, 178

William Langland (see *Piers Plowman*)

wills (*see also* inheritance), 67, 125
witch hat, 67–8
witch flight, 67
witch trials
  In England, 71–7
  In Scotland, 77–9
  In Wales, 70–1
witchcraft
  and brewing women, 5, 62, 63–79
  and brewing men accused, 76
  alewives and witch myth, 8, 11, 66–79
  appeasement with ale, 69, 77–8
  magickal practices and, 79
witchcraft pamphlets, 75–6
Women in Beer, 10, 39, 121, 122, 141, 142, 144,
  162–3, 168–9

Women of the Bevolution, 145–6
women's beer groups, 10, 39, 121, 122, 141, 144,
  162–3, 168–9
Women's Section of the British Legion, 161
Women's University Settlement, 165
Woolley (or Wolley), Hannah, 88–9, 96
World War I, 133–4
World War II, 134–7

Y

yeast, 42, 74, 92, 95, 96, 134
  and witches, 65, 73
  in recipes, 83, 87, 90, 99
yeoman farmer, 85
Young's Brewery, 136
Youngs, Deborah, 16, 24, 50

IMAGE CREDITS

The photographs on pages 29, 31, 33, 39, 42, 52, 56, 121, 138, 140, 142, 143, 162, 169, 173, 174, 175, 176, 177 were supplied by Lily Waite, lilywaite.co.uk

The images on pages 6, 19, 65 (attribution 4.0 International (CC BY 4.0)), 67, 75 and 159 are from the Wellcome Collection. (Public domain).

Page 7 is © Jim Linwood, Creative Commons Attribution 2.0 Generic Licence.

Page 14 is in Collection at the Met Museum. (Public domain).

Page 25 is courtesy of Apiwe Nxusani-Mawela.

Page 68 is from G. Wuestman, 2007, in J. Bikker (ed.), *Dutch Paintings of the Seventeenth Century in the Rijksmuseum*, online coll. cat. Amsterdam: hdl.handle. net/10934/RM0001.COLLECT.9078. (Public domain).

Page 88 is in collection at Library of Congress, Prints and Photographs division. (Public domain).

Page 102 is in collection at The Met, 91.1.141. (Public domain).

Page 108 is in collection at The Met 17.49 2(6). (Public domain).

Page 112 is © Sumit Surai, Creative Commons Attribution Share Alike 4.0 International.

Page 146 is courtesy of Ash Eliot.

Page 155 is at Yale Center for British Art. (Public domain).

Page 156 is at Yale Center for British Art, Paul Mellon Collection. B. 1977.14.4159. (Public domain).

Page 171 is courtesy of Ruvani de Silva.

Page 180 is from lacucinaitalia.com.

Page 182 is Creative Commons. (Public domain).

Page 184 is in Collection at the Met Fifth Avenue in Gallery 509. (Public domain).

ACKNOWLEDGEMENTS

I would like to start by acknowledging CAMRA, who provided me with the incredible opportunity to write this book. I am so grateful to everyone there who has helped me along the way. It means the absolute world to me. In particular, I want to thank my editor, Alan Murphy. His professional knowledge and insight have been invaluable in making this book. I would also like to thank all of the women who gave their time by allowing me to interview them. This book would not have been possible without your contributions.

I want to thank the John Gray Centre for kindly allowing me to use their fantastic data on brewing. To the team at Curtis Brown and the copyright holders of Mass-Observation, thank you so much for your help and permitting me to use *The Pub and The People* in this work. I am also deeply indebted to everyone at *Brewing Stories: An Oral History of 3 London Breweries*, for letting me use your incredible project here. Thank you as well to the *Aberdeen Registers Online: 1398-1511*, for creating such an amazing resource and allowing me to use it in my research. I would like to thank everyone at the Beer Culture Center for their support over the years. I am honoured to be among such amazing beer historians. To my PhD supervisor, Professor Terry Barry, for his professional guidance long after my thesis was finished. I cannot tell you how much I appreciate everything you have done for me.

I would like to thank my husband, Paul, for always providing me with a listening ear so that I could put the pieces together and for being my emotional rock during times of acute imposter syndrome; I never would have made it this far without you. To my parents, Bill and Bridget, for their unwavering support for my obsession with history since they took me to my first medieval ruin as a child, thank you. I want to thank my life-long editor, my mother, who has spent countless hours on the phone with me agonising over word choice or sentence structure over the decades. This book simply would not exist without your love and guidance. To my father, for his complete faith in me and for helping to remind me of life outside of work, I am incredibly grateful for your encouragement. Beth and Bill, my aunt and uncle, thank you for cheering me on from the very beginning – your support has meant the world.

I would like to thank my friend Elicia Gilreath, with whom I started this beer journey some years ago. I owe her a great debt for always believing in me. To everyone at the Beer Ladies Podcast and The Ladies Craft Beer Society of Ireland for their kindness over the years; you all kept me going and I'm so grateful for that. Thank you for listening, reading drafts, and supporting me while I wrote this book. I am immensely thankful to Emily for our discussions over the years which have helped shape this book. I am forever grateful for your advice and friendship. And last, but certainly not least, thank you to the best co-worker anyone could ask for, my dog, George. You are the very best boy.

Also from CAMRA Books

Desi Pubs
A guide to British–Indian Pubs, Food & Culture
DAVID JESUDASON

In this new book, the first of its kind, award-winning British-Asian journalist and beer writer David Jesudason travels the length and breadth of the UK, visiting desi pubs run by British-Indian landlords who have stamped their unique identity on a beloved institution and helped to challenge our preconceptions of the pub customer.

RRP £**14.99**   ISBN 978-1-85249-385-1

Cask
The Real Story of Britain's Unique Beer Culture
DES DE MOOR

This book by award-winning beer writer Des De Moor introduces cask beer to a new generation, explaining why it's still important, what distinguishes it from other beer formats, and the impact this has on the drinking experience.

RRP £**17.99**   ISBN 978-1-85249-384-4

Manchester's Best Beer, Pubs and Bars
MATTHEW CURTIS

The essential, indispensable guide to one of the UK's great beer cities. From traditional pubs serving top-quality cask ale, to the latest on-trend bottle shop bars and funky brewery taprooms, Manchester is bursting with great beer and this new book will direct you to the very best.

RRP £**16.99**   ISBN 978-1-85249-383-7

New for 2024

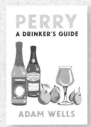

Perry: A Drinker's Guide
ADAM WELLS

Renowned drinks writer and campaigner Adam Wells has written the world's first dedicated guide to this most wondrous of drinks. Beautifully illustrated throughout with stunning colour photography, *Perry: A Drinker's Guide* takes the reader on a journey through the magical world of perry, with information on its troubled history, how it's made, and, most importantly, a guide to perry styles, regions and producers.

RRP £**16.99**   ISBN 978-1-85249-388-2

Order these and other CAMRA Books from **shop.camra.org.uk**